ArtScroll Series®

Rabbi Nosson Scherman / Rabbi Meir Zlotowitz
General Editors

MIRISH
KISZNER

Published by
Me'sorah Publications, ltd

EXTRA-ORDINARY STORIES About ORDINARY PEOPLE

FIRST EDITION
First Impression … July 2008

Published and Distributed by
MESORAH PUBLICATIONS, LTD.
4401 Second Avenue / Brooklyn, N.Y 11232

Distributed in Europe by
LEHMANNS
Unit E, Viking Business Park
Rolling Mill Road
Jarow, Tyne & Wear, NE32 3DP
England

Distributed in Australia and New Zealand by
GOLDS WORLDS OF JUDAICA
3-13 William Street
Balaclava, Melbourne 3183
Victoria, Australia

Distributed in Israel by
SIFRIATI / A. GITLER — BOOKS
6 Hayarkon Street
Bnei Brak 51127

Distributed in South Africa by
KOLLEL BOOKSHOP
Ivy Common
105 William Road
Norwood 2192, Johannesburg, South Africa

ARTSCROLL SERIES®
EXTRAORDINARY STORIES ABOUT ORDINARY PEOPLE
© Copyright 2008, by MESORAH PUBLICATIONS, Ltd.
4401 Second Avenue / Brooklyn, N.Y. 11232 / (718) 921-9000 / www.artscroll.com

ALL RIGHTS RESERVED
The text, prefatory and associated textual contents and introductions
— including the typographic layout, cover artwork and ornamental graphics —
have been designed, edited and revised as to content, form and style.

No part of this book may be reproduced
IN ANY FORM, PHOTOCOPYING, OR COMPUTER RETRIEVAL SYSTEMS
— **even for personal use without written permission from
the copyright holder, Mesorah Publications Ltd.**
except by a reviewer who wishes to quote brief passages
in connection with a review written for inclusion in magazines or newspapers.

THE RIGHTS OF THE COPYRIGHT HOLDER WILL BE STRICTLY ENFORCED.

Readers who would like to share their inspirational stories can contact the author via e-mail at kisner@bezeqint.net

ISBN 10: 1-4226-0829-8 / ISBN 13: 978-1-4226-0829-6

Typography by CompuScribe at ArtScroll Studios, Ltd.
Printed in the United States of America by Noble Book Press Corp.
Bound by Sefercraft, Quality Bookbinders, Ltd., Brooklyn N.Y. 11232

There is no way that I can adequately
acknowledge my beloved parents
for all that they did in shaping my life.
My childhood days were infused
with their noble standards, stemming from
a potent blend of love and fear of Hashem.
To them, life is about serving Him
and doing chesed with His children.

I pray that HaKodosh Baruch Hu bless you,
watch over you, and grant you much nachas.
May He shower you with His choicest of blessings
and grant you length of days
and much joy from all
your children and grandchildren.

It is with blessings that I dedicate this book to you.

Table of Contents

Acknowledgments	9
Introduction	13
Memorable Melodies	15
To Give It Your All	18
A Moment of Restraint	24
Worthwhile Compensation	29
A Grand Welcome	38
The Windfall	43
A Light Unto the Nations	52
Divine Delivery	57
The Difference	65
David	71
The Deal of a Lifetime	77
Labor of Love	83
Dissolved but Resolved	95
The Missing Key	101
Altruistic Acts	108
To Kindle a Flame	116

A Yiddishe Neshamah	121
Actions Speak Louder …	125
Last-Minute Changes	136
The World To Come from a Single Daf	142
Liberated Men	150
The Value of a Mitzvah	158
I'm Going on Vacation	163
When More Is Less	169
The Gift	174
Guardian Angels	182
Settling Accounts	188
The Succah That Remained Standing	197
Alone With Hashem	201
A Promise Kept	218
A Rose Among the Thorns	227
Flight or Fight	234
A Magnetic Change of Heart	242
The Real Thing	248
Life's Lessons	253
The Perfect Hiding Place	258

Acknowledgments

אודה ה׳ מאוד בפי ובתוך רבים אהללנו.

I am profoundly grateful to *HaKodosh Baruch Hu* for giving me the opportunity to write this book and for His constant infinite kindness to us. I pray that He continue to grant us and all of *Klal Yisroel* His blessings always.

I wish to express my deep-felt gratitude to my dear in-laws, for their encouragement, love, and support. For clipping the articles I write, for your warm words of encouragement, for all the love packages you send us, and for being there for us in every way. May *HaKodosh Baruch Hu* watch over you and grant you much nachas. May He shower you with His choicest of blessings and grant you length of days and much joy from all your children and grandchildren.

To my grandparents, who turned my childhood days into a garden of love and affection, whose pride in my work gave me the impetus to undertake more and more. May you be *zoche* to continue reaping much nachas *ad bias goel tzedek*.

Thank you, my dearest sisters and brothers, parts of myself. No words will ever do justice to what you mean to me. Your love, support, and encouragement were and are the lush groundwork for everything I do.

To my beloved sisters-in-law in Montreal, New York, and Israel, how can I thank you enough?

For enhancing my life in so many different ways, for always thinking of us, for your warmth, closeness, and care in so many beautiful ways.

In addition, I'm grateful to my aunts for their inspiration, enduring friendships, and for being a wonderful source of encouragement to me in everything I do.

To Mrs. Kviat, for instilling within me the love for the written word, for believing in my ability, for leading me to believe in it, too. Thank you for being there for me and my writing experiences for as long as I can remember.

To Chany Twersky, my *yedid nefesh*. Through thick and thin, over mountains and valleys, oceans and skies, you have remained, forever, my closest friend. Fortunately for me, you always have been a pro at reading the language of the heart.

I want to express my gratitude to Rabbi Ephraim Wachsman. I have learned so much from his penetrating insights into Torah and from his wellspring of knowledge. My life has been immeasurably enriched by listening to his lectures. May he and his family be rewarded with Hashem's abundant blessings.

My heartfelt appreciation goes to Chavi Ehrenster, talented editor of *Hamodia*, who so enthusiastically opened for me the door to the world of writing. My thanks goes to *Mishpacha* and *Hamodia Magazine* for permitting me to use those stories that originally appeared in their magazine. I am grateful to Rabbi Hanoch Teller, Devora Kiel, Chavi Shwartz, Leah Kotkes, Tzivia Tabak, and Libi Feinberg for offering feedback on various parts of the manuscript.

Many thanks to Nechemia Coopersmith, talented editor of Aish.com, for granting me the opportunity to publish the story of David that originally appeared on Aish.com, a leading Judaism website.

I am deeply grateful to all the many wonderful people who have so selflessly given of their time to offer me encouragement and support and to Sarah Shapiro, Yonina Hall, Sara Chava Mizrahi, Aviva Rapapport, Yocheved Krems, Miriam Gitty Damen, and Raizy Stern, who helped me in invaluable ways. May Hashem repay them and their loved ones with His bountiful blessings.

These notable people generously gave me of their precious time and shared their inspirational stories: Rebbetzin Weissman, Mrs. Gold, Mr. David Braun, Dalia Barnes, Miriam Swerdloff, Mrs. Direnfeld, Sara'le Taubenfeld, Esther Frimet Baumgarten, Raizy Kruger, Yocheveth Twersky, and Zahara Ashkenazi.

And most of all I wish to express my gratitude to my wonderful husband, who, with unflagging support and dedication, gave me the courage and incentive to write and was always there to advise me and to spur me on. Thank you also to my children for making my life so sweet.

ויהי נועם ה׳ אלוקינו עלינו ומעשה ידינו כוננה עלינו ומעשה ידינו כוננה.

May Hashem's Presence and Satisfaction rest upon us. May Hashem complete our effort and answer their success. May the work of our hands establish Hashem's Kingdom on earth (*Tehillim* 90:17).

With gratitude to *HaKodosh Baruch Hu*.

Mirish Kiszner

Sivan 5768
Jerusalem, Israel

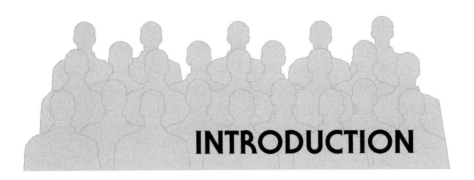

INTRODUCTION

A small note fluttered to the ground. It was a crisp one-hundred dollar bill. I stared at it. I blinked. I didn't quite know what to make of this. Was money raining down to me from the heavens? Lifting my gaze, I scanned the skies, searching for a clue.

Two more bills came tumbling down.

And then another one.

That's when I noticed Nosson standing on his balcony, seven flights above, clapping his hands in ecstasy, his eyes following the bills as they danced and twirled in the breeze. Even at this distance, I recognized him. Nosson is my two-year-old neighbor — a rambunctious little boy whose face is always wreathed in smiles that make you wonder what he's got up his sleeve.

I observed the ripples of the golden curls that framed his laughing face, and stared, dumbfounded, as he stretched his tiny hands out as far as they could go, hurling yet more bills, one by one, to the wind.

Suddenly his father appeared. The toddler's joyous giggles and exclamations of delight must have alerted him and brought him to the scene. From my vantage point, I couldn't make out the expression on Dad's face, but it didn't call for too much imagination. His young son had been playing with a small fortune, though he did not know it.

Because if you do not know you have a treasure, you are in danger of losing it.

For all of us, every action that we take makes a difference. The world needs every one of us in order to exist. We are a nation of *tzaddikim*. Infinite greatness intrinsically exists in every Jewish *neshamah*. The awareness of our greatness can inspire us to love, appreciate, and respect both ourselves and others. But beware: if we don't know the value of our people and ourselves, we may cast away that value, flinging it from us like little Nosson's hundred-dollar bills.

MEMORABLE MELODIES

I remember standing in my kindergarten classroom, a child of five, surrounded by tiny chairs and little desks, silently viewing the commotion around me.

The walls are decorated with gay banners in every color of the rainbow. Amidst all the animated voices and happy chatter, I stand alone and have no part in this excitement. I am not excited, only bewildered and confused. I wonder if a concept such as fairness exists within the vast universe.

Standing in a neat row at my left are proud little girls, all gaily decked in soft pink crepe-paper skirts and vests, with dainty rose-colored bows adorning their hair. To my right are girls dressed up as boys, equally outfitted in splendid finery, all handmade with care by the teacher. My memory transports me to that moment, and in my mind's eye, I see the teacher vividly now. I look on through an invisible bubble, as the teacher glides from one child to the next, adjusting, tightening, smoothing, and applying last-minute touches to her creations.

From the corner of my eye, I observe some daring little girls as they venture to test the teacher's patience by stepping out of line to prance around the room in childish ostentation. I feel so conspicuous and so perplexed.

I swallow hard, attempting mightily to retain the tears that are threatening to spill over my face. I feel engulfed by a peculiar new sensation and I wonder why my face is contorting strangely as I struggle with my feelings of envy. What about me? Where is *my* rose-colored bow and pretty costume?

Hesitantly, cautiously, I peek down at my drab attire — my own Shabbos housecoat that I had brought along with me to school today and that had appeared so lovely before this morning. Where has its prettiness fled, leaving me alone amid a sea of softly shimmering costumes, to stand out in the crowd in humble eccentricity?

How dismal, how sadly unfortunate. Why am I so quaintly dressed and so … different from everyone? Why has the world allowed this to occur? And why am I banished from the crowd, cast aside and abandoned?

It is soon time. The mothers are beginning to trickle in. Eager anticipation spreads visibly across their proud faces and I watch them from afar as the lights dim and the mounting excitement in the air slowly settles down.

The pink girls begin the performance as they raise their sweet voices in song. The melodious tunes cascade across the stage in ripples and waves. I long to sing along, to join with them, to be a part of everyone else — and envy, secretly harbored, threatens to erupt in my heart.

The song has ended. Enthusiastic hand-clapping vibrates throughout the room. The "boys" begin their performance. Their childish voices unite in chorus as the song takes off with ardor and fervor. A harmonious blend of sound resonates so passionately through the air once again.

Alone, in the center, standing between the two lucky groups, I gaze in awed silence at their solemn faces and masterful performance.

Then, the mother in the scene steps out to enact her part. Shyly, tremulously, her thin voice reverberates across the room. To the rapt audience the little girl appears duly dressed to fit her role as mother; in a lovely housecoat and elegant head covering, she softly sings her lines that further unfold the drama of the play.

The shining eyes of her own mother, amongst all eyes that are upon her, transmit a pure pride toward this very earnest soloist. The other children look on, each wishing that *she* had been chosen to be the "mother."

The song ends, the drama is over. And I, the lone soloist enacting the role of the mother, step back into place.

Not until many years later did I come to realize that on that night, each little girl played her own unique role to complete the drama. My own role, I came to understand, was no less important than that of the pink little girls or the elegant "boys."

In the drama of life, every one of us plays a significant role and contributes to the world's perfect symphony; using our voices, through our own unique songs — our divine gifts from Hashem.

Numerous accounts of triumph and victory exist within us all. The stories in this book reflect the greatness inherent in every member of the Jewish Nation. They are stories of you and me; of human beings who cry and laugh, fail and triumph, struggle and succeed, and — when the occasion demands — rise to a higher calling, transforming the ordinary into extraordinary, the mundane into the spiritual.

All the stories are true; however, some character names and story settings have been changed to shield the privacy of those involved. Some fine points have been interwoven to enhance the impact of the message.

May we truly know, understand, and utilize the strengths that *HaKadosh Baruch Hu* granted each of us.

TO GIVE IT YOUR ALL

*T*he medical team of physicians, interns, radiologists, and other hospital personnel huddled around the elderly patient. One nurse adjusted the IV tube and measured blood pressure, while another thrust a thermometer into the patient's mouth, simultaneously checking the pulse on her frail wrist. To the doctors discussing the patient's prognosis in clipped tones and medical jargon, Ben Sherman, the patient's son, seemed to be entirely invisible.

Just as Ben began contemplating the idea of getting himself a fresh cup of coffee from the cafeteria, the team turned on their heels and left as pretentiously as they had arrived. Ben tenderly leaned over his mother, caressed her ashen cheeks, and smoothed her blanket. He headed to the nurse's station to request an update on his mother's condition. That's when Dr. Allen Dodson, who from the start had displayed more compassion than the others, returned to the room. He hadn't forgotten about Ben, after all.

After a warm handshake, Dr. Dodson addressed Ben in a somber tone. "We have done the best we could, Mr. Sherman. Your mother is extremely ill and her health is waning drastically."

Ben Sherman nodded solemnly, not quite comprehending the immensity of those words. He knew Dr. Dodson well and appreciated his serious, no-nonsense manner, complemented by his kindness and understanding. As the two men stood opposite each other in the gloomy hospital room, the doctor's eyes seemed somber and defeated.

The doctor cleared his throat and brushed his hand through his graying hair. "Unfortunately, there is nothing we can do for her here," he said quietly.

Ben, at a loss for words, simply stood in his place, motionless. What could he possibly say?

Dr. Dodson had contended with scores of patients and had witnessed the diverse reactions of numerous family members. Yet the strength and quiet dignity this gentleman exuded in the face of adversity was a novelty to the seasoned doctor.

"I suggest, Mr. Sherman," the doctor added, the sympathy in his voice evident, "that you find your mother a comfortable senior citizens' home to make her last days as pleasant as possible."

With a look of utter disdain, Mr. Sherman stared at the doctor, narrowed his eyes and whispered, "An old-age home? I will never do that. I should discard *my* mother like the peel of a squeezed-out orange? To allow her to sit in some unfamiliar atmosphere at the mercy of some apathetic nurses? Sorry, Doc, not me! Not *my* mother."

The doctor eyed him in silent consideration for a few moments. The man standing before him, wearing an immaculate gray suit, wasn't a youngster himself anymore, probably in his upper 50's or so. Yet the respect he always displayed toward his mother was legendary among the hospital personnel. How unfortunate it seemed that, due to hospital regulations, they could no longer accommodate his dying mother. On the other hand, the patient's condition required sophisticated equipment and she needed constant care. "Mr. Sherman," Dr. Dodson pressed, "there are many fine homes around. Your mother can be well tended to. You know as well as I do that she needs round-the-clock nursing. You have got to be sensible."

Ben gazed intently at an invisible spot in the distance, pointedly ignoring the doctor's reasoning.

This was his mother they were talking about. All his life, she'd been there for him. With utmost care, she had tended to his every need. Every minor scrape or bruise had been treated as though it were of monumental importance. Every tear had been wiped with love and devotion. How much understanding, how many pearls of wisdom and life lessons had his mother imparted to him throughout his school years and then later, during his yeshivah days! And it hadn't ended there. Her kindness, wisdom, and care had grown and developed along with his own growth and development.

Nostalgic thoughts of his mother, once a strong and vibrant woman, washed over him as he stood at the foot of her hospital bed. Small in stature, but tremendous in virtue, his mother had presided over the house with an aristocratic bearing. Though she remained at home to care for her family, she always seemed to be a top professional, elegantly dressed as she stood in the kitchen peeling vegetables, slicing fruit, and cooking wholesome, nourishing food for her family.

Her numerous acts of kindness never came at the expense of her family. Quite the opposite: Ben had been an integral part of her endless *chessed* projects, swept up in the joy and love of the mitzvah that his mother radiated. Food packages were affectionately prepared together. Ideas and suggestions of ways to help their neighbors in need were invariably discussed mutually. His mother had always treated him like an adult, with respect and consideration. There was no way in the world that he would treat her any differently.

"Doctor Dodson," he said finally, "isn't there some way it can be done; a way to bring my mother home to me and to care for her in the comfort of family and familiar surroundings?"

The doctor adjusted his spectacles and scratched his forehead. "Theoretically, it can be done, Mr. Sherman," he said. "But quite frankly, it will be an unbelievably costly process. Your mom will need special machinery that costs tens of thousands of dollars! It is not very practical; I think you should give this decision some thought." After another firm handshake, he turned to leave; then he paused and faced Ben.

"You know," the doctor said, retracing his steps, "most people never imagine their parents getting old and incapacitated. We have this way of believing that our mothers and fathers are indestructible. Your reaction is totally normal, Mr. Sherman. Give yourself a few days to adjust to this new reality."

Ben stared after the doctor's receding back. *Theoretically, it can be done.* The doctor's words reverberated in Ben's ears. There was no question in his mind. *If it can be done, I'll do it!* Money wasn't a consideration.

Though by no means wealthy, Ben Sherman had established himself moderately well, financially, yet his lifestyle was modest. His mother had taught him the detrimental effects of raising children to expect luxuries, and he had prudently followed her advice. His wife, too, had agreed, so they had never splurged on unnecessary lavishness and extravagance. Now, when he needed those funds, they were available.

For the next few years, Ben Sherman tended to his mother in his own home, with supreme devotion. Every need was fulfilled, and everything that could make his mother more comfortable was seen to. Freshly cut fragrant flowers decorated the room where his mother rested, well-contented. Ben hardly gave a thought to his dwindling savings; could money be better spent than on his mother?

When a mother departs from the world, no amount of preparation is enough. Whether after a prolonged illness or a sudden tragedy; whether young or old, when a mother passes on, the sorrow and anguish are intense.

There was an overcast sky that day, drizzling rain and wet roads everywhere, when Ben's mother breathed her last breath. Pained and heartbroken, Ben nevertheless headed towards the funeral chapel to make the necessary arrangements for the *levayah*.

"My mother's last wish was to be buried in the holy soil of *Eretz Yisrael*," he notified the mortician, Mr. Lieber.

"All right, we can certainly accommodate you," Mr. Lieber replied, leaning back in his leather swivel chair behind the desk. "However, I'm not sure you are familiar with the law here in California regarding the procedure of transporting a body outside of the country. Let me explain …." Mr. Lieber briefed Ben on the required procedure that was a legal prerequisite for taking the deceased out-of-state; a procedure that was absolutely counter to Jewish Law.

"What? What are you talking about? You're going to do that to my mother? *Chas veshalom*! I will never permit you to do that," Ben Sherman exclaimed, much alarmed.

"Mr. Sherman, if I don't do it, I can lose my license," he said, shrugging, his hands sweeping the air in a resigned gesture. "That's what I must do in order to transport her to *Eretz Yisrael*, you must understand."

Ben leaned over his desk and with a determined expression gazed directly into the eyes of the mortician. "Mr. Lieber," he said in a deliberate, even tone, "I want you to know that all my life there wasn't anything that I would not do for my mother. I've given everything I've ever saved, all my assets, to care for my mother properly. In fact, I exhausted my last penny for that purpose." He paused, allowing his words to sink in, before plunging ahead.

Pulling his chair closer, Ben lowered his voice, "I have only one thing of value left," he said with fervor.

"Mr. Lieber," Ben suddenly raised his tone a few octaves. Pointing at the mortician, he implored, "if you send my mother to *Eretz Yisrael* in accordance with *halachah* …"

"Look here, Mr. Sherman," the mortician was getting impatient, "this is …"

"… if you fulfill her last wish, I'll give you my house!"

"… the only way I can …." Mr. Lieber stopped short. Had he heard right? His HOUSE?

The mortician's jaw dropped open and his eyes grew several inches in diameter. HIS HOUSE? He gaped at the man sitting calmly opposite him. *It must be my headache,* he mused.

"It is a rather stately home, sir; you will be most delighted," Mr. Sherman was saying.

Mr. Lieber raised a questioning eyebrow, coughed uneasily and asked, "I'm sorry, what did you say, I'm afraid I missed that. You said you would give me your … house?"

"You heard me, all right," Ben replied. "Can't you find a way? It would mean so much to me …." Despite his sorrow, he couldn't help but smile as he looked at the man's face. He observed the rapidly changing expressions passing across Mr. Lieber's features, and he knew that his impassioned plea had hit its mark. He remained silent, not wishing to ruin the moment.

The room was absolutely still. The mortician, thoroughly overwhelmed at the dramatic gesture, could hardly speak. In the course of his long years at his job, he'd never come across a selfless act of such cosmic proportions. *Now this is a person of high caliber,* he ruminated. *This is a man with values and principles. For a human being like that, I'll find a way!*

Rising, the mortician strode around his desk to face his client. "You know what?" he said dramatically, placing his right arm around Ben's shoulder. "I'll do it!"

"And you know what else?" he added. "Your house shall remain yours!"

A MOMENT OF RESTRAINT

*H*ow did it all begin? Nobody could remember. What everybody did know was that Chaim Becker and Tzvi Leitner were not on speaking terms. In truth, Chaim and Tzvi were fierce enemies, each one harboring deep-felt hurt, anger, and animosity.

At first the flames smoldered quietly, crackling with a few words of gossip here and there. But once the tiny embers were ablaze, it didn't take too long for their enmity to escalate into a destructive fire. Like an unrestrained flame, the blazing hatred did not remain contained between these two individuals alone. It soared, singeing and searing wives, children, friends, and neighbors as the fire of dispute devoured the very timbers of their hearts.

And then, one day, Tzvi went too far ….

The shrill sound of the telephone woke Tzvi from his slumber. The time: 2:45 a.m.

"Who's this?" he managed to ask in a croaky whisper.

"This is Sergeant Michael Donovan from the 57th precinct. Is this Leitner?" The breezy voice coming through the telephone belied the time and import of an early-morning call.

Throwing off the covers, Tzvi shot up from the bed, his heart hammering.

"Yes?" he half-shouted, clutching the receiver in a tight grip.

"I am calling to notify the owners of Leitner and Co. that the fire alarm went off this morning at the precinct and at the fire Department. I'm calling the emergency number listed on the building. Our men are at the scene, and the firemen are doing their best to control the blaze. We suggest you come down immediately."

The frigid morning wind whipped against Chaim's face as he steadily made his way to shul. In a feeble attempt to shield himself from the cold, he walked with his head slightly bent, which effectively hid the deep lines of worry etched into his forehead. He dug his hands deeper into his pockets, his mind racing, as he searched for solutions to the myriad business problems that were plaguing him. As soon as he successfully tackled one predicament, two more would spring forth out of nowhere, it seemed, to take its place.

Deep in his heart his conscience nagged at him. *Come on, Chaim, you know the reason you are having problems*, the voice in the back of his mind whispered to him. *Ein kli machazik berachah ela hashalom* — no vessel can hold blessing as does peace. That persistent voice inside him wouldn't let up, much as he tried to silence it by rationalizing, even pleading with it. He presented every possible excuse, real or invented, that would confirm his innocence, but that voice never relented.

Chaim now dug his chilled hands deeper into his pockets, vainly attempting to bury his tormenting thoughts deeper in the recesses of his mind. *Nonsense*, he told himself with a shake of his head. *Just take a look at Tzvi. He's a successful entrepreneur, owns a thriving business, and has a large number of satisfied clients. That's all the proof I need that my troubles have nothing to do with the dispute. Besides, all this strife and discord are entirely his fault to begin with ....*

He knew it was a lame excuse. It didn't even convince him. He was painfully aware of how large his own part was in their bitter dispute. Nevertheless, he managed to brush his introspective mood aside as he entered the warm shul.

Chaim made his way adroitly through the aisles — by now he had become quite skilled at avoiding Tzvi even as he moved right past him — to get to his own seat. Today, though, his inner dialogue had pricked his conscience and somewhat reduced the intense dislike he usually felt for his rival. He sneaked a glance at Tzvi.

Tzvi, always on the alert when Chaim was around, had been observing him from the corner of his eye. The long years of disharmony had laced his mind with a touch of paranoia. Covertly, he studied Chaim, mindful of every subtle movement he made.

There is a hint of a smile on his lips today, Tzvi thought, leaning forward to get a better view. He even went so far as to look directly at his enemy's face, something he hadn't done for a long time. *There is laughter in his eyes!* Tzvi was incensed. Instantly he shot out of his seat. *What a heartless, ruthless man,* his heart cried out. *To laugh at my tragedy like that, to openly gloat at my misfortune, how could he?*

The early-morning fire in his office, his disturbed sleep, and the perceived slight all took their toll on Tzvi's benumbed brain. He burst out in an unprecedented tirade. His angry voice reverberated across the holiness of the quiet shul. Stridently, he roundly denounced Chaim, heaping insult upon insult on him, in front of the whole congregation. The silence that followed was deafening; all heads turned to look at Chaim.

Chaim's blood drained from his face. For a moment, he stood rooted to the spot, his tongue cleaving to the roof of his mouth. The shocked look on the faces of the shul members wasn't lost on him, and Tzvi's stinging words struck him like resounding slaps. This was too much to bear.

Instinctively, and without another moment's thought, Chaim charged over to Tzvi. The precious fragment of goodwill Chaim had felt but moments ago vanished without a trace. He searched for the most cutting words he could inflict on his nemesis now. *The chutzpah of this brazen man! Who does he think he is? I'll show him!*

"You scoundrel … you …."

Suddenly, Mr. Gewurtz, a quiet, unassuming man, who was visiting from out of town, rushed forward. In an instant he had planted himself directly between the two.

"Wait, wait! *Please* … hold it … wait one minute. Listen to me … please!"

A deep purple shade flooded Chaim's cheeks. He was livid; every fiber of his being trembled with volcanic fury, ready to erupt in an instant. With his face contorted in pain and anger, Chaim turned to face Mr. Gewurtz.

Absolute silence reigned; all eyes focused on the unfolding drama.

"Please, I beg you," Mr. Gewurtz implored. His voice, shaking slightly, was barely above a whisper. "I have a son …. Listen to me!"

A faint look of interest flickered in Chaim's eyes. Encouraged, Mr. Gewurtz rushed on, the words tumbling out of his mouth.

"He doesn't have any children, my son …. He is married for *nine years*! Can you imagine the pain and anguish of his every waking moment? He is childless! Do you know how his empty hands long to cuddle his own child? To hold it close to his heart?

"Let this moment of restraint be a *z'chus* for my long-suffering son. Please, take hold of yourself, control your … this … excruciating moment of anger … may it be for the merit of a broken-hearted couple …."

Chaim wrestled with his temper, struggling to gain control of his emotions. He stared at Mr. Gewurtz, a kind, diminutive man, whose dark-brown eyes now glistened with tears.

Slowly, Chaim regained his composure and lowered, first his clenched fists, then his eyes. The congregants' collective sigh of relief echoed loudly in his heart, and he quietly turned away in shame and remorse.

Mounds of chick peas, stacks of succulent fruits and a rich variety of nuts were making their way around the room, compliments of C. Becker and T. Leitner, Incorporated.

Chaim Becker and Tzvi Leitner had become partners in a new and promising business venture. Together, they were hosting Mr. Gewurtz's simchah. The sounds of tinkling glass and hearty "*L'chaims*" blended smoothly with the lively tunes the men were singing. The well-wishers congregated around Mr. Gewurtz and his radiant son, extending warm handshakes and heartfelt blessings at the *shalom zachor*.

"Mazel tov, *shalom aleichem*, Mr. Gewurtz!"

"Mazel tov! Mazel tov!"

"May you be blessed with much *yiddishe nachas*!"

Overwhelmed, Mr. Gewurtz found a moment to step outside surreptitiously, ready for a short break from the tumultuous celebration. He'd arrived in town just that morning in honor of his new grandson's *shalom zachor* and he was tired.

In the solemn beauty of the night, the stars sparkling up the sky, he closed his eyes for a moment. The scene of two angry people standing at either side of him rose fleetingly his mind's eye.

Mr. Gewurtz shook his head in silent wonder. *Just one year ago* ....

WORTHWHILE COMPENSATION

"TONY, get over here," Rudolph's voice boomed across the work floor. The other workers averted their gazes from their boss's crimson face. Their machines whirred at a quickened pace and their chitchat ceased abruptly.

The tall Italian mechanic weaved his way through the rows of machines manned by dozens of workers. They were fond of their fellow workman, and they squirmed uneasily as Tony approached the irate boss.

"The central bottling machine didn't start up this morning. I want to know WHY!" Rudolph roared, his callused finger indicating a colossal contraption about the size of a square block.

Tony shrugged. "I'll take a look at it, sir," he answered.

With scores of men in his employ and dozens of job hunters seeking work daily, his employees knew that Rudolph had no compunction about firing men at will. There were plenty of willing applicants at that time, shortly after World War II. Refugees from war-torn Europe streamed to the shores of the United States, many of them electing to live in Williamsburg. Their lives shattered, their hearts torn, they desperately sought to build new, ordinary lives again. Yet a decent job was exceedingly hard to come by, especially if you were Jewish. Any religious Jew who showed up at Schimmler's Brewery in search of work was categorically denied employment. Rudolph Schimmler, president of the brewery — the largest in Brooklyn — was of German descent and had little regard for Jews.

Tony tinkered with the tangle of wires, chains, bolts, and nuts for a while, but he made no headway at all. This time the breakdown was beyond his expertise.

Rudolph reached for the phone with one hand, the other flipping through the address book on his light oak desk. He needed a more skilled mechanic.

The next few days saw a succession of engineers and technicians traipsing in and out of the factory. They came and meddled, bolt and unbolted, wired and rewired; nothing changed. Not a cog moved.

Days passed and the production line ground to a halt. Rudolph's temper grew shorter. Every local newspaper carried a large classified ad soliciting qualified master mechanics to come in to repair the bottling machine.

"Good morning, good morning," Rose Cohen greeted her two visitors happily. "Come on in. It's cold out there."

"The wind nearly blew us away," Sadie Goldstein said gratefully, blowing on her fingers in an effort to warm them.

"We figured we would pop in for a minute on the way home from the greengrocer. You know, to warm up a bit," Bessie Klein said, looking around for a place to set down her shopping bags. Her eyes surveyed the room and stopped at the huge, black, wood-burning stove, which Rose fed each morning. On its far corner stood an aluminum kettle, whistling shrilly. The stove's large, flat surface was just the right place for her bags, she decided, placing them on it.

The threesome moved into the small parlor off the kitchen. Rose removed a blackened piece of metal from one of the chairs. With her foot, she shoved a greasy steel cylinder to the side of the room. An assortment of grimy black machine parts lay scattered across every available space of the room. Meyer, her husband, was a talented mechanic. With his golden touch, Meyer's hands could fix almost anything. Rose sent a glance around the room to ascertain that all was in order and then went into the kitchen to prepare a snack for her guests.

The women sat over tea and home-baked cookies, freely distributing advice to each other, sharing their troubles, triumphs, and favorite recipes. Soft strains of music played in the background after Rose started the record-player.

"Did you see the ad in the *Daily News?*" Sadie asked. "Schimmler's Brewery is looking for a mechanic. Right away I thought of your husband." Sadie rummaged in her large handbag, emptying its contents bit by bit onto the table. Odd bits of paper began to pile up, along with letters, bills, several candies, a couple of handkerchiefs, a folded brown paper bag ....

"Ah, here it is," Sadie called out triumphantly. "See here, a thousand dollars they're offering! What do you say to that?"

Rose put on her glasses and leaned forward. She scanned the eye-catching advertisement Sadie held out. "Seeking," the large, bold letters of the headline screamed from the page.

"Technician to repair Mass Flow Rotary Filler.
Model #H2vV. German parts.
No interview required.
Apply at Schimmler's Brewery, South 9th Street.
$1000 in cash to successful applicant!"

Rose gasped in amazement.

"Didn't Meyer see this? Everyone is talking about it."

"Meyer?" She stood up to crank the old Victrola. The old-fashioned machine didn't play for long, and every now and then Rose remembered to restart the music.

"Since when does my husband have time to read the newspaper?" Rose shrugged. "My Meyer is always busy running around helping people. The man has a heart of gold, what can I tell you."

"Everyone knows Meyer and his good deeds," Bessie concurred. "No one really knows how many people unburden their hearts to him every day."

"He doesn't talk about the things he does. He does it all quietly although he did mention something about it being hard to find a job today," Rose said.

"They don't fire Jews because of being Shomer Shabbos so much anymore, do they?" Bessie asked.

Sadie took another sip from her cup. "No, thanks G-d," she said through the sugar cube held fast between her teeth. "They have stopped doing that now, with the five-day work week. Still, many employers, even the Jewish ones, don't like us because we're religious. They claim there is no need for religion in America."

"*Nebach*," Bessie said, shaking her head.

"What about the non-Jewish factory owners, don't they hire Jews?" Rose asked, wiping up some tea that had spilled.

Sadie looked at her in surprise. "What do you expect from them? They have always hated us. And that Schimmler," she paused, adjusting her glasses to look at the advertisement again, "he never, and I mean *never*, hires a Jew. Everyone knows that."

"The problem is that we need them more than they need us," she added, cradling the warm mug in her hands. "There are loads of other immigrants looking for work now too."

"And all those war refugees looking for work," Rose sighed, "are desperate to earn money for bread, for a roof over their heads …."

"I am so glad they're coming to live in our Williamsburgh," Bessie said sarcastically."

"You didn't think they'd go live in the East Side! Not even refugees want to live in those dilapidated tenement houses."

Bessie refilled her cup and leaned back in her chair. "Remember what those houses look like? One bathroom on each floor for four families .... Who can live like that today?" She shuddered at the thought. "And imagine having the bathtub down the hall, outside the apartment! And the terrible crowding! Families live one on top of another. Sure they're coming to Williamsburg. Why shouldn't they? The apartments are much larger — and prettier too."

The friendy conversation and hot tea warmed the women. It was pleasant to be together. After some time, the distinct fragrance of baked apple wafted through the apartment. Rose was surprised. Where was the smell coming from? All three of them hurried into the kitchen. A quick survey of the room apprised them of the source of the aroma. It was Bessie's bag of apples that she had placed atop the black stove; they were now baked apples.

"Oh, no," Bessie cried between her giggles. "That was just the lunch I had planned. And now it is all prepared."

Their laughter rippled across the room.

The lack of comforts never marred the simple joy of living, and the women drew happiness from the plainest things: a child's carefree laughter, a full pot of shelled peas, and even a bag of prematurely baked apples.

Rose Cohen stood on the landing of her fourth-floor apartment and waved good-bye to her friends just as her husband Meyer arrived.

Meyer, she knew, cut a comical figure on the streets of Williamsburgh. The clothes covering his short, thin frame were always mottled with soot and grime due to the long hours he spent toiling over old equipment. The undulating brim of his black hat somehow complemented his straggly beard.

Despite his outlandish appearance, Rose held her husband in high esteem. Beneath his sullied outer garb, she recognized his pristine character. To her, Meyer Cohen was a *tzaddik* and she treated him with great respect.

Rose was quick to notice the new lines etched onto his forehead. "Something is troubling you, Meyer?" she asked.

Meyer placed his toolbox on the table and put his hat on the chair. He sighed.

"I spent the morning at the Weiss's. Tried to do something with their battered old boiler — their house is freezing cold."

"He didn't find a job yet, Mr. Weiss?" Rose asked. She lifted a basket of wet laundry and carried it to the window leading to the fire escape, where her laundry line looped out over the courtyard below.

"They don't have it easy, these Holocaust survivors," Meyer said. "Some of them are, thanks G-d, doing well, but some of them are desperate for work. They need to rebuild their lives, and they've lost so much. Everything is so new to them here. The language, the people … think about it, Rose."

"They are hard-working too," she said, clipping a dish towel to the line. "Look at all the yeshivos and shuls they've organized so fast. They set goals for themselves and they do whatever it takes to reach them."

Rose pinned a tablecloth to the line. She gazed with pleasure at the long-sleeved dresses, white Shabbos aprons, and *tichels* fluttering on the neighbors' laundry lines around her. How different the face of Williamsburgh had become since the refugees had arrived!

Her husband sat lost in thought. She knew that his heart ached for his downtrodden brethren.

"You know, Meyer, Bessie showed us a newspaper ad today. Schimmler's Brewery is looking for an experienced mechanic. But she also said that they never hire Jews, so I guess it's not for us." She leaned out to move the laundry line forward. "They are offering a huge reward. A thousand dollars, I think."

Rose's head reappeared inside. "I think they are looking for a mechanic to fix some kind of machine. What a shame they never hi —"

"A mechanic, you said?" Meyer abruptly rose from his seat. "They need a mechanic?" He reached for his hat. "I am going there right now."

"Where?"

"To Schimmler's, of course. South 9th Street isn't far from here."

"What are you talking about? Why on earth are you going to Schimmler's?"

"To try my luck!"

"What do you mean? Schimmler'll never hire a Jewish mechanic! Don't go, they'll laugh at you. You will make a fool of yourself."

"I must go and at least try."

Rose sighed. She recognized the determination behind his quiet words. "May Hashem be with you."

The strong smell of beer, mingled with the stench of grease and perspiration, assailed Meyer immediately as he entered the imposing building. The Schimmler Brewing Company was a huge enterprise. Meyer looked around, trying to get his bearings. To his right, behind a glass partition, sat a woman entering numbers into a ledger.

"Mr. Schimmler, please," Meyer pronounced firmly. The woman looked up. Without saying a word, she raised one eyebrow and gave him a questioning glance. "I am here to repair the filler machine," he said confidently.

Barely hiding a smirk, the secretary spoke into her intercom in a nasal voice, "Mr. Schimmler, someone is here to repair the rotary filler."

"Go right in, sir," she told Meyer after listening to the reply, and pointed to an inner door.

Two men were sitting there, one on either side of a huge

desk. Each wore a sharply pressed suit, white shirt, and tie. They looked at Meyer in astonishment, then glanced at each other and burst into laughter. His disheveled appearance certainly did not indicate competence.

"Any experience?" The older gentleman asked. His distinct German accent was heavy with condescension.

"I am an expert mechanic, sir," Meyer replied, his back straight.

"*Was solch ein kleiner Jude kann wissen?* [What can a little Jew know]" the younger man said, rolling his eyes in mockery. "It is a waste of time, Rudolph. Send him home."

"Just try me," Meyer said quietly.

Rudolph's clear blue eyes darted back and forth between the bizarre-looking Jew and his colleague. At this point, he was clearly desperate and was willing to try anything.

"All right," he said after a moment. "Have a look at the machine and we will see. Come with me."

Rudolph led Meyer directly to the huge, silent apparatus. "Make sure you don't damage it even more," Rudolph warned, pointing an admonitory finger at him.

With a prayer for success directed heavenward, Meyer swiftly got to work. The mammoth machine dwarfed his small figure. The minutes speedily ticked by, but Meyer's nimble hands worked even more quickly. After only half-an-hour, the engine suddenly stirred into life. Huge puffs of thick smoke began spewing from the exhaust pipe as the cylinders whirred into action, and in minutes the whole machine was clanking away in full working order.

Meyer Cohen emerged from behind the apparatus. Rudolph stood rooted to the spot; red blotches appeared high on his cheeks. He seemed somewhat embarrassed.

Nevertheless, he remembered his commitment and walked over to the "little Jew." Reaching into his back pocket, Rudolph withdrew a black leather wallet. He reckoned it would salvage his pride before all the spectators if he presented the promised money on the spot.

With a flourish he handed ten crisp one-hundred-dollar bills to Meyer.

Meyer shook his head in silent disagreement. A collective gasp rippled forth from the onlookers.

"Wh ... what's the matter?" Rudolph spluttered. "Do you feel it is not enough? Will another hundred satisfy you?"

Meyer shook his head again.

"Two hundred? Two twenty-five? How much do you want? I will see to it that you leave here satisfied."

"Are you sure?"

"Of course I am sure. One hundred percent sure. That was a great job you did."

"Well then, what I would really like is a guarantee that the Schimmler Brewery will hire religious Jews."

Rudolph blinked. His mouth suddenly felt very dry.

"That will be my payment, sir."

The proud, arrogant businessman stood rooted to the spot. His mind raced with the anti-Semitic songs and slogans he'd absorbed since his youth. The picture of Jews he'd envisioned until this moment didn't quite fit with the inner nobility of the strangely-dressed man standing before him.

Slowly, hesitantly, he took a step forward. For the second time, he extended his hand to Meyer, but this time he offered equality, not arrogance.

"Come down to the office, sir," he managed to say. "I will give that to you in writing."

A GRAND WELCOME

Melissa looked down at the cherubic face of her one-day-old daughter and felt certain that she held the prettiest baby in the world. Peering at the newborn nestled peacefully in the crook of her arm, a sudden rush of fierce love seemed to encompass her entire being. She sat mesmerized as the baby's mouth opened wide and she yawned.

"How did you know how to do that?" she cooed to the tiny one. But the baby merely shut her eyes in total tranquility and was fast asleep again.

Melissa stroked the silken skin of the angelic face and a contented sigh escaped her lips. *Will I do justice to this innocent little human being?* she questioned herself. *Am I fit to be a mother?*

Endless doubts and uncertainties raced through her mind, questions for which she found no answers within. This wasn't a subject she had tackled at Oxford during the six years of her studies there, nor did graduating summa cum laude help her now. Her advanced degree did not give her a clue about mastering the utter bewilderment she felt at this formidable task called motherhood.

Exhausted, she carefully placed the baby in her bassinet and laid her own head back against her pillow. Her doubts over her abilities in her new role gnawed at her heart. The rest of her hospital stay was spent contemplating her responsibilities as a mother, fantacizing about her hopes and dreams for her daughter's future, and observing with wonder the powerful new feelings of motherly love that coursed through her veins.

Finally, they were ready to take the baby home. Max arrived bright and early, carrying a brand-new car seat, and waited patiently for the nurses to fill out their discharge papers.

As soon as the new threesome was comfortably settled in the car, Melissa presented her request. "Max, I really hope you won't mind, but … can we please make a stop at the synagogue?"

Max's eyebrows shot up and he glanced quizzically at his wife. "Synagogue?"

"Uh huh. The Beth David Reform Synagogue on Cheshire Avenue."

"What do you need a synagogue for?" he asked incredulously. Neither of them had stepped into a synagogue since the High Holidays eight months earlier. He might have expected a stop at the pharmacy to pick up some odds and ends, but why had his wife suddenly decided she needed a synagogue? *Did all new mothers suddenly go nuts? I really don't have enough experience in this new-baby business.*

"Perhaps you just need to rest a little," he replied soothingly.

"No, Max. I will rest just as soon as we get settled at home. But first, I must go to the synagogue."

"All right, if that is what you want," he shrugged. "But can you tell me why?"

"I want to hold the baby up to the Ark. I want her to kiss the *Aron Kodesh*."

"Hmm."

"I also want you to bless the baby." She continued to reveal her plan. "You are a *kohen*, remember? You can say the Blessing of the *Kohanim*. You will place your hand on the baby's head right there in the synagogue and recite the blessing."

Max was amused at the absurdity of her request, but he was agreeable and drove right up to the caretaker's home next door to the synagogue. Mr. Davidson, a compliant elderly man, opened the door for them.

They quickly found a prayer book and their mission was soon accomplished. Both of them felt surprisingly uplifted by the experience, and they promised each other to perform this rite for any future children as well.

———◆———

Grandpa Stan had landed in England in 1945, where he quickly established himself in business. "Stan David's Timberware" was open every day of the week, expectantly awaiting customers. One day, a couple entered the shop and put together a rather large order. As the impressive numbers on the bill were tallied, Stan's heart beat with exhilaration at this unexpected windfall so early in the year. The couple bent their heads over the counter as they reviewed the bill. Suddenly, the wife said loudly, "Wait a minute!"

She turned to her husband with a look of disgust and said firmly, "He is Jewish!" The two turned around and walked, stone-faced, out of the store.

After that, Stan changed his name and the name of his shop. Now the freshly-painted sign on the door announced, "Thomas Smith — Timberware," and he relegated anything associated with his old Jewish identity to the dusty corners of his mind. He couldn't endanger his livelihood with those ancient practices. He would not live in destitution; the memory of his poverty-stricken childhood was too deeply engraved on his weary bones and beaten spirit.

He often thought of his mother. *She had been such a devoted soul, my mammeh, may she rest in peace, a true Yiddishe Mammeh. And she cared for me with boundless love.* She would never have approved of the way of life he had carved out for himself. In an effort to please his mother and to placate his conscience, he attended the local Reform temple with his family each year for the High Holidays. *At least the children will have a glimpse of their heritage.*

From the start, his son Max had displayed an open affinity to anything Jewish. Stan remembered the copious tears his mother had always shed at candlelighting time. However, no candles were lit in his home in England. Nor did he observe any of the other ancient rites that he sometimes permitted himself to think about with nostalgia.

Then Max married Melissa. They tried their best to raise their children with a proud Jewish identity. Unfortunately, they did not have much knowledge to impart, because they knew so little themselves.

When the children were older, Max felt a need to be more connected to Judaism, so he began giving bar mitzvah lessons to the Hebrew School children. He toiled over his books, trying hard to learn what the children should know. Superficial though his growing knowledge was, the holy words of the Torah wormed their way deep into his *Yiddishe neshamah*. One day he recognized the folly of his position. *I teach the children all about observing Shabbos and I myself head straight for work on Shabbos morning! I teach the kids about the commandments, and I myself do nothing.* His own hypocrisy disgusted him.

Henceforth, he resolved, he would keep Shabbos. He stayed home from work, with Melissa's encouragement, and in their limited way, without much information, they went about observing Shabbos. Melissa embraced their new life with enthusiasm and joy. Slowly, with the help of some kind individuals, they advanced in their Jewish studies.

Their children, however, were already young adults, raised outside the Torah framework. They were all well-established in their way of life. Could this new way of life now be imposed on their children? They probably would resent their parents' interference and come to despise Judaism.

Melissa's dilemma plagued her. It gnawed at her heart and gave her no peace. She wanted to take the right step. Yet, she knew one wrong move, an erroneous word, and her fragile house of cards — so cautiously and delicately constructed — would come toppling down. If she approached the subject casually, they might shrug her off; if she was too overbearing, they would rebel.

"Pray!" the rebbetzin advised. And pray she did. Fervently, she implored Hashem to lead her children on the right path.

Her earnest *tefillos* were answered, her sincerity was rewarded. With trepidation, she measured and weighed her words when sharing her newfound Jewish outlook on life. *Bechasdei Hashem*, all four of their children followed Melissa and Max in their quest for a Torah-true life, continuing in the exalted path of their ancestors.

Perhaps their unique welcome ceremony — that first glimpse of the *Aron Hakodesh*, at the tender age of two days — represented the tiny seed of Yiddishkeit that had been implanted in their *neshamos* right from the start.

THE WINDFALL

Set amidst a sprawling expanse of a 250-acre property, the Victorian-style mansion boasted thirty-five extravagant rooms, which from every angle looked out over panoramic landscapes. Aside from the sounds of the cascading waterfalls that fell into the picturesque streams dotting the exquisite estate, only the twittering of the birds punctuated the silence.

Dennis Marks, the proprietor of Marks Manor, rarely set eyes on the exotic gardens. Nor did he find the time to tread the cobblestone pathways that led to the sizeable swimming pool and nine-hole golf course.

In truth, the Vancouver-based tycoon's most traveled path spanned the distance from one end of the large conference room to the other, where his footfalls fell silently into the depths of the plush carpeting. His bass voice proclaiming strategies and plans to a select group of VIP personnel, coupled with the constant flipping of project outlines at the overhead projector, was his workout.

If there was anything that Dennis valued above his work, it was his son, Seth. The business magnate felt certain that if ever the need arose, Dennis would drop everything to see to the lad's needs. Surely, if the youngster would so much as articulate a wish,

Dennis would rush to please him. But Seth seldom expressed an interest in his Daddy, the big man, whom he rarely saw and hardly knew. Though his father would tell him, on those rare occasions when they did meet, that one day he would help decipher his son's math problems and let his entire business empire wait, Seth knew that the day would never come.

Seth was also aware that his mother seldom caressed his cheeks or bandaged his boyhood bruises. Cynthia Marks had more important matters to take care of, he surmised, and between her parlor meetings, hairdressers' appointments, and shopping excursions, Seth hardly managed to catch a whiff of her soft perfume. Occasionally, he would watch her blow him a kiss, if she happened to notice him standing at the window, watching her hurry away. If it bothered Seth that he caught only glimpses of his mother, he never revealed it to anyone. Not even to Jeannette, his nanny.

Twelve-year-old Seth stood on the lush grass behind the mansion, gazing with pleasure at his beloved Robinson. The deafening sounds of the motor didn't faze him at all; the earphones he wore protected him well. The central hinge of the rotor head began to tilt left and then right, and then it swiftly picked up velocity. Seth liked to think of the sleek helicopter's propellers as a cute teeter-totter — whenever one rotor went up, the other came down — and he often imagined himself sitting atop the machine. Still, the interior of the helicopter was decidedly more comfortable, and he loved to fly.

"Ready to climb on board?" Henry, the family's private pilot, shouted to him over the din.

The boy never needed a second invitation. In a flash, he leaped inside the Robinson and slid in next to Henry.

Henry fastened his seat belt and began the ascent into the light-blue skies, filling himself and his solo passenger with a unique sense of freedom. "With a cruise speed of up to 130 mph, the two-bladed piston helicopter is any pilot's dream," Henry told him. Seth wasn't surprised. He'd read up on helicopters and he knew that the Robinson was simple to fly and that its unique technology allowed for easy descents and climbs.

Seth sensed that, as a helicopter pilot, Henry aspired to see every nook and cranny of Planet Earth. He too, shared that dream. Since his father hardly glanced at the helicopter and his mother was afraid of heights, he knew that Henry didn't have much opportunity to fly. Now that he was old enough to enlist Henry's services, they were both closer to realizing their dream. Fearless and adventurous, Seth requested a weekly tour, thoroughly delighting in their aviation adventures together.

"One day I will be a pilot just like you," the youngster often informed Henry.

"Say, you are one ambitious guy," the pilot would fondly reply.

"You'll teach me how, won't you, Henry?" was Seth's oft-repeated mantra.

Henry would merely shrug. Seth knew that only the best pilot instructor would do for him. Still, he admired Henry, who would always listen good-naturedly to his elaborate plans.

"You'll be proud of me yet," he let Henry know. "It won't be too long in coming. One day you'll hear about the brave pilot who flew off the naval ship near Guatemala, joined the fire service in Alaska, and rescued climbers on Mt. Everest." The wheels in his young mind could spin as fast as the Robinson's rotors. Henry merely chuckled in reply.

The red ball of fire gradually made its descent before nobly dipping below the horizon. Seth, now eighteen, was dressed in a collared khaki-and-beige shirt that accentuated his tanned face.

He sat mesmerized; his favorite scene, the sight of the sunset painting its striking colors across the sky never failed to inspire him with profound awe. The cool, late-afternoon breeze tousled his hair, and the deep, velvety blue waters gently lapped at the sides of his luxurious yacht, lulling him into a tranquil stupor.

His companions, too, sat leisurely viewing the sunset while enjoying cocktails and hors d'oeuvres. They were sailing the Regatta Lake in celebration of their forthcoming trip to Europe, Maguire Academy's annual football tour.

"Say, Seth, you will have someone look after her while we are gone, won't you?" Nat asked, stroking the yacht. Seth looked over at the lanky boy who had interrupted his silent reverie.

"That's all taken care of, buddy," Seth rejoined, reaching for his cocktail on the tray at the side of his seat.

"Oh, good," Nat said. His long fingers caressed the polished wood of the cruiser. "She'll be nice and ready for us when we return from the football tour out there on Europe's soil."

"Well, actually …" Seth began. Slowly he lifted his gaze from the water. The familiar impish grin returned to his face. "I'm not sure I will be joining you on the return trip."

Nat's hand paused in its reach for his drink. Stanley's inquisitive eyes opened wide with curiosity as the glass of wine in his hand remained suspended in midair.

"You don't say! Don't tell me you've decided to stay in an exclusive European university. Or that you got sick of your ol' friends here at Maguire Academy," Nat said, looking intently at Seth. "Do you think you will find better friends over there?"

"Don't make a federal case out of this," Seth said. "It is just that Dad asked me if I can hop over to Israel after the football tour. I won't be there for very long. Maybe one night … or two. Dad wants me to represent him at this award dedication dinner; it's just one of those boring events. He can't attend it in person, but wanted to be part of it anyway, that's all," he concluded plaintively.

"What did your father donate this time? "To whom?" "Where will this dinner take place?" his friends demanded.

"Dad donated a tree grove to the Jewish National Fund," Seth replied. "The dinner will take place at the Garden Luxury Hotel in Jerusalem. It's really no big deal."

The glow of twilight enveloped the boat and they began heading back to shore.

Seth Marks, however, did not come back two days after the rest of his football team returned. Neither did he arrive two weeks or even two months later. "My place now is right here, within the walls of this yeshivah building," he wrote to his parents.

Back in Vancouver, Dennis Marks' blood pressure climbed to unprecedented heights. The enraged business magnate threatened to file a suit against the Jewish National Fund — it was their dinner that had allegedly instigated his son's decision to remain in Israel.

Cynthia Marks merely shrugged. "If Seth is happy, so am I. It is his life to live as he sees fit," she confided to her seamstress while the latter fitted Cynthia's new evening gown one morning.

Seth's friends remained calm, sure that he'd be back soon.

His Dad's fury and his mother's indifference notwithstanding, Seth's encounter with Rabbi Meir Reisman at the dinner had altered his life. Rabbi Reisman's words opened his eyes to a way of life entirely different from the one to which he was accustomed. The black-hatted and black-suited Rabbi wasn't in the least the fanatic lunatic he had supposed religious men to be. On the contrary, the wisdom that he poured forth with his words left Seth entranced. At Rabbi Reisman's suggestion, and without the slightest hesitation, Seth attended every introductory course at Yeshivas Toras Chaim.

The dynamic discourses delivered by the rabbis thrust him into a world he had never known existed. Words of crystal-like clarity that echoed across the study halls delighted his soul and beckoned to him to delve deeper into their teachings. Ordinary life faded into the background as Seth, oblivious to all but Torah, plunged into its depths. The invigorating words of Torah resuscitated his soul and filled him with life.

Summer turned to fall and frosted into winter. Numerous business associates tried their hand at appeasing the irate Dennis Marks, but to no avail. He forgot his longstanding philosophies of "live and let live," "my child before business," and "charitable acts never go to waste."

The business magnate who presided over a veritable financial empire refused to send his son a single penny.

Seth remained oblivious to his father's altered philosophy and to his frequent threats to disinherit him. His commitment to bear the yoke of Torah was not limited only to the hours he spent poring over his *sefarim*, studying Torah. Seth, now Shlomo, sincerely sought to conduct his entire life according to the precepts he learned. Whether it was in cultivating *yiras Shamayim*, praying with proper intent, or perfecting his character traits, Shlomo felt obligated to conform to his status as a Torah Jew. He viewed his father's actions as a test, and he further strove to enhance his performance of *mitzvos*.

The erstwhile coddled child now subsisted on the bare minimum, gaining sustenance from his new surroundings and beloved lifestyle. Kind Aunt Marsha sent him care packages, imploring him to keep them secret. Gradually, however, the efforts of some benevolent individuals prevailed. With Hashem's help, they succeeded in defrosting the icy chill that had settled upon Dennis's heart. By the time Shlomo was engaged to Sarah, two years after he had first settled into the yeshivah, his father declared a "cease-fire." A sliver of regret had warmed the father's heart and melted some of its frostiness.

The wedding was a splendid affair, with more than 3,000 people in attendance. In the midst of all the clattering dishes, blaring music, and joyous dancing, Dennis Marks, the father of the groom, rose to his feet. He had an announcement to make.

The sight of the entrepreneur standing poised at the podium brought an abrupt silence to the ballroom.

"Honored guests," he began, "thank you for coming. I will get to the point right away. All of you know that my son Seth has chosen his unique way of life, one that is the antithesis of the lifestyle in which he was raised."

Some people in the audience squirmed. Marks cleared his throat and continued. "He has also chosen to live in a different continent, in the Middle East, a place with ongoing hostility.

"As you all know, both his lifestyle and choice of residence caused a rift between my son and me. Now, during our celebration of his marriage, I wish to present an offer to my son."

Dennis surveyed the crowd staring at him with rapt anticipation. No one stirred as the culinary delights were all but forgotten. Their trays hovering in the air, the waiters stood off to a side at the far end of the ballroom, for fear of shattering the silence. Seth sat motionless, his eyes cast downward.

"I hereby offer my son, Seth Marks, fifty million dollars," he announced. A cacophony of voices erupted in the ballroom. Dennis raised his right hand. "On one condition …" he began.

The noise in the room died instantly.

"On the condition that he and his wife remain right here in Vancouver, Canada — the place where he was born and bred."

A collective gasp reverberated across the wedding hall. After a moment, the multitude of spectators exploded into animated discussion and heated debate.

Shlomo remained seated, his head bowed as if he were focused solely on the pattern of the tablecloth. So many thoughts raced through his mind as his heart vacillated between the two options.

Should he acquiesce to his father's request? $50,000,000! No small treasure! Surely that would be enough to keep him comfortably at his Gemara. Not merely for a couple of years, but

The Windfall 49

for a lifetime! Besides, he knew quite well that his refusal would mean chipping away at the underlying layer of coldness that still remained between father and son.

How happy Sarah, his bride, would be! What an act for the sake of peace this could be! He could attach himself to the small enclave of Orthodox Jews in Vancouver. Perhaps he could even increase Torah and spread its holy light.

Shlomo lifted his face; his dark eyes roamed across the room, the air laden with suspense. The scene before him suddenly blurred. Another crowd, a crowd in a distant world, seemed to merge with the guests sitting before him.

In a small, cobblestoned side street in Jerusalem, a flock of people had gathered on Simchas Torah. The exuberant men were dancing with true, uplifting ecstasy. Faster and faster went the circle. Dancing and leaping, their *tzitzis* flying in the air, the black-garbed men exulted with their Creator and His Torah. The air was thick with unadulterated happiness and joy.

Shlomo blinked; the vision vanished — but the poignant memory tugged at his heartstrings. The words of the Sages resonated in his ears: *Im ata nosen li kol kesef vezahav vaavanim tovos umargalios shebaolam eini dor ela bimkom Torah!* — Even if you were to give me all the silver and gold, precious stones and pearls in the world, I would dwell nowhere but in a place of Torah (*Pirkei Avos* 6:9).

No, an inner voice screamed, *I cannot remain here in Vancouver. This is not the place for me. I must return to my yeshivah, to my Rabbi, to my esteemed chaverim, as fast as I can.*

He stood up and slowly walked, as if in a dream, to where his father sat waiting for his response. An anxious hush fell over the wedding hall. Hundreds of necks craned to get a better view; all eyes were focused on the unfolding drama before them.

Dennis Marks observed his son's approaching figure with smug satisfaction. He'd known his son would come forward. No one could afford to forgo an offer like this one. A huge smile spread across his face, and his black eyes sparkled with pleasure.

Shlomo sat down next to his father. "My dear father," he spoke in a subdued tone, choosing his words carefully. "I would like to use this auspicious occasion in my life to thank you for everything you have given me from the moment of my birth until this very splendid moment."

The sincere words touched a tender chord in the hearts of many in the audience. They dabbed at the corners of their eyes. Some began coughing nervously, while others cried unabashedly.

Dennis Mark swallowed hard, blinked back unshed tears, and actually reached out to caress his grown son's cheeks. A feeling of warmth surged up from deep within. *In another instant he'll get to the point and promise to remain in this beautiful country,* he gloated silently.

Then, hesitantly, with trepidation evident in his voice, Shlomo resumed talking. "Dad, I will … I will cherish this offer in my heart forever, but …" he fell suddenly silent. It was obviously difficult for him to continue. All eyes followed as Dennis Marks raised a questioning eyebrow at his son. Time seemed to stand still.

Shlomo took a deep breath and forged ahead, his voice cracking, "I am so sorry to say this to you, Dad, but unfortunately, I must decline your offer. I must return to the place where I now belong …."

A LIGHT UNTO THE NATIONS

It was still dark as the inmates slept on the three-tiered planks of unfinished wood. A gusty wind blew through the cracks in the wall. A soft, haunting voice rang softly through the darkness, "*Eizehu mekoman shel zevachim* …."

Yosef stirred. Through closed eyes he listened, mesmerized, drinking in Binyomin's melodious morning prayer. In the short time they'd been together, it became obvious to Yosef that Binyomin's wellspring of hope and faith would never run dry. Yosef's own natural strength of character attracted him to Binyomin's fortitude. To Yosef, Binyomin seemed like a brick wall, his principles and values rock-solid.

This morning, as every other morning, the sound of Binyomin's prayers allowed Yosef to temporarily forget his sordid surroundings, his miserable existence, carrying him way above the squalor, dirt, and lice that pervaded the barracks. Yosef marveled at the way Binyomin recited those prayers from memory. It was hard to focus when one's stomach relentlessly begged for just another morsel of food, yet that prayer was a small ray of light amid unfathomable pain, brutality, and degradation.

Streaks of dawn shone through the dirty windows; it was 5:30. The barrack door crashed open, and the *blockführer*, aided by the block senior and subordinates, shouted at them to get dressed, threateningly thumping the bunks with his truncheon.

A rush of panic followed, and through a haze of despair and bewilderment the inmates hurried to get ready, straighten their "blankets" in military fashion, and march toward the queue for breakfast. If one person felt too tired to move, sticks and truncheons would rouse him into the grim reality of life in Auschwitz.

After the extended morning roll call, amid shouts, curses, and random beatings, Yosef hustled into line for a cup of ersatz coffee. He closed his eyes as he drank the dirty, warm liquid, unwilling to see its contents. A piece of bread mixed with sawdust, hard and moldy, was tossed his way. This was to be his entire food ration for the day. Sometimes he saved it for later, after the hours of physical labor would take their toll. But today his gnawing hunger got the better of him and he chewed on it immediately.

"You!" bellowed the *blockführer*, pointing towards Binyomin. Binyomin froze, almost choking on his bread.

The Nazi looked around and then shouted, "And you!" This time his finger was directed at Yosef. "The two of you will not go out to work today!"

For one heart-stopping second, Yosef waited to hear the reason, if it would be forthcoming at all. Then with some choice curses hurled down at them, they were ordered to remain and clean the barracks.

Thousands of camp inmates looked longingly at the two who stayed behind while they were forced to stand outside for hours and hours for the second roll call, until the *haupsturmführer* would arrive with his dog and hustle them to their work sites.

Until his arrival, they would be subject to the tortures of the Nazi guards, who took great pleasure in tormenting their prisoners as they stood in line, five abreast, to be counted, selected, or simply made to suffer. One never knew what awaited him in the *appellplatz*. Punishments could be handed out at whim. The Nazis meted out lashes, blows, or sadistic tortures. In the frigid weather, the SS men would traipse around in their warm coats while the inmates shivered in the cold. In withering heat, the prisoners would be made to stand or kneel, motionless, for hours — the most horrific torture of all.

But today, Yosef and Binyomin had been given a temporary reprieve. They had commenced work, cleaning the latrines and sweeping the muddy wooden floor, when Yosef noticed a small floorboard that had been pried loose to create a hiding place. His eyes widened in amazement; he stood motionless, unable to move.

Outside he could hear the shouts of *"Schnell! Schnell!"* ("Fast, Fast!") as their fellow inmates were marched off to work in squads, the camp orchestra playing in the background. Some men went to the *steinbrochen,* the stone-chopping corps; others to the *strassenbau,* the road crew who swept the road and kept it clear of snow and debris; and the rest went to the *eisenbahn,* the railroad corps, carrying heavy tools on their broken and battered backs.

"Binyomin," Yosef called, his hands trembling, "come look what I've found." Swiftly, Binyomin rushed across the room to see what his friend's excitement was all about. He, too, was stunned by the sight that met his eyes.

Nestled among the dirt and grime was the unbelievable sight of a real loaf of bread.

A loaf of bread in Auschwitz!

In the ditch of despair and depravity, in a world gone mad with mercilessness and malice, one morsel of bread in Auschwitz could mean the difference between surviving another day and succumbing to starvation.

The ravenous prisoners, living on starvation rations, tried at every opportunity to find something to eat. Some even resorted to rummaging through the refuse bins outside the kitchens. If they were lucky, they would find raw peelings and rotting vegetables to somewhat appease the relentless hunger pangs.

As he faced the Nazi officer, Leon Goldman remembered just two weeks before, when he had descended from the train and stepped onto the blood-soaked soil of Auschwitz.

Theirs hadn't been a cattle car. The French Jews — the aristocratic families — were treated with the Nazi's deceptive silk gloves, until the final moment, when it was too late. Transported by regular railway, Leon and the others were led to believe that their elite group of wealthy landowners and prosperous businessmen were simply being relocated until the peril of intensive bombing passed.

Leon tried to regain his bearings amidst the shouts of the SS men milling about the platform, barking out orders while brandishing their guns and whips. Still sporting his silk top hat and fur coat, Leon lugged his designer suitcase and stylish baggage. But the chaos all around was swiftly closing in on him. Straight ahead, he could see the thick, dark smoke curling up toward the grey sky. A Nazi thrust a rifle butt into his back, and Leon was initiated into the life of Auschwitz, completely stripped of anything resembling civilization.

Now, dressed in prisoners' striped garb, deprived of human dignity, trembling from hunger, cold and fear, the once world-famous banker slowly reached into his pocket.

Leaning calmly against the wall of the barracks, smoking a cigar, with a supercilious sneer on his face, the SS officer studied Leon's every move. The erstwhile banker removed a black velvet pouch and emptied it into the Nazi's outstretched palm. A handful of precious diamonds fell into his hands. The diamonds glinted in the sunlight as the Nazi threw a loaf of bread into Leon's face and strode arrogantly on his way.

———•◦•———

That was the value of a loaf of bread in Auschwitz. And now, in the barracks, Binyomin and Yosef eyed the bread that was more valuable than bags full of diamonds, their hunger tearing at their innards, silently entreating them for even a crumb.

Binyomin turned towards Yosef. "I know whom this belongs to," he said quietly. "It belongs to the Polish prisoner. You know him, he is always ranting and raving against the Jews."

"You mean Yanek, that rabid Jew-hater who is always blaming us for his troubles?"

"Yes, yes, it is his bread. Actually, I saw him prying open this board when I awoke this morning."

The two fell silent, steeped in thought, each waging a silent battle against the Nazis, the Poles, the hunger, and the thirst. Auschwitz was designed to destroy the Jewish people, body and soul, to remove every vestige of their essence, the *tzelem Elokim*, the Divine image, and twist them into creatures of instinct whose only concern was about themselves and their immediate preservation.

After an interminable moment, Binyomin looked at Yosef, "Let's leave the bread!" he said emphatically. "Let the gentiles know that Jews do not steal!"

Neither horror nor hardships, hunger nor hostility, could defeat the gentle yet indomitable soul of the Jew.

That evening, when the work squads returned from their forced labor, Yanek barged into the barracks like an untamed tiger let loose from his cage. Snarling raucously about the injustice of doing forced labor while the Jews got to stay behind, pummeling and shoving anyone in his sight, Yanek ran over to his hiding place and yanked at the floorboard. There, in all its grandeur, lay his precious loaf of bread. Yanek's eyes widened in astonishment, surprised that the Jews had not stolen his bread while in the barracks. Meekly, like a defeated animal, he retreated to his plank and wordlessly nibbled at his bread.

From that day on, at every opportunity, Yanek went around saying, "Did you know that Jews don't steal? Take my word, a Jew will not touch that which does not belong to him!"

DIVINE DELIVERY

*I*t was his gait that gave it away. One glimpse at her husband as he half-staggered through the door, and Avigail knew. It hadn't gone well.

"Come sit down," she told him gently.

"It's no use," he said, collapsing into the nearest chair without so much as glancing up to face his wife.

Avigail quietly placed a steaming cup of tea onto the table in front of him and took a seat facing him. She keenly felt his pain and understood his disappointment. The business her husband had toiled at for the past fifteen years was disintegrating in front of their eyes. SunLight Soap had hit rock bottom.

It had been a good enterprise, the soap industry and Yonatan had invested all his energy into building it up from scratch. SunLight Soap Company had prospered and its massive sales had provided them with a comfortable livelihood. Over the past year, though, business had unexpectedly shifted, swiftly heading downhill. One deal after another fell through, and sales plummeted until almost none of their formerly faithful customers were left.

"So they did not accept your offer?" Avigail asked softly. This much-anticipated appointment had carried with it some measure of hope. When the meeting failed, Yonatan's last remnant of optimism had vanished along with it.

Yonatan lifted his face at last and looked at his wife. Her sea-blue eyes exuded oceans of compassion and glistened with warmth and admiration. His taut features relaxed and he raised his cup toward his lips.

"*HaKadosh Baruch Hu* will help us," he replied with a sudden fresh wave of confidence. "Something will come up, you'll see."

Avigail felt relieved. *So the situation isn't that bad*, she thought, grateful that her husband wasn't despairing. Her husband was usually the pillar of strength in their home; always cheerful, always optimistic and encouraging.

"I am so thankful to Hashem," Avigail finally said as her husband placidly sipped his tea. "Until now, while we always knew that Hashem provides, still, in the back of our minds, we'd be thinking 'SunLight Soap Company.' Sure, Hashem / Sunlight Company fulfilled our requirements — the business was turning out vast profits. All of a sudden, Hashem took SunLight from us and we now have the ability to discern that it's not from SunLight that we obtain all our needs, but rather from Him alone."

"Absolutely," Yonatan concurred. "The illusion of SunLight is undeniably gone. But Hashem knows what we need and He cares for us more than we can ever care for ourselves. By placing our complete trust in Him, we surely won't lack for anything."

As the months passed, the savings that Yonatan had amassed spiraled out of their bank account. The family, now measured and weighed each potential purchase with prudent deliberation.

Avigail became a more proficient cook. She learned how to use the simplest of ingredients to concoct many tasty dishes. She did not mind the long hours these time-consuming meals demanded. She did not complain and she continued expending her efforts towards stretching the modest provisions they still managed to afford. This period in their lives was far from easy.

Their overdraft at the bank climbed steadily. Shortly after Purim, their overdraft reached its limit. They lived from day to day and struggled desperately to notice the many miracles they witnessed daily. It became a frequent occurrence for some shekels to miraculously appear, and they would be able to buy some bread, with perhaps a bit of chumus for the day.

Yonatan and Avigail bravely wrestled with their situation. It became difficult to remain above the mire of depression and despondency that kept pulling them down like quicksand.

In the morning, when Avigail opened her eyes, she would use the solitude of those tranquil moments to explore all the gifts that were hers regardless of the situation, and sincerely thanked Hashem for his abundant kindness.

"Thank you, Hashem, for the seven beautiful children that you granted me. Thank you, Hashem, that we're all healthy; that we can see, hear and walk …. Thank you, Hashem, that they are doing well at school. Thank you for giving me a roof over my head, for the kind neighbors, for the wonderful breeze drifting in through the window …."

In the hushed stillness of those precious times, she would consider every positive aspect of her life and proceed to thank Hashem for the minutest of details. It became her habit, her lifeline, and proved to be her most potent weapon, helping her fight against the deep pit of despair that beckoned, and it kept her afloat.

"Ima, it is Rosh Chodesh Nissan today," Eliyahu informed her one day. "Let's have pizza and falafel, okay? Remember when Abba and you and everyone would all go to Hadar Falafel on Rosh Chodesh? Can we go?"

Avigail regarded her son for a long moment without responding. Suddenly, without any warning, Eli whirled the next question at her.

"Ima," he lowered his tone conspiratorially, "are we poor?"

Avigail moved towards her son and embraced his thin shoulders, lovingly stroking his cheeks.

Divine Delivery 59

"We are not poor, Eli. Our Father is a millionaire!" she replied.

Eliyahu's jaw dropped open and his large brown eyes bulged in their sockets.

"He is?" he whispered.

"Yes, Eliyahu, my dear, He is," Avigail nodded, pointing to the sky. "Our Father in Heaven is even richer than a millionaire. Everything in this world belongs to Him. He can give us anything He wishes. All we have to do is ask Him. Daven to Him, Eli, He will give you everything you need."

Eli skidded away, *tzitzis* flapping as he ran. This was something he had to report to Ari, his neighbor. His Father was a millionaire.

Avigail watched his receding back before turning her eyes heavenward, whispering a silent *tefillah* to her Father, the millionaire.

Yonatan, in the meantime, did not sit idly. Every day, without fail, he would set off, making his rounds to various meetings, appointments, and interviews. Each evening he would return home with rejections, apologies, and empty promises for the future. Times were difficult. The economy was at a low and unemployment rates were high — an inauspicious time for employers to expand their payroll lists.

Then, right before Pesach — the season of renewal — the answer to their prayers appeared, dispatching hopeful sunrays into the lives of Yonatan and Avigail. Yonatan met with Yuda Safrin, a former business associate. Yuda required an office clerk and valued Yonatan's business acumen. Yonatan was enthusiastic and the future looked somewhat promising.

Nonetheless, Pesach was swiftly approaching and Yonatan had no way of paying for all the holiday provisions.

"Abba, when are we going to the supermarket?" eight-year-old Shira wanted to know. "Ahuva told me that they already bought all their Pesach food and her mother is cooking everything today."

"Yeah," Eliyahu joined in, "let's do the shopping today, Abba."

"We need to buy lots of grape juice," Nechama said, removing her thumb from her mouth just long enough to say what she had to say. "Morah Dina said that everyone makes Kiddush at the *seder*, even the *kinderlach*."

"I hear that it takes hours to stand on line in the supermarket these days." It was Elisheva who said that. Eleven-year-old Elisheva was a sensitive child. She sensed the financial difficulties her parents were encountering. She turned to her father, an earnest expression spread over her innocent face. "Abba, are we ... will we be able to go shopping this year?"

Yonatan crouched down to face his young daughter. "Elisheva," he said with conviction, "if we really have *bitachon* that Hashem is going to help, He will. You will see."

Straightening his back, he reached for his attaché case and headed for the door. He had to go to another crucial meeting with Yuda. There was no time to squander.

As Yonatan stepped across the threshold of his home, he was met by an incredible scene. Cartons and cartons brimming with kosher for Pesach food were sprawled at his doorstep. What was going on here?

"Avigail, please come here," he called. "What is this?" he said, pointing to the boxes. "Did you order this?"

"No, of course not," was her reply. "All this? When was the last time there was so much food anywhere in the vicinity of our home?"

"Well, there must be some mistake here." Rummaging through the first box, he said, "Let's look for a phone number or a name."

The two were instantly joined by the rest of the family who stared, wide-eyed. Eliyahu waltzed around the hallway. "Hashem is here, Hashem is there, Hashem is truly everywhere," he sang as he clapped his hands to the tune. "You see Abba, our millionaire

Divine Delivery 61

Father doesn't have any problem. If He wants, He sends all this food for us!"

Awed, Elisheva stood rooted to her spot. Her deep hazel-brown eyes scanned the boxes, then darted to her father and back to the boxes. "Could this really be happening?"

Nechama stood sucking her thumb with such fervor it was a marvel it didn't come off.

"Hold on, everybody," Yonatan shouted over the din. "No one said it is ours. There may have been a mix-up in the delivery."

For a moment stunned silence reigned in the hallway.

"Hashem is here, Hashem is there, Hashem is truly everywhere ..." Eliyahu continued his mantra once again. "Hashem will help, you will see," his clear voice rang out in childish glee.

There was no name or phone number anywhere on the cartons. Yonatan pulled them all to one side and hurried off to his meeting. They would have to wait until someone would call and tell them what to do with the packages. Avigail carried on with the scrubbing and cleaning, the children all pitching in.

Sure enough, the phone rang a few hours later.

"Hello," a deep voice said into the phone. "This is Mr. Barone. I believe you have our order. The delivery boy from *L'Maan Achai* mistakenly delivered it to your address at Givat Mordechai 31 instead of Pisgat Mordechai 31."

"Oh I see. The order that arrived here this morning is yours. All right." Avigail replied. "I am sorry we couldn't phone you earlier; we couldn't find any information on the box."

"Unbelievable!" said Mr. Barone sounding angry. "Well, can you bring it to us? It's our Pesach order, you know."

Avigail knew. She also knew that she could not possibly deliver the order to him.

"Why don't you call the supermarket and have them come pick it up? I have no way of getting this over to you."

"Oh, all right, I'll do that," said the irate caller.

Exasperated, Mr. Barone hung up the phone. What a nuisance.

Why did he need this nuisance at the busiest time of the year? He had so much to do, yet he had promised his wife to help her peel the mounds of vegetables that she needed to prepare for her cooking. But their grocery order had never arrived.

Annoyed, he punched the numbers of the supermarket into his phone.

"Hello, this is Mr. Barone. I just spoke to you about my order. Yes, I succeeded in tracking it down, but they won't bring it to us. Please send someone immediately to pick it up at Givat Mordechai 31 and deliver it to us."

"What? I don't understand," the clerk shouted over the din in his store. "You want us to go pick up the order from the other end of town and bring it to you? Do you realize it is three days before Pesach? Do you know what's going on here? With the traffic, it would take us a couple of hours to do that, and that's time we don't have."

"Do you realize how long we've been waiting for our order?" Mr. Barone's voice rose several decibels. "You call this service?"

The clerk was exasperated. "Let me transfer you to the manager. Hold on, please."

The manager came on the line and Mr. Barone let go a string of complaints dating back over the past few years. "… and if you do not deliver this order immediatly," he said, ending his tirade, "you can be sure that this will be the last time we'll ever shop in your store. I have had enough."

"Mr. Barone," the manager suavely replied, "I understand your frustration. I will see to it that we pack up the identical order and have it delivered to you immediately. Your order will be at your door within a half-hour. My clerk simply meant that it is just too much of a bother to send our men to the other end of town and bring it to you. Again, we apologize for the inconvenience this has caused you. You can be sure it will not happen again."

Somewhat appeased, Mr. Barone relented. "All right," he

Divine Delivery 63

mumbled into the phone, "Half-an-hour and not one minute longer."

"You have my word. And … um … Mr. Barone," the manager added as an afterthought, "Can you just do me one favor?"

"What is it?" Mr. Barone rolled his eyes.

"Just do me one favor. Call up the other family, the one on Givat Mordechai. I am really pressed for time and you have their phone number handy, don't you? Please phone them again and tell them they can keep the order, courtesy of *L'maan Achai* Minimarket."

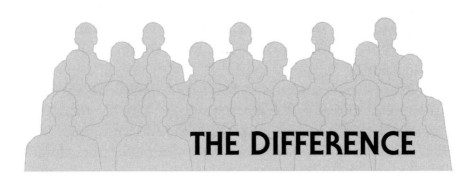

THE DIFFERENCE

Stories of *tzaddikim* lead to many destinations. Some stories show the wondrous workings of *tzaddikim*, some capture the morality and holiness of righteous individuals, and still others echo the words of the Sages: *Tzaddik gozer veHaKadosh Baruch Hu mekayeim*, "A *tzaddik* decrees; the Almighty fulfills." The following story is a story of *emunas chachamim*, one that depicts the pure faith in the heart of a *Yid*.

This purity is not one that can be mimicked or imitated. It has to be real. When a *Yid* approaches his rebbe to ask for a *berachah*, it is his sincerity that counts.

"Oh here you are, Sarah'le! I was looking all over for you," Chaya exclaimed. Sitting next to her on the little red chair, Chaya peered closely at her friend.

"Daydreaming again?"

"Uh huh. The nicest dream. Wanna hear it?"

Chaya nodded.

"I'm walking down the street wheeling a beautiful baby carriage," Sarah'le gushed, barely catching her breath between words. "A real one! And there are tons of little girls with red ribbons tied in their hair. Blonde hair that shines in the sun." She paused for a moment, seemingly to relish the memory of her fantasy. "They were all mine," she added as an afterthought. "And they were holding on to the sides of the carriage and skipping along."

Sarah'le's eyes sparkled and her friend looked on dreamily, savoring each thread in the tapestry of the story her friend was weaving. Hours passed by in this way, the two little heads bent close together as they whispered their dreams of their future, filled with children and laughter.

As the years advanced and their reveries developed into more sophisticated hopes and aspirations, dreaming remained their favorite pastime.

When Sarah married, she immediately designated one room in the apartment as the "children's room," investing all her spare time into its interior design. In a way, her mind was constantly within that room. One day, on her way home from work, she passed a garage sale and instantly spotted a rocking horse. Without the slightest hesitation, she purchased it and then joyfully lugged it home. At another occasion, she came across a charming piece of fabric at a bargain shop. Her next few days were spent bent over a borrowed old sewing machine. With a faraway look in her eyes, she whimsically designed and sewed dainty little curtains for the "children's room."

Time passed. One year after another. The glint in her eyes faded, as did the cheerfully painted walls in the room of her fantasies. Each week, as she dusted the toys on the shelf, she tried to dust away the heartache that seemed to have settled in a corner of her soul.

Menachem, her husband, stood by her side, a constant pillar of strength, and attempted to soothe his wife's aching heart. He, too, longed for a family to call his own. "Soon it will come to be," he would gently intone. "With Hashem's help we will be parents soon, you will see."

When the intense pain threatened to envelop her completely, she would escape for a brief respite and run to visit her childhood friend, Chaya. For hours, they would sit and unspool their dreams in childlike animation. Chaya proved to be a genuine support and keenly felt Sarah'les pain. The sincere empathy and heartfelt understanding that Chaya felt was truly sincere ... for Chaya too had thus far remained childless.

As their tenth anniversary drew near, Menachem resolved to travel with his wife to *Eretz Yisrael*. There they would spend Pesach and participate at the seder of his Rebbe, the Vizhnitzer Rebbe, Reb Chaim Meir.

A large table, dotted with numerous Haggadah's and silver kiddush cups, stood in the center of the large room. Lavish Pesach dishes graced the long table, the exquisite cup of *Eliyahu* majestically dominating the center. Chassidim in *shtreimlech* and black frocks milled about as they waited for their venerable Rebbe to enter and begin the seder.

Finally, the Rebbe arrived, surrounded by a small entourage of faithful Chassidim and promptly began. "*Kadesh* ...."

Menachem slowly inched closer toward the spot where the Rebbe had placed the Afikomen matzah. As he reached it, he stretched out his trembling hands and in one swift movement deftly grasped the outer fringe of the matzah cover. The prized treasure found a temporary haven within a safe fold of his frock coat. Then he held his breath and waited. He waited while the sweet voice of a child melodiously recited the *Mah Nishtanah*. He waited as the Rebbe chanted the Haggadah, pausing at timely intervals to brilliantly expound on certain phrases. Menachem waited for the meal to be served. With a great deal of apprehension, he waited.

At long last, the anticipated moment arrived. The Rebbe was asking for the Afikomen. Menachem edged his way from among the throngs of Chassidim, slowly advancing toward the Rebbe. All eyes were upon him and the silence in the room was palpable.

Too soon, he was standing respectfully at his Rebbe's side. "I have the Afikomen," he whispered into the hushed stillness. The Rebbe nodded. "But I want something in return," he added, a tremor in his voice. The Rebbe smiled, as if to say, *Go on, don't be afraid.*

Encouraged, Menachem continued. "I want a child. Please …"

"*Children!*" His wife's voice sounded in his mind. She had implored her to make his request properly. She would not be satisfied with merely "a child." She wanted *children.* When the Rebbe would beseech Hashem in heartfelt prayer, his pleas would reach the Heavenly Throne. She wanted the Rebbe to pray that she be blessed with a family of children, not just a single child.

The Rebbe closed his eyes and raised his hand. "May the *Ribbono Shel Olam* grant that you be blessed with healthy children, *zara chaya vekayama,* and may you raise them to be *marbeh kvod Shamayim!*" The precious *berachah* reverberated across the room and some Chassidim were seen dabbing at warm, sentimental tears.

With a song in their hearts and joy-filled faces, the couple returned to their hometown. Sarah rushed to her friend's home. Breathlessly she related what had transpired at the Rebbe's seder. Chaya was skeptical, but she kept her dubious thoughts to herself, not wanting to mar the newfound joy her friend radiated.

True to the Rebbe's word, within a year, Sarah held a beautiful child in her arms. *And this is just the beginning,* Sarah repeated to herself as she devoted every fiber of her being to caring for her precious infant.

Chaya was amazed. "Perhaps we, too, should try this method," she implored her husband, Shimon. "Let's also travel to *Eretz Yisrael* for the seder." Shimon, however, remain unimpressed. Only after he grew tired of his wife's endless pleadings did he agree to travel with her, on the condition that his wife not build up her hopes too high.

The following year, the duplicate scene replayed itself at the Rebbe's court. The childless couple returned and waited. The months grew into a year and the year into two, and still they waited. No change occurred in their situation — Chaya's arms remained empty and Shimon's eyes retained their vacant stare.

Shortly after Sarah gave birth to her third child, Shimon finally acquiesced to his wife's numerous entreaties to travel to the Rebbe once again and ask for an explanation.

When Shimon entered the Rebbe's study and approached his mentor. "As of now, we have not yet merited to see the fulfillment of the Rebbe's *berachah*," Shimon explained. "Why did it turn out differently for them?" he asked, after reminding the Rebbe of Menachem's identical request.

A shadow crossed the Rebbe's face. His eyes expressed profound sadness, and a deep sigh escaped from the core of his *neshamah,* a sigh that spoke of the compassion and distress he felt for the suffering *Yid* standing before him.

"The difference," he said gently, "is that Menachem and Sarah *believed*. And that is why you have not yet seen your salvation."

In all our deeds, "*Rachmana Liba Ba'i*," Hashem desires the intentions of the heart. A story is told about the Satmar Rebbe. At a wedding he attended, he was approached by a very talented *badchan* (a jester who traditionally entertains at weddings) who asked the Rebbe's permission to mimic the Rebbe's renditions of the prayers of Hoshana Rabbah to entertain the *chassan* and *kallah*. The Rebbe agreed and soon the audience in the wedding hall were doubling over with laughter.

In the midst of this amusement, the *badchan* noticed out of the corner of his eyes that the Rebbe was crying! Devastated, the *badchan* rushed over to the Rebbe. He was extremely distraught, believing that he had hurt the Rebbe's feelings.

"Rebbe, Rebbe," he pleaded, "please forgive me. This was not what I meant. I did not intend to hurt the Rebbe's feelings. Will the Rebbe please forgive me?"

The Rebbe gazed at the *badchan* through tear-filled eyes. "No, no," he said. "That is not why I am crying. I am crying because I see that you imitate me so well, and I am wondering — perhaps when I pray, my prayers aren't really sincere. Maybe *I* imitate myself too …."

A Rebbe's blessing is not merely a *segulah* (a spiritual remedy). One has to really believe that the Rebbe is an emissary — a *tzinor* — that draws down the blessings from Hashem. That faith cannot simply be imitated in a superficial manner.

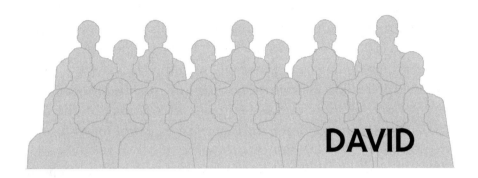

DAVID

Without exception, everyone who endured the tremendous trials and tribulations of the Holocaust has a story to tell. Yet through all those years since liberation, my grandfather could rarely bring himself to tell of his own painful account of survival. Gradually, despite his reluctance to talk, and through bits and pieces of information, a remarkable story of faith and surrender to the Divine Will emerged.

Ironically, the sun was shining on Europe that day. The calm skies were a beautiful shade of blue. That such a phenomenon was possible seemed inconceivable to the weary group of inmates placing one foot in front of the other in their desperate march for survival. Yet the clear skies served as a small reprieve to their exhausting ordeal. For days it had snowed relentlessly on their shivering, thin-clad backs, their ragged striped uniforms their only protection against the elements.

It was hard to believe that the sun was capable of shining, that the world continued to exist, and that humanity was capable of going on with its carefree lives. It seemed as though the death march passing before the citizens of Europe was just a pesky nuisance to their own peaceful lives.

Amongst this forlorn group of shattered victims was David, a youngster of sixteen, precariously clinging to life. Stumbling along, weak with hunger and exhaustion, he felt his strength beginning to ebb. It seemed to David that he had been walking for an eternity. That the only thing he had ever done in his life was walk; one foot forward and the other following numbly, step by step. Each agonizing step a triumph, with the Heavens as a silent witness, applauding his victory, lauding him on. His bloodstained imprints on the snow mingled with the bloodstains of the age-old *Galus Yid* treading down the long road of a prolonged history of adversity.

The shouts of the SS troops blended with the cacophony of the sounds of the Jews' tormentors throughout the ages. The sounds of blood libels, Cossacks wildly stampeding through villages, drunken peasants with torches in hand, all combined into a deafening crescendo. It was the perpetual dance of hatred, anti-Semitism, and bloodlust.

In quiet contrast, David was struggling to overcome his hunger pangs, and transcending the painful sensations of human suffering. His lips uttered the eternal words of Tefillas Minchah as he forged ahead. He did not know it at the time, but those were moments so Divine that many years later he longed to relive that incredible feeling of elevation. To have the *z'chus*, to be capable of davening such an exalted Minchah once again. That tefillah of Minchah had been such a wonderful and inspirational *taanug ruchani* that words simply fail to define the experience.

Yet, despite his inner strength, physical reality was threatening to take over. He felt himself succumbing to the ravages of his tortured body. His body simply failed to respond to the lofty aspirations of his mind, which impelled him to keep going.

Unexpectedly he suddenly felt the strong presence of two escorts, one at either side, protecting him and encouraging him on. He knew at once, beyond a shadow of a doubt, that those guards were true heavenly angels — direct messengers from Hashem. Though he could not explain the phenomenon, neither then nor later, the experience was unmistakably real and the words of *"Ki malachov yetzave loch lishmorcha bechal derachecha,"* flashed across his mind. "For He commands His angels concerning you to protect you in all your paths" (*Tehillim* 91:11). Suddenly it became clear to him that these guardians had been there beside him throughout the whole grueling experience, assisting him and aiding him all along.

Indeed, after the war the Belzer Rebbe remarked that every survivor of the Holocaust had been protected by two *malachei hashareis* standing by his side and guarding him throughout his ordeal.

There is no doubt that all those who survived this devastating *churban* can recall many wondrous events of extraordinary *nissim geluim* throughout their unfathomable experience. Much has been written about it, yet those who were not there have been unable to grasp even a glimmer of comprehension of the actual gruesome experience they endured. Yet, like flashes of lightening in a dark forest, these unmasked displays of *chasdei Hashem* flickered in their hearts and kept them going when they no longer felt it possible. *A poor person and one who is broken ... Hashem illuminates their eyes ...* (*Mishlei* 29:13).

There were other miracles, too, that David encountered during those traumatic times and during which he strongly felt the hand of Hashem leading him and directing his every move.

One frightful episode occurred when David left his barracks briefly in order to daven Minchah behind a tank standing outside. He returned to a dreadfully eerie silence. Gradually his mind registered the appalling sight greeting his shocked eyes. As comprehension set in, his entire body gave way to violent trembling when he realized that every one of his fellow inmates was lying dead before him. The Nazis, it seemed, had paid them a visit while he was outside conversing with *HaKadosh Baruch Hu.*

Another incident took place in Auschwitz. There had been a *selektion* and he had been shoved to the left, slated for the gas chambers. It came as no real surprise. David was a frail-looking boy; his slender frame was not likely to deem him a worthwhile resource for the Nazi work machine.

Soon afterwards he found himself in the dreaded Block 25. Block 25 was notorious as the last chapter in the tragic saga of Auschwitz. David was among those condemned, awaiting his end, resigned to the fact that within twenty-four hours he would be killed in the crematorium. David felt no fear, no dread, and no anguish, only a strong sense of serenity. He was completely at peace with himself.

That evening David thought about his young life and his mind led him back, over the dismal moments and past the dark tunnels of his recent past, carrying him in sweet nostalgia to the memories of his beautiful childhood. His father's kind face, his mother's loving smile, the laughter and happiness of days gone by. He was entirely swept away from his morbid and melancholy surroundings to an enchanting setting created by memories of the past. He inhaled the heavenly aroma of freshly baked delicacies and the sweet smell of wine at the resplendent Shabbos table; he heard the distant echoes of the melodious strains of Torah in a home filled with peace and harmony.

From childhood, David, the youngest in a family of *Talmidei Chachamim*, had been nurtured with *kavod haTorah* and surrounded with the melody of Torah study. David had imbibed a passionate love for Hashem's mitzvos and the meaning of *emunah* and *bitachon* from his cradle. Every bone and sinew was infused with a combination of love and awe for Hashem, coupled with a longing to serve Him with joy. The words, *vechai bahem*, "and you shall live with them [the words of the Torah]," were a real part of his essence. Torah was life and life was Torah. The walls of his home spoke of a higher purpose and reverberated with the sounds of Torah, *Avodah*, and *Gemillus Chassadim*.

He had a sense of pride in his family of Torah scholars. The legendary tales related to him about his forebears made him determined to remain steadfast in the high standards of *avodas Hashem* set by those distinguished ancestors.

But now it was all over. All his hopes and aspirations would be gone in a few hours, when the showerheads would emit their poisonous chemicals. He had no misgivings — if that was the will of the *Ribbono Shel Olam*, it would be his will as well. Like a faithful soldier he was obedient, standing ready to serve his Creator by returning his life to his Maker with love and acceptance.

A sudden skirmish for the slush of watery mixture called soup shook him from his reverie. He sat still, regarding his fellow inmates as if he were viewing the scene from behind an invisible curtain. He suddenly recalled a story he had heard repeatedly throughout his youth. It was the story of how his grandfather and uncles had abstained from eating so that they would appear sick and thus avoid conscription in the army and forestall the consequent spiritual demise that would surely follow. They had kept themselves alive by breaking their fast in the evenings on some dry crusts of bread and black tea, keeping to this austere regimen for an entire year!

David sat in silent rumination, pondering his own current circumstances. He was young, yet he had tried hard to remain loyal to whatever possible vestige of *Yiddishkeit* he was able to uphold in this *gehennom*. He had considered the problem of kosher food, and he had decided that he would eat whatever he could in his attempt to stay alive. Now, though, since he was slated to be exterminated the following day, this reasoning was no longer valid, so he preferred to forego his ration of *treife* soup.

Softly he whispered the *viduy* prayers and went to sleep in peace. He felt ready for his journey to meet his Creator. Soon he would be together again with his dear father and mother, his sisters and his brothers ....

It was the astonishing dream that jolted him awake, shaking him from his calm passivity and galvanizing him to act. In uncharacteristic urgency, his glance darted quickly around the room, searching for a way out. His father had appeared to him in a dream.

"Run, my child!" he had urged. "Escape!"

Amidst the stillness of sleeping inmates, he made out some whispering sounds of a small group of boys huddled together in hushed conversation. Silently he inched his way closer until he was able to catch some snatches of their anxious consultation.

"The chimney …."

"How can we succeed …?"

"… the guard?"

Slowly, through bits and pieces, he managed to form a clear picture. Apparently the watchman had unexpectedly fallen asleep and those dauntless boys were planning their escape through the chimney!

Spurred on by the image of his father, now fresh in his mind, he felt compelled to join them in their risky venture. He reckoned there was nothing to lose. *It would be either the bullet or the gas*, he supposed.

One by one the boys grasped at their last chance for life. Each boy climbed deftly, in surreal silence, up through the narrow chimney of formidable Block 25, while the next in line, in a mixture of trepidation and courage, waited for his turn.

Each individual made his (literally) narrow escape skyward through the chimney and then the daring leap from the roof down to the ground, after which they fled into the neighboring barracks and mingled with the other striped-pajama-clad inmates.

Seven boys made it out on that fateful night. Seven boys received a new lease on life. Sadly, the eighth one was shot. David was the seventh boy! His saintly father had received permission from *Shamayim* to come to his son in a dream, to rouse him and drag him from the ashes.

THE DEAL OF A LIFETIME

"Neal Rosen from Prudential is on the line," the secretary's voice on the intercom called out. "He claims he has an offer you can't miss!"

Ah, a breath of fresh air, Ephraim thought, pushing aside the work in which he had been engrossed. He reached for the phone and retrieved the pencil from behind his ear, ready to jot down any relevant information.

"Good evening, Neal."

"Hi, Ephraim. I'm calling with the deal of the year. We're talking big. You know that Florida is a hot market, right? Anyway, I have this 155,000-square foot, food-anchored shopping center. You need to invest only $30,000 to put it through. What do you say?"

"Send me the details and we'll take it from there."

Ephraim replaced his pencil behind his ear, crossed his legs, and swiveled comfortably in his chair. Neal Rosen was an enthusiastic young agent. He possessed vibrancy and charm and presented every deal in the most glowing terms. He would probably follow up on his phone call pretty soon. It was the way he worked — with a consistency that challenged indifference, yet a politeness that neutralized resentment.

Rosen delivered on his promise and quickly e-mailed the precise facts and figures. Ephraim liked the deal and immediately forwarded the information to his lawyer.

His attorney, Leo Savoy, gave him the go-ahead in record time. In fact, he urged Ephraim to fly down to Miami to look over the situation himself and clinch the deal at once.

"The deal looks good. It is a go," Ephraim informed Rosen when the latter called to find out.

"I suggest you schedule a meeting in Miami right away," Rosen replied. "Stay on the phone. I'll get the seller on the other line and see if we can coordinate this."

Ephraim drummed his fingers on the polished surface of his mahogany desk while he waited for Rosen. It was a great deal. With all the offers coming his way these days, he had to sift through them carefully to discover a real gem. This one promised to be just that.

Purchasing the Solomon Plaza in downtown Miami would give him a return of over 100% — in only one-and-a-half years! This was one terrific deal. The location was optimal, the return on his money remarkable. The investment would open up a new avenue for more great projects to come. When Rosen's voice came back on the line, Ephraim suddenly realized that he had shifted to the edge of his chair.

"Mr. Lerner. Tuesday morning at 50 Pine Street in downtown Miami. Is that good for you? A Mr. Maroony will wait for you at the airport and escort you to the hotel."

Ephraim Lerner waited impatiently on line at the Delta Airlines counter. With boredom edged out by agitation, he watched as the clerk checked in the middle-aged couple ahead of him.

Finally the couple was directed to the correct gate and Ephraim stepped up to the counter. With just a small carry-on bag, check-in was a breeze and the clerk cheerfully handed him his boarding pass. "Please proceed to gate B23," she said in clipped tones. "Boarding time is at 11:10, sir. Delta Airlines thanks you for choosing Delta. Have a nice flight. Next, please ...."

Ephraim slung the strap of his bag over his shoulder and accepted his boarding pass and passport from the clerk, keeping them in his right hand ready for inspection.

Never one to patronize the gift shops sprawled across the vast airport, Ephraim headed straight to the gate to await the boarding call. His mind was completely occupied with his deal.

He scanned the large overhead screen that showed arrivals and departures. He prided himself on being an expert in time management. Characteristically, he had arrived at the airport with little time to spare. He could not imagine waiting around. Yet, he always allowed adequate time to get himself oriented — rushing into an already full plane while panting and gasping for breath was anathema to Ephraim.

Ephraim took a seat on a black couch in the waiting lounge and placed his carry-on bag in front of him.

"Good day," he greeted the Jewish gentleman seated beside him.

"Uh hum," was the laconic reply.

Ephraim twisted around in his chair to get a better look at this unhappy guy.

"Ephraim Lerner," he said cordially, extending his hand in greeting. "And you are?"

"Chaim Gavriel."

"Nice to meet you."

"Yeah."

Ephraim watched as the man sighed heavily, a deep, wrenching sigh that seemed to come out from the deepest part of his being. The profound sadness that cloaked the unknown traveler evoked Ephraim's sympathy.

He leaned toward Chaim Gavriel, "You don't seem to be traveling to a simchah; are you?"

The Deal of a Lifetime

"Nah," the man answered, averting his eyes.

For a moment Ephraim hesitated. Who was he to probe another's sorrow? Everyone carried his own burdens.

Still, he could not help but think, *Do not stand idly by while your brother's blood is being spilled* (*Vayikra* 19:16). With a quick prayer for Heavenly assistance, Ephraim decided to try again.

"There is something troubling you, Chaim Gavriel," he said, careful to keep his tone devoid of emotion.

The man fidgeted in his seat.

Ephraim sank back into his seat. *Try again,* he said to himself.

"Flying to Miami?" he asked nonchalantly, his eyes focusing straight ahead.

"Got myself some business to take care of," Chaim Gavriel said finally.

From the corners of his eyes, Ephraim observed the man's expression. The latter's mouth opened and closed as the battle between talking and guarding his story apparently stormed within. Ephraim's instincts, honed from years of his own struggles, prodded him on.

"And that is?"

"The last thing I ever dreamed of."

"Hmm …?"

Chaim Gavriel turned to face Ephraim. He saw care and concern reflected in two deep pools that stared back at him. Then, suddenly, he decided to share his pain.

"It's my son. The tests just came back. The only option we have is surgery. I tell you, I would rather die than knock on a door and beg. But it is my son that is dying, not I. And I cannot allow it. No one should ever know this kind of shock. The pain. The all-consuming worry. We haven't slept since we heard. My wife's tears could fill an ocean. But Hashem has been so kind to us …

"All it takes is thirty thousand dollars to buy him a ticket to life, *be'ezrat Hashem*. I was advised to go to Miami to ask for a donation from a rich man there. For a man like me, who has never been outside the halls of Torah, it is hard to fly somewhere to collect money. But I have to ask — saving one life is like saving the whole world, you know."

The leaden words, which had been bottled up for some time, spilled forth in a rush of pain and apprehension. They seemed to hover in the air as Ephraim fell into deep contemplation.

Thirty thousand dollars! Exactly the amount he had carefully placed in his bag that morning; the amount that would give him a share in the 150,000-square foot shopping center in downtown Miami. An investment with a return of over 100% in only one-and-a-half years.

Here before him was truly a great deal — an investment for eternity. Money comes and goes. Saving a life would give him substantial luggage to present at the check-in counter in Heaven.

The turmoil raged in his heart. Was he obligated to give up this money to help a stranger? He wasn't responsible for solving the world's problems. Besides, no one had asked him. Still, what was the Miami deal all about? More money? All that paled in comparison to saving another person's life. *Hashgachah* had dropped another kind of investment opportunity right into his lap. Was he to shrug it off like a pesky fly and be on his way?

Ephraim opened his carry-on bag, revealing the packets of crisp bills.

What about his lawyer and Neal? They would say he was crazy, impulsive, rash.

On the other hand, was he here to impress them or his Father in heaven?

Ephraim bent closer to Chaim Gavriel.

"You need $30,000?" he whispered. "Here, take this."

"What?"

"It's $30,000. Take it, please."

"Whaddayamean?" Chaim Gavriel was stunned.

"Just take it," Ephraim insisted.

The Deal of a Lifetime

Slowly, Chaim Gavriel reached out and wrapped his fingers around the bundles of bills.

"Good," Ephraim exhaled in relief and sank back into his seat. "I was afraid that I would not have the strength to fight my *yetzer hara*," he said, and his eyes sparkled. "May your son have a speedy recovery."

LABOR OF LOVE

My grandmother is an extraordinary woman, a precious reminder of the past, with a discerning eye to the future. But most of all, she is a woman who knows how to live in the present. This is her story.

Clinging to the last vestiges of sleep, Chaim listened to the whistle of the kettle, the clinking of the coffee mugs, and his parents' voices as the two drifted comfortably in and out of conversation. The soft voices floating into his bedroom from the kitchen wrapped him in a mantle of coziness.

In the semi-darkness of his room, he could picture his mother hovering about his father in her usual energetic manner. He could hear her now as her voice rang with decisiveness. "You look tired, Duvid. Have another cup, and here are the sugar cubes."

"It's not the coffee, Chana." His father sounded weary, Chaim could tell.

"What is it then?" Chaim discerned the worry in her tone.

"I don't know," he sighed. "It's not how I thought it would be."

"Our new business?" His mother's voice seemed to relax. "These things take time, you know. You only just started. Give yourself a few months before you start fretting over the loans you can't repay yet. With Hashem's help, everything will work out fine, you will see."

"You are right that it takes time, Chana, but …" his voice trailed off.

"Is it your learning that's bothering you?"

"Um. Hm. When I worked for Yehudah, I was free of pressure, free of worries. I would come home from work and head straight to my beloved *sefarim*." She had been right; Chaim marveled at his mother's keen perception. How did she always read other people's minds so well?

"But you are still learning, Duvid; what is the problem? You haven't given that up. You start learning at four in the morning. Then, in the evening you go back to your learning. If you add up all your hours, you clock in eight hours of learning each day." Chaim heard the hint of pride in his mother's voice. "Just like any *kollel yungerman*," she added.

"You're right, Chana. But it's just not the same. Now my mind is filled with numbers. All these new ideas …. And I am tense. I worry — *Will I make it? When will I be able to repay the loan?* When I sit down to learn, my head isn't all there, don't you see?" The pain in his voice hung in the air.

As the sun dispatched its bright rays through the windows, Chaim's brothers and sisters awoke and padded into the kitchen.

Chana rushed to serve them a nutritious breakfast. Healthful, nourishing meals measured high on her list of priorities. Duvid looked on with pride. *What a caring mother she is to the children*, he thought.

Little Leah wiggled her way onto a chair. "Be careful not to get dirty, Leah," Chana said, slicing a tomato. "You know why? Because you're wearing a nice dress. You have to take care of it and look like your special self." Duvid noticed how she did not say, "Because I cannot clean so much, or because it is not nice to have a stain on your dress." She always seemed to choose just the right words to use.

She placed some cups on the table, then turned to the refrigerator and removed the milk and a bottle of orange juice. "Children," she said gently, "we have one bottle of juice and everybody will share."

Shimon sat, swinging his legs back and forth, munching on his bread. "Abba," he said between bites, "my friends told me that you earn huge amounts of money. Is that right, Abba?" Duvid smiled into his beard. How should it dawn on this young child that his mother counted her pennies? He seemed quite sure that his father was a millionaire. Certainly, that's the feeling Chana gave the children.

"We have everything we need. Hashem takes care of us," Chana responded to Shimon's question.

"But the Davidson's always have watermelon. How come we never have any?" Duvid, who knew that his wife would not answer, "Because we don't have money," waited for the answer with the same curiosity evident in his young brood.

Chana looked up from buttering Gedalyah's bread and gazed at her family with a sparkle in her eyes. "It is not important to eat watermelon. It is important to eat fish. Bread, eggs, and chicken are important foods. Why should we buy something that is not important?"

Duvid was reluctant to leave the exciting chatter at the kitchen table. He loved his children; they represented the embodiment of his boldest dreams. But his sense of purpose drove him on. "Have a good day, children, and learn well." With his attaché case in one hand and a friendly wave of the other, Duvid opened the door of his warm home and stepped into the rigorous, harsh life of the outdoor world.

Chana never sat idle for a moment. An industrious woman, she kept an immaculate home, making do with the little that she had. After she had washed, starched, and pressed the simple cloth she used to cover the dining-room table, it became transformed into elegant table linen. Not only were the old linoleum floors polished to a gleam every day, but each pair of the children's shoes was buffed to shined every night, the shoelaces washed, and every dress and pair of pants neatly pressed.

Moving quietly, Chana attended to her daily tasks with efficiency. It was Thursday and she had a great deal of work to do before the children would be home from school. While the baby slept and quiet reigned in the small house, she used the time well. She worked quickly, sifting the flour, cracking the eggs, and then kneading the dough by hand to bake a batch of yeast cakes for the children's lunchboxes.

My dear mother, how did she work so hard? she reflected, momentarily overcome by a flash flood of memory.

What a carefree child I was, the youngest of five children, doted upon by loving parents and siblings. I never noticed how much toil and effort my mother put into her home. She didn't merely knead 5 kilos of dough like I do; she would knead 50 kilos of flour at once and stand over the hot oven for hours, turning out many loaves of fresh bread. She was always properly dressed, in a neat suit and well-coiffed wig.

Thoughts of her mother invariably led to the most painful memory of all. She had probably relived the ghastly experience thousands of times.

The cattle cars rumbled to an agonizing stop on the rails inside the Auschwitz compound. The doors were violently thrown open by the SS soldiers, their machine guns at the ready. Chana gripped her mother's arm in terror.

"Raus, raus!" ("Out, out!") the Nazis shouted at their human cargo. Bewildered, Chana followed her mother as she rushed out, attempting to avoid the strikes and blows of the soldiers, the snapping jaws of the barking German shepherds. Families were separated immediately, but Chana desperately clung to her mother. She refused to part from her. The air was thick with the deafening, confusing sounds of the Nazi's orders, children wailing, and gun shots punctuating the turmoil.

Chana's mother knew that only the young and fit would be allowed to live. Though Chana was only fourteen years old — below the minimal age for survival — she stood a chance to live only if she went her own way. Suddenly, a Nazi jerked her mother's arm, pulling her into a line that was slowly forming. With the strength of her motherly love, she gently shoved her daughter away.

Chana suddenly noticed that she had been crying. She could never erase that excruciating moment of separation. In her entire life, she had never felt such searing pain as when mother said good bye. Each time she relived that scene, the acute pain stabbed at her again.

Alone now, Chana was marched off to the head of the ramp to be inspected by an SS officer, his uniform impeccably tailored and pressed, shiny black boots belying the brutal heart beating within. Through a haze of tears, Chana watched how Josef Mengele, yemach shimo, the Angel of Death, moved his white-gloved finger to indicate the direction to which he selected each prisoner to go.

"Links, rechts," left or right. Those he deemed healthy enough to work were herded off to one side. Those who were too young, too weak, or too ill to work were shoved to the other side, to die.

From out of nowhere, a woman she had never seen before suddenly approached her.

"How old are you, my child?" she asked kindly.

"Fourteen."

"No," the unfamiliar woman hissed into her ear. "You are sixteen."

Chana stared at the woman, uncomprehendingly. What did that woman want from her? Who was she? What did she care whether she was fourteen or sixteen or twenty-five? The raw pain of separation, the shouts and barking, and the horrible stench, all assaulted her senses. Not for one minute did she dream of death. Her young life stretched out before her. Soon she would be reunited with her mother, his sisters, her father. Soon all this horrible nonsense would come to an end.

"Links, rechts ..." *The line continued to move forward, the same woman suddenly appeared again.*

Labor of Love

"How old are you?"

"Fourt ... sixteen," Chana stammered.

"Sixteen!" The woman repeated.

"Links, rechts ..." The finger kept pointing. Again she appeared at her side. "You are sixteen, you are sixteen, you are sixteen," she repeated dozens of times, drilling it into her young mind.

"You will say you are sixteen, do you hear me?" she said sternly.

All too soon, Chana stood before the Angel of Death himself. "How old are you?" he asked.

Chana straightened her shoulders as far as they would go, "Sixteen!" she said. "Rechts." And she was pushed to the right. To life.

Who was this woman? Chana wondered. She would never know. But in the death factory of Auschwitz, this brave woman had fought her own silent war against the Angel of Death as she played the role of the Angel of Life.

Chana's tears wouldn't stop now. *In the camp too, I cried non-stop. My friends chastised me, "We will throw you out of here, if you keep on like this."*

Yet, now as she thought about it, she realized that her ability to cry had kept her alive. The tears had whittled out a tiny crevice in the monumental wall of sorrow. They provided relief — a smidgen of relief — of the unbearable anguish that threatened to hurl her into a pit of despair. And despair was precisely what she could not afford if she wanted to live.

Many a time, in that gruesome kingdom of human misery, she would close her eyes and dream. She would picture herself together with her mother again, her sisters, her home, but she wouldn't allow herself to think about the chimney, the stench, or the fear that lurked in every corner.

Duvid sat behind the gray steel desk, hunched over a thick ledger, scanning the numbers. Outside his office, the whirring of sewing machines, manned by expressionless laborers, droned on.

He looked up from his books and gazed unseeingly at his sparse office, the new calendar on his desk, the revolving card-index file that he had painstakingly filled with important numbers. Abruptly he rose from his chair and sighed.

On the one hand, he felt grateful to Yehudah, his brother-in-law. His mind brought him back to the day he had approached Yehudah, a few months ago. Before that Yehudah had employed Duvid to sew winter caps in order to eke out a living.

He knew that Chana struggled daily with the paltry wages he managed to bring her and he so wanted to ease her plight. After giving the matter some thought, he had finally resolved to seek the advice of his brother-in-law, Chana's brother.

"I think you should open up your own business." Yehudah had offered without the slightest hesitation. "I'll help you, of course."

Duvid had looked at his brother-in-law in shock, but Yehudah didn't seem to notice. "I think it's a great idea. We'll find a place, I'll give you all my contacts and connections, some start-up cash — and you'll be in business. In a few months' time you'll be earning enough to live comfortably."

Yehudah was as good as his word. He had helped him find this small factory on Havemeyer Street, told him about all the ins and outs of the business, and spent the first few weeks with him, making sure that the venture was off to a good start.

Engrossed in thought, Duvid began to pace back and forth. He stopped near the window that overlooked the bleak street below. It was an overcast day, one that matched his mood, and a slight drizzle had begun to fall.

Yet, he brooded, there was a price to pay for owning a business of his own. With his whole heart and soul, he longed to spend every spare moment engrossed in his Torah studies.

He was consumed with an all-encompassing desire to learn Torah. That was when he became alive. For him Torah was not just the spice of life; it was life itself. Indeed, that was the legacy of his parents, his older brothers, who had all perished in the war. As the descendant of great *talmidei chachamim*, his earliest childhood memories revolved around the palpable joy of the Torah that permeated his home. Those earliest memories were an integral part of him, woven into the fabric of his soul.

When he had worked for Yehudah, his mind was free to delve into the lofty words of Torah while his hands operated the sewing machine. The Gemara, the *Tosafos*, the *Rashis*, would transport him far beyond his immediate environment of dozens of nondescript laborers, producing hundreds of nondescript winter caps.

It wasn't that Chana had ever objected to their meager income. On the contrary, he never heard his wife demand more money or pressure him to try to work faster, put in more hours, or find a better job. In fact, she wouldn't even ask him, "So, how much money did you manage to bring home this week?" Whatever he put into the gray strongbox at the end of the week — that was what she used to run the household. And she used it wisely, thoughtfully weighing her priorities, budgeting the money with skill.

Chana was a wonder woman, he felt. A warm and caring wife, always placing the other person before herself. A true *eishes chayil*. It was she who enabled him to pore over his beloved *sefarim* day and night. Lovingly and with incredible devotion, she chiseled out for him a haven of peace and serenity so that his mind was always free to learn.

The heavenly aroma of the yeast cake baking in the oven permeated the small home. Chana's fingers clutched the iron as her hands vigorously slid it back and forth over the tablecloth's smooth surface. Her mind was far away, in a distant country, in a different time and place.

Another selektion. A request came in for strong, healthy laborers to operate the sewing machines in a nearby factory. Those who were deemed fit enough to work would be sent on a transport to the sewing factory. All others would be sent out through the chimney.

Again it was Mengele presiding over the selection process. Standing tall and erect, while a sea of misery in the form of exhausted and starving inmates washed up at his feet, he pointed his finger, pronouncing judgment on those who would live and those who would not.

Earlier in the week, Chana had burned one foot when a scalding pot of soup had spilled. The camp infirmary, with its pitiful lack of medical supplies, was often the final station before the gas chambers and a dangerous place to enter. Yet Chana knew that her injured foot required treatment. A sympathetic nurse had somehow fashioned a "bandage" and applied it on the injury. Now, in anticipation of the selektion, Chana tore off the dressing and tried to hide her reddened foot.

Mengele, with his cold smile, granted her one glimpse. She was emaciated due to the starvation diet, and her friends had warned her that she was as good as dead. Apparently, Mengele felt the same way. Nonchalantly he pointed to the left, to death, and turned to the next girl in line.

For one interminable moment, Chana's heart stopped beating as the SS women began shoving her toward the group of girls slated for the gas chambers. But suddenly she felt herself becoming infused with an overriding desire to live, a renewed surge of vitality coursing through her every limb.

Without batting an eyelash, she turned to face the "Angel of Death" himself.

"Please," she said, concocting a story on the spot. "We were a family of ten children, and only I stayed alive. Can you let me go along?"

A gasp rose among the girls. The world seemed to stand still. Everyone waited with bated breath to hear the verdict. The arrogant Nazi deigned to gaze down at Chana from his pompous position of power.

"You go along," he pronounced.

Chana darted to the group of girls and quickly mingled amongst them. Even the woman SS guard was taken aback. She rushed over to Chana and thrust her stout finger at Chana's face, "You are a lucky girl!" she said.

As the group of girls waited to board the truck, they applauded her courage. But Chana felt drained. On a whim, Mengele suddenly decided to ride his motorcycle. Round and round he circled the group, relishing the pleasure of taunting the trembling girls. Each time he approached her, Chana's heart fell, but Mengele soon whizzed off again.

The command was given to climb aboard the train. "Relax, we are on our way," the girls told her. But she couldn't. Mengele could change his mind any minute and drag her off the truck. Finally, the truck began to rumble through the gates of Auschwitz. Only then, did Chana relax her taut nerves and the tension subsided.

Then the war had finally come to an end. Standing in the woods where the Nazis had herded them, the group of girls waited for the final shot to end all the misery. Suddenly the rumbling sounds of American jeeps were heard, and in a stupor they watched as their captors, like frightened animals, ran for cover. Of the hundreds of children in Chana's block, only a small number survived.

Rising from the ashes, Chana struggled to makes sense of her life, salvage the shattered pieces, and forge ahead. Recuperation was a slow process in the aftermath of the war. With the realization that she'd never again feel the soft touch of her mother's hand, no longer laugh with her older sisters, Chana felt that her tears would never run dry.

Together with a group of young survivors, she was taken to Sweden. Various groups of people with foreign ideologies approached her and offered the shattered orphan golden promises of happiness and security if she would join them in their way of life. Yet, in her heart, Chana clung fast to her father's words, "Never sell yourself short by sweet words. There is no substitute for *halachic Yiddishkeit*."

Only Hashem's kindness soothed her wounds, and with time she managed to smile again. With iron resolve, she brushed off the cinders of Auschwitz, and her indomitable spirit and youthful vitality emerged once again.

Soon she began to dream again of establishing a home and holding her own young children in her arms. Many matches were proposed. Handsome boys with charismatic smiles and young men who'd managed to regain some of their family's former wealth all wished to win her hand.

Still, Chana knew the type of person with whom she wanted to rebuild her shattered life. She knew what her father would have wanted. To the surprise of her friends, she became engaged to a penniless young refugee — emaciated, weak, slight of frame, and short of stature — with nothing but the shirt on his back

But he was a *talmid chacham*, the first student to enroll in a post-war yeshivah. His life was saturated with a love of Hashem and love of Torah. When the new yeshivah relocated to Antwerp, Chana proudly traveled at his side.

One day, Chana often told herself, she would have a beautiful home. She would envision the finest furniture adorning her dining room, imagined serving gourmet meals on the best china dishes.

But for now, her discriminating European taste would have to be placed on the back burner. For she owned but one spoon, which they took turns using. The one watch they possessed between them, a wedding gift, was stolen. And every night she would wash her one pair of stockings. Joyfully she looked on as her young husband made his way to the yeshivah every morning and returned late at night, exhausted but fulfilled, with a weary smile on his face. A dream home? Fine-looking jewelry? Its luster would be lost if they would come to her at the expense of one minute of his Torah studies.

Eventually they came to the shores of America. Since the family had grown, Duvid, quiet and unassuming, headed to work every morning in order to be able to provide for his family. Earning a livelihood, he felt, was also the will of His Creator. And as with everything else he did, his heart and mind constantly clung to Him, like a faithful soldier always poised to serve his Master.

As soon as Duvid entered his home, he was surrounded by the shining faces of his beloved brood. A steaming, wholesome dinner awaited him as usual. Chana had a flair for serving the simple, nourishing dishes with the grace and finesse of royalty, he thought with appreciation. Here was a woman who, by virtue of her sense of duty and vibrancy, was a regal and aristocratic woman.

Now too, she put down the dishcloth she had been using, and greeted her husband like a royal guest. She took her seat by the table and, not wishing to pry, she waited quietly for her husband to begin talking about his day.

They sat in silence. Duvid's thoughtful expression did not escape her.

"Duvid," she said, her voice soft and tender, "close the business. It is not important. You will go back to your former schedule. You will have more peace of mind for your learning. Go ahead."

Duvid looked up at his wife. He felt torn. How he wished he could adorn his *eishes chayil* with the finest of jewelry.

"Chana, you work so hard. I know it is not easy for you to stretch every dollar. And what about the dinette set you would love to have?"

She leaned forward, the warmth in her eyes reaching out to her husband. "Go back to your Gemara, Duvid. I have everything I need."

DISSOLVED BUT RESOLVED

Edith was shocked to find Nosson doubled over in agony. His large, dark eyes silently implored for relief and his little face was contorted in agony. Yet the six-year-old was bravely struggling to control his pain and stifle his cries. Waves of fear surged through Edith's body, and in one swift movement, she scooped up the little boy and ran out the door.

It was clear to her that Nosson was suffering from excruciating pain. She knew too, that Nosson's tough exterior sheltered a sensitive little heart that often suffered in silence. Hurriedly she shut the door behind her and flew down the stairs and into the streets of Lower Manhattan to hail a cab.

Less than ten minutes later, her pediatrician was advising her to go straight to the emergency room of the nearest hospital. Not surprisingly, the doctor's uncertainty over the diagnosis intensified the pounding of her heart, and as the taxi sped toward the hospital, she tried to keep her distress in check. Not for single moment did she take her eyes from her child. Nosson sat next to her, his slight frame arched over in a strange curve, his hands clenched at his sides, his face ashen, not making a sound.

As the car drew up at the ER entrance, Edith hurriedly carried Nosson from the taxi, having paid the driver a block in advance.

The customary flurry of activity in the emergency room did not in any way impede Edith's sense of purpose as she headed straight toward the nurse and firmly requested that her son be examined at once. The nurse conjured up a doctor out of nowhere, it seemed, and he began the examination. A few minutes later, he arranged to have little Nosson admitted to Room 310.

Roberta, the nurse on duty on the third floor, normally did not waste a moment's thought on any visitor to the ward. Busy dealing with a multitude of patients each day, she hadn't a moment to spare. Today, though, she found herself thinking about the little boy's mother, Edith.

Though the woman was simply dressed, she seemed almost regal. Roberta saw the distress and extreme anxiety drawn on her face, yet at the same time noticed the powerful determination flashing through her eyes. The nurse noticed that although the woman spoke English with a heavy European accent, punctuated with many words in a language unfamiliar to Roberta, she made herself perfectly understood. There was something about Edith that set her apart from all the other anxious parents Roberta normally saw in the ward.

What was it about the quiet dignity of the woman that aroused her curiosity? How had she managed so effectively to evoke a sense of urgency quite unlike the screams, shouts, and hand-flailing of other distressed parents? Roberta wondered about all this as she acted on the physician's request to call additional doctors to Room 310. Evidently the boy's condition was complicated, and the physician wished to consult his colleagues.

What annoyed Edith most was that Dr. Troper hadn't said a single word directly to her, neither during the examination nor after all of the whispered consultations with the other doctors. Dr. Troper's gray eyes stared straight past the mother of the patient as if she did not exist.

In the end, they agreed that Nosson was suffering from acute appendicitis. Unfortunately, the diagnosis was a bit late in coming, and by then his appendix had ruptured, which further complicated his condition. The orderly wheeled Nosson hastily into the operating room, accompanied by his mother's heartfelt prayers.

After the surgery, Nosson's tiny figure lay in the oversized hospital bed, connected to various tubes, which would help to clear the toxins that the ruptured appendix had let loose in his body. No food was allowed, as it could prove to be dangerous and might thwart the cleansing process.

Edith, naturally, stayed by his bedside throughout the entire ordeal. Other visitors came as well, bringing little gifts and happy chatter along with them. Roberta, the nurse, also came to check up on the little one's progress and always stopped to chat with Edith. She admired the intelligent, fastidious woman. In addition, she adored the child, marveling at his clever comments and cheerful spirits.

"That child sure has got a head on his shoulders," she would repeatedly comment to Edith as she left the room, chuckling with amusement.

When Aunt Bella visited, she would sit at Nosson's bedside and chat with Edith in a foreign language. This was, after all, 1950, and adults still believed that their conversations were not meant for little ears to hear. Nosson, however, had a special knack for languages and silently followed every word. He did his best to keep up with the fast flow of adult conversation.

At one point, Aunt Bella suddenly seemed to remember that she had come because of Nosson and begun rummaging about in her elegant bag. Happily, she produced a piece of candy from the depths and dangled it enticingly in front of Nosson, waiting with great anticipation for his little hands to reach forward and grab hold of this rare treat.

Nosson hesitated, his bright eyes the only indication of inner conflict. Then, his tiny chin quivering and in an almost inaudible voice, he bravely asked the question he wasn't sure was polite and yet to him, was essential. He had to know the answer before he could accept the proffered treat.

"Mama, is it kosher?"

Aunt Bella tilted her head back and laughed heartily, while Edith assured him that it was. In those days there were few widely known kosher brands of candy on the market, and Nosson needed to find out for himself.

But kosher or not, Nosson knew he could not enjoy the candy yet. He was forbidden to eat any food until the toxins were cleaned out of his body. With care, he placed the piece of candy in the top drawer on the little bedside chest and relished the taste of happy anticipation.

At last, after some days in the hospital, Roberta finished checking his chart and happily pronounced that he was free to eat some soft food.

"Go ahead, Edith, go buy him a milkshake in the cafeteria," she urged.

Edith did not need a second invitation. In an instant she was on her way downstairs. She wasn't sure who had found the fasting period more difficult, she or her young son. For herself as a Holocaust survivor, it had been an extremely arduous experience. The last thing she wanted was for one of her children to feel the hunger pangs she knew so well and wanted locked up and forgotten somewhere in the recesses of her mind.

Furthermore, eating properly meant good health, and that ranked quite high on her chart of good parenting. Along with all the other Torah values she had absorbed in the "old country," she still retained the memory of her own mother forgoing her own food in order to ease the hunger of her children in those dire days. To her, food was a tangible expression of motherly love. She was sure that proper nourishment represented the epitome of good child-care and deep affection.

Edith returned Room 310 shortly, disappointment marked clearly on her face. She had found nothing kosher downstairs in the cafeteria. Entering Nosson's room, she was stunned to find Roberta, with her back to the door and a milkshake in her hands, pleading with the youngster.

Perceiving his mother's presence in the doorway, Nosson looked up with a fiery sparkle in his eyes and a dogged expression on his face.

"It is not kosher, Roberta. I won't drink it!" It was the tender voice of a child, but the words were spoken with a finality, genuine sincerity, and total conviction that rang out clearly.

Roberta swung around to face Edith. "He has got to get some food down," she reasoned, and tried to carry on with her self-appointed mission.

"It's okay, Nosson," Roberta urged, unaware that she was playing a major role in an unfolding drama before the eyes of curious onlookers. Astonished silence reigned in the large hospital room.

"This will help your recovery, so it is okay for you to drink it — just like medicine." Roberta was sure that all Nosson needed was some gentle prodding and then he would yield to this tantalizing treat.

Nosson remained calm and unruffled as he politely but consistently declined the entreaties of the doctors and nurses who tried their hand at convincing him to drink.

The milkshake, completely melted in its cup, remained at his bedside on the little chest. The doctors and the nurses left if there all day. It served as a mute reminder of the courage and spirit of a six-year-old Jewish child.

"This kid knows his own mind, all right. He will make a fine physician one day," Dr. Troper remarked to Edith when he made his rounds. "You should really send him to medical school when he grows up."

Edith shook her head in silence.

"You surely wouldn not allow a brilliant mind such as his to go to waste," the doctor persisted. "He has the making of a great doctor, er, like me. Such intelligence, already apparent at this age, coupled with his amazing self-discipline, is just what he needs to study medicine!"

"Doctor, I have full respect for the world of science. We need skilled physicians and erudite scientists. But not for my child," said Edith politely. "I would prefer that he attain his Master's degree in the Torah study hall. With the help of Hashem, he'll grow up to be a Torah scholar."

"Torah study hall? Ah, he'll be a rabbi, you mean?"

She nodded.

"So then he will be like Maimonides, the great *Rambam*." Somewhat mollified, Dr. Troper adjusted his glasses, and almost reverently studied Nosson's chart for a long moment.

It felt good to be caring for a potential *Rambam*.

THE MISSING KEY

Nechamah opened her eyes slowly and tried to focus her mind. She had a strange feeling that something was not right.

What was it? Somewhat befuddled, her exhausted mind could not at first make sense of the rapid pulsation of her heart. As the cobwebs of sleep gradually left her, she suddenly bolted upright.

Naftali! Where was he?

She glanced at the large red numbers on the digital clock staring at her silently in the darkness. Four in the morning! A cold chill made its way up her spine. Where could he be at this unearthly hour on *Leil Shabbos*? Why hadn't he come home? What could have happened to him? A million questions swirled in her brain like pesky flies swarming about, clouding her thoughts.

She squeezed her eyes shut in an effort to remain calm and think constructively. Breathing deeply, she tried to recall what had transpired before she had gone to sleep.

After the Shabbos meal, Naftali had left to join his *chavrusa* in shul, just as he did every Friday night. The baby had cried and cried until she had finally fallen asleep in Nechamah's tired arms. It had not actually been so late, considering the hours her baby generally liked to keep. It had only been 9:30, too early for

Naftali to come home from shul, and she had wanted to go to sleep. They had agreed that she would leave the key downstairs so that Naftali would be able to come in without having to wake anybody. Before retiring, Nechama had made her way down four flights of steps with the key in her hand.

She admired her husband's diligence. Having made an early start with a few hours of Torah study each morning, he put in a long, taxing day at his business. In spite of that, at every opportunity, he still retained the energy and zeal to delve into his Gemara with the eagerness of a young yeshivah *bachur*. She knew he especially enjoyed studying with his *chavrusa* on Friday nights. Neither had ever missed a session.

Nechama had hung the key to the outer door carefully on a hook hidden behind a cement column and climbed the stairs again. Leaving the key to the apartment under the doormat, Nechama entered her apartment and turned the little knob to lock the door from the inside. Although she was thoroughly exhausted, she knew she would wake up at the sound of the key turning in the lock when her husband would return. She always did.

But tonight there had been no key turning in the lock. What could have happened to him? Frightening images filled her mind, one rapidly replacing another. What should she do? What *could* she do? It was Shabbos; she couldn't use the phone. But what if it were a case of *pikuach nefesh*? But how was she to know if it was? Should she go out and search the streets? Where would she start?

She would just go. Perhaps Naftali needed her help somewhere out there. But the children! How could she leave two tiny tots alone in the house? The baby would probably wake up soon, as she was due for a feeding, and her cries would quickly awaken the toddler. No responsible mother can leave two wailing children alone in a house, completely unattended; she would have to stay home. Perhaps she would go down to the ground floor and just look outside.

She was frantic, but she could think of no other solution.

Naftali left the shul at 11p.m., deeply absorbed in conversation with his study partner. The peaceful Friday night streets were dotted with *shomer-Shabbos Yidden* heading home after attending a *shalom zachor*, ending a study session, or making a social visit. At the corner, the two parted and Naftali headed home.

His stride was swift and firm, portraying him as a man who knows where he is heading in life and has a clear goal in mind — and an equally clear strategy of how to get there.

Naftali was content and feeling the satisfaction that goes hand in hand with that special feeling of accomplishment. The crisp wind blew against his face as he contemplated the *sugya* he had just resolved with his companion in the *beis midrash*.

As he neared his home, his thoughts turned to his young family. A new baby had recently joined the family, and his tired wife probably would be sleeping by now. Living in an area without an *eiruv*, on Shabbos they always left the key to the outside door of the building hidden in a place where it would not be found easily by intruders. He would be able to let himself in without having to wake any of his neighbors. He knew Nechama would have left one key for him outside in its secure nook and the key to the inner door upstairs under the mat.

Reaching out his hand to the hidden nail, expecting to feel the cold, smooth metal of a key, he felt only the sharp edge of the protruding nail. There was no key. He was horrified to realize that he was locked out. His wife could not possibly hear his knocking way up on the fourth floor. And it was far too late to knock on the vestibule door and wake his neighbors. Besides, the residents on the ground floor of the building were an elderly couple whom he would not dream of disturbing. They were Holocaust survivors who had no children.

He tapped very lightly on the door on the off-chance that one of them might be awake. The stillness of the night was his only answer.

It did not take too long for shock to give rise to frustration. *How could Nechamah have forgotten? She knew I was relying on her to leave the key out for me, what was she thinking?*

Naftali struggled to control himself, to stop the accusations and questions that were swirling around him like pesky mosquitoes. *Let me be skeptical in my assumptions,* he ordered himself firmly. *There is no reason for me to play the blame game here. Nechama has a lot on her mind, with a newborn baby and a toddler — what do I want from her?*

But the hour was late and he longed to be within the warm confines of his home. Giving anyone the benefit of the doubt at this late hour was a tremendous struggle.

Wistfully, he eyed the fourth-floor window. Barred from entry, he felt like a pitiful vagrant, and once again reproachful thoughts assailed his tired mind. *Why couldn't Nechama be more responsible? What does she think?* She knew he couldn't get in without a key and that he could not carry the key with him.

Hold it, hold it, he told himself. *I cannot be sure that my wife is at fault. But what I can be sure of is that my line of thinking is faulty,* he chided himself. *"Al tadin es chaveircha ad shetagia limkomo." How can I pass judgment on her when I don't know it all? There must be another side to the story. Besides, all my accusations will not open the door.*

Naftali was not one to dwell on a problem; he preferred to look for the solution. He would not allow himself to wallow in self-pity and blame any longer. After another quick glance at the windows on the fourth floor, he decided to make his way back to the shul. He would simply have to sleep on a bench.

He would not be comfortable, but he could think of no other solution.

Mrs. Guttmacher was tired. As she cleared off the table after the Shabbos meal she reflected sorrowfully that there were only two settings to clear. How lonely they were. While most of her friends were enjoying the company of children and grandchildren who came to join them around their Shabbos tables, she and her husband sat alone. Deftly brushing the last crumbs of her home-baked *challos* into her silver-plated crumb shovel, she thought about the young family living on the fourth floor.

How she loved the impish smile of their precocious toddler. It was an open secret that the child enlivened her life; she adored that little girl. When little Chayale would come downstairs for a brief social call, the Guttmachers' quiet home would suddenly be filled with the delightful chattering of a precious child. How she cherished those sweet sounds, their charming echoes fading gradually long after Chayale had gone home. Mrs. Guttmacher doted over the child, indulging and coddling her "wonder-child," as she had dubbed her tiny friend.

Out would come the little white footstool from underneath the table and the child would sit herself down unceremoniously on "my chair." The cookie jar would make its appearance next, and Mrs. Guttmacher would revel in the sight of the dainty little hands fumbling in the jar, searching for the very best one. Then she would be rewarded with the most winning smile, surpassing the most eloquent words of appreciation. When her friends would talk, as they predictably did, about the antics of their wonderful grandchildren, she would regale them with tales of her little Chayale.

The soft knock on the door broke her from her reverie. Her husband was home from the *shalom zachor* he had attended. They would retire early. Mrs. Guttmacher went outside to make sure the outside entrance door was securely locked. Lately she needed to check and double-check — not just the lock but also the fire on the stove, the open windows. Her fear of intruders in the middle of the night had intensified with the years, and since they lived on the ground floor, it had almost become an obsession.

Automatically, she fingered the hook beside the doorpost where they kept a spare key. It was difficult to see in the dark, and her eyes were not so young anymore. She just wanted to make sure her husband had remembered to take the key inside with him for the night. *Good, the hook is empty.* But her hands brushed unexpectedly against cold metal. Surprised, she bent to peer more closely at the offending object. It was a key hanging on a second nail.

Ah, those young neighbors. Surely they must have forgotten to take the key in for the night. It seemed to her that young people were just not careful enough in this frightening world of hoodlums and robbers. How could they know how dangerous the world is? They had never witnessed the barbarity of a world gone mad, as she and her husband had in the Holocaust. It was up to her and her generation, with the wisdom born of experience, to protect and guard the young ones. She suddenly felt very old and weary at the thought of carrying such a huge responsibility.

She thought of her sweet Chayale. The image of her cherubic face, so vulnerable and unprotected, rose before her eyes as she contemplated whether to leave the neighbors' key outside, an open invitation for strangers to use. Benevolently, she took the key off its hook and carefully pocketed it. She would return it to them in the morning and remind them to be more careful about taking it in for the night. It was a righteous act done with the sole intention of protecting all the residents, who were blessedly unaware of their danger.

She could think of no other solution.

Nechamah checked on the children once more, whispering a prayer to He Who slumbers not. Then she flew down the four flights of stairs.

At the same time, back in shul, Naftali rose from the hard bench and straightened his sore back. He would try again. This was probably his fifth attempt; he had stopped counting after the third. He had returned home each time and stood outside, gazing wistfully at the fourth-floor windows before returning to his bench in shul. It was now four o'clock in the morning and he was standing outside his apartment building once more. Without warning, the door suddenly flew open. On the threshold stood his wife in wide-eyed shock, her face ashen.

"What happened?" they cried out in perfect synchronization. Each stared at the other with unmasked relief. Frustration, fear, worry, and anger soon melted as the darkness faded and gave way to the rising sun.

Naturally, explanations and clarifications ensued; the next day, heartfelt apologies were accepted. There had been another side to the story.

Sunday morning, as Mrs. Guttmacher refilled her coffee mug, she suddenly heard a knock on the door. Cautiously, she peered through the peephole in the door. Her eyes widened.

"Oh, my goodness," she muttered, unlocking the triple locks on her door. There at her doorstep stood Naftali and Nechamah, smiling good-naturedly. Nechamah held a tray with a large chocolate cake. It was shaped like a key.

But little did Mrs. Guttmacher know that the icing on the cake remained with them. For Nechamah and Naftali had experienced a lesson for life — the *key* to *shalom bayis* now rested in their hands: Giving each other the benefit of the doubt.

ALTRUISTIC ACTS

euven Walkin, deeply immersed in thought, didn't feel his knees trembling, though they shook like saplings in the wind. But he struggled to still the beating of his heart as he paced the length of the floor. A sudden ominous rumbling outside on the street below startled him and he jumped in fright. Squinting warily through a corner of the window, he caught sight of a motorcycle with the Nazi insignia zooming past, and the magnitude of what he was about to do sent a fresh surge of terror coursing through him.

In slow motion, his entire life passed before his eyes. Memories of laughter and innocence from the not-so-distance past engulfed him. He was so young. Was it all to end in a little while? There was no time to think, however. It was his life or the life of the Rebbe. A soft knock on the door broke through his reverie and his already overtaxed heart took another leap of fear. His breathing was becoming labored.

"Are you ready, Reuven?"

Ready? Am I ready?

Germany, early 1920's ….

As soon as Hitler had joined the National Social Democratic Party, he immediately set forth in a frenzy of activity. With unmatched gusto he took charge of the party propaganda, rallying thousands of people, spewing forth his doctrine of hate.

The Rebbe of Belz understood exactly the outcomes of Hitler's evil plans and he urged the people to escape.

To those good, innocent Jews, the madman's anti-Semitic tirades did not seem real. Their hearts and minds could not accept the possibility of a world going crazy.

As the propaganda machine continued the vicious blaming of the Jews for all of Germany's problems, most Jews reasoned that the Nazi's rise to power was merely a passing phase. While the masses of Nazi membership increased, the Jews sadly clung to the belief that such insanity would shortly pass over.

The Rebbe, however, acutely sensed the persecution. When the ominous reports of the initial horrors — perpetrated by Hitler and his cohorts in the pre-war years of the 1930's — trickled in, the Rebbe suffered tremendously.

At first, the Rebbe had opted to remain in Belz rather than to abandon his flock. The Jews gathered around him. He infused them with strength, showering them with the warmth and compassion of a loving father. He immersed himself in special prayers which lasted all day long, fasting till late at night.

The community leaders pleaded with him to flee before it would be too late. As a compromise, the Rebbe agreed to keep a horse and wagon ready for a last-minute escape.

Then, late in 1939, the Nazis invaded Belz. Before doing anything else, they rushed to capture the *Wunder Rabbiner*, as was their regular course of action. Upon the invasion of every town, the Nazis would immediately single out the rabbis or anyone who seemed to be one. This time too, the *Wunder Rabbiner*, famous for the miracles he performed, ranked high on their list of prime targets for persecution, humiliation, and execution.

But the Rebbe had, at the last possible moment, managed to escape their vicious clutches. On Simchas Torah, after the *hakafos*, he had departed on the very last horse and wagon to leave Belz.

During most of the war, the Rebbe and his brother, R' Mordechai of Bilgorai, hid from the Nazis, miraculously escaping from one place to another.

Reuven raised his eyes heavenward, silently pleading that Hashem send him the right thoughts, a spiritual raft to allow him to stay aloft in the deep waters of fright.

Then, out of nowhere a vision emerged — a white tallis. He recognized the tallis. It was the very same tallis that his father had wrapped him in on his first day of cheder. A sudden peace enveloped him.

"I am ready," he declared. Ready to put his life on the line for the sake of his beloved Rebbe, he took a deep breath and stepped out of the room.

Hundreds of selfless individuals risked their lives to save the Belzer Rebbe, with *mesiras nefesh* and substantial sums of money. Undeterred by the formidable task, they promised to save their Rebbe at any cost and constantly pushed ahead with their single-minded mission of extricating the Belzer Rebbe, despite all obstacles.

From Belz, they journeyed to Sokal, then Premishlan, then to the Kraków ghetto, and from there to the Bochnia ghetto.

Bochnia Ghetto ….

A fearsome silence hung heavily around the two young boys as they gingerly made their way in the direction of the Bochnia ghetto walls. In the street, the darkness was total and tension ran high as they imagined a Nazi lurking behind every corner, ready to leap out at them. Moving stealthily, the thunderous pounding of their hearts rivaled — to them — the deafening sounds of their faint footfalls. The wooden fence that stood like a silent sentry wasn't too far away, yet to the boys the distance seemed infinite.

Guards, patrolling police officers, and Gestapo agents were virtually everywhere. Inside the barbed-wire-enclosed ghetto, the Jewish Militia kept a tight surveillance lest any escapees cause them to lose their lives; outside, the anti-Semitic Poles were always ready to swoop down on a hapless Jew and hand over their prey to the Germans.

The two youths reached the fence at last. A small commotion at the other end of the fence attracted the Polish police and they dashed off in that direction. Working quickly, the young boys ignored the thumping in their hearts and deftly pried away several heavy wooden boards.

When the work was completed, a policeman who had stayed behind signaled a silent go-ahead. The Bilgoraj Rav noiselessly edged his way past the fence, and, together with his attendant, assisted the Belzer Rebbe, frail and in a weakened condition, to slip out of the ghetto. The two brothers, disguised beyond recognition, were wordlessly greeted by R' David Shapira, who by luck of his working in a factory outside of the ghetto had not needed to resort to this perilous escape.

Under the moonlit sky, the threesome hurriedly made their way to the home of Baruch Mordechai Tartner, who lived adjacent to the ghetto. They arrived not a moment too soon — the Polish patrol had returned.

From the Tartner home, in the early morning hours a horse and buggy whisked them all off to the neighboring Baczkow village. Once there, they spent the day hiding in the home of a Jew who owned the Baczkow workshop in which ghetto inmates performed slave labor for the Nazis. Here the three Jews were to meet their smuggler, Captain Shtaier, a Hungarian counter-intelligence agent who was friendly to the Jews.

This was their most dangerous escape attempt — when the brothers were to be driven out of occupied Poland and into Hungary. The Rebbe, his brother, and his attendant, shorn of their beards, were disguised as Russian generals who had been captured at the front, being taken to Budapest for questioning.

On the road ….

"Did you see him?"
"See whom?"
"The Rebbe."
"The Rebbe? What are you talking about?"
"What do you mean 'what am I talking about'? That was the Belzer Rebbe and his brother who just passed us. The third man must have been an attendant."
"Where? Where is he?"
"In that buggy. Didn't you notice?"
"Are you wearing your eyeglasses, brother? Those were two Russian generals."
"I am telling you that was the Belzer Rebbe and his brother. I saw him with my own eyes. I recognized his face. You have never heard of people disguising themselves?"

Like wildfire, the whispers circled rapidly among the Jewish slave laborers marching to the German factories where they worked all day long.

Many times it seemed as if the Angel of Death had finally caught up with them. Yet each time, the Belzer Rebbe inexplicably evaded his grasp. Throughout, the two brothers were accompanied by countless extraordinary events that kept them constantly one step ahead of the Nazis.

Meanwhile, in the Bochnia Ghetto …

Scores of army vehicles bearing the Nazi emblem suddenly descended upon the streets. The sight of a single German soldier was enough to provoke terror, and the streets speedily emptied of startled passersby who rushed to hide behind locked doors.

Duvid Landau, who had initiated the labor camp in the Bochnia ghetto, soon learned the reason for their appearance. The Gestapo had heard that many Jews were forging signatures and obtaining false documents, and they had chosen this fateful day to conduct a search among the inhabitants of Buczkow and other villages surrounding the ghetto. Only "foreigners" with legal citizenship papers were permitted to reside outside the ghetto walls.

The Rebbe, his brother Reb Mottele, and the attendant would surely be discovered hiding in Buczkow.

Duvid's heart pounded thunderously, but his mind worked feverishly. Frantic with apprehension, he contacted *Lagerfüehrer* Muller, the head of the labor camp.

"The SS men who have arrived this morning have come to liquidate this labor camp," he said. "Aren't they aware of how our factories and workshops are benefiting the German war effort? Who will clean and alter all the army uniforms if you close this ghetto? My best workers will be evacuated and the German staff will be sent to the front!"

"It is the Kraków Gestapo. What can I do to stop them?"

"Why don't you invite them to your house?" Duvid offered, his heart pounding. "Prepare a royal bash; they will be dazzled. Then you can prove to them the value of this camp's labor to the German Wermacht." Then, lowering his voice, he added, "Don't worry about a thing, I will personally arrange for excellent food and drinks to be served at the party."

"That is just what I will do, Landau," Muller approved wholeheartedly. He harbored no qualms about hosting an elaborate party at the Jew's expense.

And *Lagerfüehrer*," Landau added, "do not forget the prestige that will be yours if you show them how essential your camp is to the war effort. Surely the Gestapo will amply reward your exertion."

Thus *Lagerfüehrer* Muller invited the Gestapo agents to a festive meal. While they wined and dined as the party stretched on all day, a nervous group consisting of the Belzer Rebbe, his brother, and the Hungarian officer, filed into a tiny vehicle bearing the official insignia of the Hungarian government and barely escaped with their lives.

A mere half-hour later, the German troops stormed into every home, searching every corner, looking for Jews with forged documents. Their feast had ended.

However, there remained a tremendous obstacle to overcome. It was imperative that the rumors of the Rebbe's disappearance, which had started among the forced laborers, be quelled. The loyal Chassidim shuddered to think of what would happen if the Germans were to discover the Rebbe's daring escape.

But Reuven Walkin was ready. Taking a deep breath, he donned the Rebbe's silk kapota, white socks, and half-shoes. With a prayer on his lips and with trembling fingers, he placed the Rebbe's tefillin on his forehead and arm. Yes, he was ready. Ready to take his life into his hands by disguising himself as the Belzer Rebbe.

As Reuven wrapped the holy Rebbe's *tallis* around his body and his head, a feeling of awe and respect replaced the fear and trepidation. Slowly, reverently, he took a seat in the Rebbe's chair beside his *shtender*, facing the wall. Despite the harrowing danger of being discovered by Gestapo informants or members of the *Judenrat*, Reuven played his theatrical part to perfection.

At midday, Salo Greiber, a policeman, strutted into the apartment, ostensibly to verify the truth of the rumors about the Rebbe's escape. A wave of cold fear washed over Reuven; he felt totally exposed. Since a closed door would have invited suspicion, the door to the "Rebbe's" room was left ajar. But he appeared remarkably calm, swaying back and forth as though absorbed in prayer or study.

With a pretense of bravery, Yechiel Mechel Green, who'd assumed the role of the Rebbe's attendant, called to another assistant, "Simchah, the Rebbe is calling," and Simchah rushed to appear before the "Rebbe."

All day long men entered and left the apartment. Yechiel Mechel accepted visitor's *kvittlach* (petitions for blessings) with alacrity and hurried to present them to the "Rebbe." But not all the visitors came to receive a blessing. Many appeared to check out the rumors of the Rebbe's disappearance that were buzzing all around.

And then, the fateful moment arrived. Muller learned the truth. In a rage, he summoned Duvid Landau to his office.

"What does this mean?" he shouted, clambering to his feet, his face twisted in fury. "What happened to your Wonder Rabbi?"

A surge of fear coursed through Duvid. Though he had been well aware that he would have to face the inevitable and had done his homework, raw panic now threatened to overcome him. Relax, do not fall apart now, he commanded himself. With trembling fingers he reached into his pocket, groped around for a tense moment, and gingerly removed a three-carat diamond, placing it on the table.

"*Herr Lagerfüehrer*," he said in a controlled voice, "this is for your wife's birthday."

Muller's face underwent a dramatic change. The steel-blue eyes that moments ago had projected an icy glare softened as they gazed at the diamond, his tight jaw had gone slack. "But where is your *Wunder Rabbiner*?" he repeated, this time speaking softly, almost respectfully.

"I don't know what happened to him." Duvid shrugged. "He is called the 'Wonder Rabbi,' so miracles happen to him. Besides, he left me behind as well."

Fingering the precious diamond, Muller nodded his head in agreement. "My wife will be pleased," he said.

After a minute passed, Duvid resumed breathing again.

TO KINDLE A FLAME

"Thank you *so* much!" Susan cried out. Overcome with joy, she clasped her hands around her mother's waist in an exaggerated show of childish delight and hugged her tightly.

The dollhouse, perched on the floor amidst yards of multicolored wrapping paper, seemed to be the fulfillment of everything one could possibly desire in life, especially at the age of six.

Gail, Susan's mother, reveled in her daughter's elation and hoped that this costly new toy would serve well to appease her little girl and distract her from all the nonsense she was bringing home from kindergarten. Gail had chosen the day school at the YMHA for its fine reputation and its affiliation with the upper echelon of the society to which she belonged. She had certainly never entertained the idea that her daughter would find those old-fashioned relics of the past appealing.

Yet Susan would come home starry-eyed as she recounted to her mother all she had learned. It puzzled the child that she had never seen in her own home the Shabbos candles or the Shabbos table that the teacher had described so vividly at school.

"Mom?" Susan began one day.

"What is it, sweetie?"

"Why don't we light Shabbos candles?"

"Oh, that? Well, that is because it is something you *learn* about, not something you *do*, darling. It is fine, we are still Jews, but nowadays we do not do that stuff anymore. Now run along and play, okay?"

But it was not okay with Susan, who was eager to implement everything she had learned. She wanted to experience the magic of the Shabbos candles, the peaceful feeling of Shabbos that Mrs. Harris, her teacher, had described in such glowing terms.

"So then let's light our Chanukah lights," Susan implored. She remembered the colorful Chanukah candles her father had brought home the year before. "Please, Mommy, pretty please."

"How about if we go out and get you some nice, colorful birthday candles?" her mother tried.

Susan declined the offer. She wanted the real thing; she longed for it with a kind of yearning she wasn't sure she could explain to her mother or even to herself. The holiday lights decorating the non-Jewish neighbor's home across the road twinkled and shimmered in a kaleidoscope of dazzling colors, and every time she caught a glimpse of them, this unexplained longing gripped her little heart with all its intensity.

Gail could not understand her daughter's desire. Every time her daughter mentioned the word *Shabbos*, Gail felt her blood pressure rising. Though she struggled to maintain her composure, her insides would churn at the very idea.

Sometimes, when Gail entered Susan's room at night and she gazed down lovingly at her daughter's sleeping face, she would wonder. *Why did the thought of Shabbos cast her into turmoil? What lay behind her tight-lipped refusal to a seemingly benign request? What was it that caused this request to tear at her heart and activate her conscience?*

But Gail would not entertain these thoughts for too long. After everything that had happened, her religious father ... the tragic accident ... it was all too painful to contemplate. The brick wall she had built between herself and those painful memories kept religion locked out as well. At such occasions, when the image of her father would rise before her, she would shake her head as if to clear her troubled mind and resolve to be strong in the way she thought it proper to raise her child. She was the mother, after all.

Susan's father, Brent, mulling over their predicament, had a brainstorm. He determined that an elaborate new toy might just do the trick to distract Susan and fill her mind with youthful play. When the proprietor of the local toy store talked her into purchasing a dollhouse promising hours of pleasure, Gail felt as if a stone were lifting off her chest. Brent wasted no time getting to work, enthusiastically setting up the dollhouse.

Indeed, Susan lost herself in endless hours of delightful play as she maneuvered the charming little dolls and miniature furniture to fit the make-believe scenes her imagination conjured up.

With a steady rain patting against the windowpanes one day, Susan sat crouched on the floor in the coziness of her carpeted bedroom, enchanted as usual. Placing the little girl figure in a new spot on the second floor of her mini home, Susan's hand abruptly stopped in mid-air. It struck her all of a sudden: Somebody up *there* was moving *her* around as well.

She jumped up from the floor, excited, adrenaline surging through her body. Somebody was moving her around!

"Hop, two, three," she danced and whooped and bounced around the room with youthful exuberance until her energy was spent. But she was not finished. Her forehead puckering into tiny lines, her chin set squarely, she stretched her hands and feet and neck. Then she knew it. There *was* Someone up there! Someone was moving her around.

Life went on; the dollhouse served its purpose well, and the rigors of school and friends and everyday life took over.

Susan was nineteen when she felt she needed to get away. Though she could not discern the reason for it, a distressing restlessness and deep disquiet plagued her. A great void filled her heart, and an unidentifiable yearning was her constant companion. She felt like a tightly wound-up bobbin, and she ached for a way out of her tangled emotions. Her pure *neshamah* was calling out to her in a foreign language.

Susan chose Germany as the place to continue her college education, trusting that the change would be the solution to her torment.

Her new school was situated in a quaint old castle on a charming little island nestled between a river and a picturesque rural landscape. Surrounded by green hills, with a wooden bridge running across the waters beneath, the restful setting of the school promised serenity-filled days ahead.

Outer beauty notwithstanding, Susan was assigned to an uncomely dorm room, sparsely furnished with a tiny window in the corner and a hospital-like bed. Its melancholy atmosphere made her feel almost like a prisoner.

Susan responded by making a little shopping excursion to a nearby flower shop. She selected a pleasing array of flowers and paid for her purchase. As she was leaving, her eyes caught the gleam of a pair of white candles perched atop a tiny set of lovely silver-plated candlesticks. The sight made her catch her breath. The precious candles were duly wrapped up, and she made her way back to her dorm room.

The next few days saw a whirlwind of activity as Susan quickly acclimated herself to the new school, new country, and new surroundings. Soon the end of the first week was upon her. Sitting in her little room on Friday afternoon, her thoughts led her back to home, and she allowed herself to indulge in the sweet reminiscence of her childhood.

As the fading rays of sunshine peeking through the tiny window dwindled and twilight made its way into her room, she remembered her fascination with candles.

Inspiration hit her when she realized that the day was actually turning into Friday night. She stood up as if in a trance and headed for the table to light the candles she had purchased earlier in the week. As she struck the match, some vague recollection of a blessing beckoned to her, but she could not recall ever reciting or even hearing the blessing for Shabbos candles.

And then, as if breaking through the cobwebs of her memories, she unexpectedly remembered the blessing for the Chanukah candles!

Improvising a bit, she changed the last word of the blessing from *shel Chanukah* to *shel Shabbos*. When she was done, she stared at the candles, completely mesmerized by their warm glow. She was filled with an inner tranquility she had never experienced before, and she felt uplifted, as though she were transcending mundane, everyday life, and had been transported into a different world.

As the lights of that precious mitzvah glowed and sparkled, the light in her *neshamah* was kindled and soon took on a new glow and sparkle of its own.

The radiant light of this one mitzvah became a beacon of light illuminating the path on a new road leading to a treasure chest filled with beautiful gems.

A YIDDISHE NESHAMAH

It was close to Pesach, and Ellen, our trusted babysitter, had just informed me she was leaving. Living in a small out-of-town Jewish community, we had found it difficult to find a Jewish caretaker. Now we would have to start looking all over again.

The search began. Our inquiries met with no success. Anyone I could think of who could possibly help was duly telephoned. Even the plumber, who was summoned to our home due to my daughter having "bathed" her doll (and its subsequent demise down the toilet), was subjected to intense questioning.

At last, wonder of wonders, a neighbor, who was moving into a retirement home and no longer needed her housekeeper, called with the good news. After interviewing the housekeeper and contacting her references, we were happy to have Zissel taking care of our children. This reprieve lasted only a short while, however. Zissel was eager to further her education, and she left us.

Our search resumed. So did our prayers. I had read about a great *tzaddik* who was heard whispering a prayer that the maid should return to work in their home. Convinced that he had great holy *kavanos* behind this prayer, his students mustered up the courage to ask him what his *tefillah* was really for.

"Whom should I ask if not Hashem? He is the One Who grants big requests as well as small ones. In the same way that I ask Him for the big things in life, I ask Him for the small things."

We seemed to be at a stalemate. The children were shuffled from house to house for babysitting while I tried to hold down my part-time job and finish my frantic Pesach preparations. Occasionally we interviewed a candidate, only to discover that the specific time we needed her would not work out. Most of the applicants wanted to work five days each week, while we needed help only four, as I did not go to my office on Fridays.

And then we found Nadya. She came warmly recommended, so we interviewed her. Her schedule corresponded to ours, so we hired her.

There was one thing that nagged at my conscience and pulled at my heartstrings. Nadya wasn't Jewish — or so she claimed. During the interview I had asked her numerous times and she always answered, stubbornly it seemed to me, that no, she is a Ukrainian from Kazakhstan. Accounts I had read of the terrible Ukrainians during and after the Holocaust flitted through my brain and constricted my chest. Yet somehow those stories and her personality didn't seem to go together.

Her nobility of soul, her genuinely refined manner, were so impressive. This was not an imitation "this-is-my-act-to-make-a-good-impression" kind of thing, because when one tries to make a good impression that is the impression they make. The smile on her face was real. Her kindness was authentic. She exuded a special air, something that implied aristocracy, and my children were attracted to her warmth. In her spare time, while the children slept or played contentedly, she would wash the floors, iron laundry, or take care of any of the myriad household tasks. She was any working mother's dream.

I never tired of asking her, "Nadya, are you sure you are not Jewish?"

And she never tired of answering me, "Oh no, I'm Ukrainian!" Once, she confessed that her children had begged her to become Jewish, since they had admired the Jewish children they had seen.

One *Erev Pesach* I called Nadya to come and give me a hand with the housework. If she was available she would always agree to come, even if I asked her to work outside outside of her official hours. The table was laid for Yom Tov, and gleaming silver candlesticks had pride of place in the center. As soon as Nadya set eyes on them, she couldn't avert her gaze. She stood glued to the spot, staring, oblivious to anything around her.

"Nadya," I said softly, "did you ever see candlesticks like these before?"

"Yes," she whispered, as if in a trance. "Grandma had candlesticks like those." Then, breaking out of her reverie, she was quick to add, "But she lived far away, and she died when I was very young."

"Oh," I said. This was a rare moment; I knew I had to proceed cautiously. Then, as if it were an afterthought, I asked casually. "Was she your mother's mother or your father's mother, that grandmother?"

"My mother's mother," came the answer. "But Mother married a Ukrainian man, so *I* was no longer a Jew."

So that was the answer to the riddle. The age-old Jewish story came out then.

After Nadya's grandfather's death, the shattered widow remarried. Her new husband, a Ukrainian, often shouted at his wife, calling her "dirty Zhid," and, in a drunken stupor, threw her out of the house. Nadya's mother desperately sought to protect herself and her future children from her bitter experiences and married a gentile, believing that her children would thereby be safe from anti-Semitism.

I explained to Nadya what I had always known in my heart. She was a Jew according to *halachah*. She seemed amused to hear it.

A Yiddishe Neshamah

What could I do to help her? How can one be of help to someone who doesn't even know she needs help? The only thing I could do for this poor *neshamah* was to pray for her and for the countless other lost *neshamos*. I often wonder what illustrious ancestors she must have had. Her noble personality is a reflection of their greatness.

ACTIONS SPEAK LOUDER ...

"Dear Mindy," Malka was penning her thoughts to her friend overseas.

"They call it the 'big vacation' — *chofesh hagadol.* Well, I can tell you that it is vacation 'big time.' Vacation from school, vacation from routine, vacation from structure.

"Vacation also means that there is no school for the girls and half-day day camp for the boys — which means that after you turn around, the first boy is home. After you eat breakfast, the second one is home. And before you can straighten your snood ... the third one is home. Everyone is ordering his special menu for the day. If they would only let me prepare it without chairs around blocking my every move. By the time the last one is eating his lunch, the first one is already running around the place, busy doing who knows what. So you see, life is pretty hectic around here and I am somewhat out of breath. That's 'vacation time' for those of us across the ocean, so many miles away from you.

"This is also the time when many families take a two-week vacation; others only take a mini vacation for 3-4 days. Remote farms, attractive hotels, or an interesting settlement area (*moshav*) are good choices. Then, of course, there are those who make do with *tiyulim* — day trips. So today, when Shimmy had an appointment at the pediatrician, the whole family came along for a *tiyul*! What fun that was. Who's to say that a ride in some amusement park is more thrilling than a roller-coaster ride in the taxi? Not my kids — they all had a wonderful time!

"I will assume you are wondering if we're planning a vacation in a hotel too. The truth is, we have stayed in one already! "Hadassah Hospital Hotel." It all began when the baby had a virus. I took Surela to the clinic when she was sick, and the doctor on duty at the clinic reached a "professional" medical decision. He informed me that the baby needed to be x-rayed. I was then urged to RUSH to the hospital.

'Can I make a stop at home?' I ventured to ask the grim-looking doctor.

'I cannot in good faith allow you to go home; you must go right now!' the doctor rejoined.

"Off we sped to Hadassah Ein Kerem, to be relieved upon arrival, when a pulmonologist in the emergency room took one look at the x-ray I brought along and stated unequivocally that there was nothing wrong!

"But it was too late. As someone told me recently, the doors to the hospitals open wide, but their exit doors are quite narrow. Once you are admitted, they don't let you out before subjecting the patient to a whole battery of tests. Throughout the night we went running from one pavilion to the next, enduring all the pricks and stabs of the needle. It wasn't until 2:00 a.m. that we were given the release papers for a happy, smiling, hand-and-feet-kicking little girl who had apparently pined for some *chofesh hagadol*."

Malka looked up from her writing and smiled to herself as she watched Moshe sneaking up to the countertop and grabbing a cookie from the shelf, gliding away as noiselessly as he had come.

"I am looking forward to hearing all the delightful antics at your end! I am sure you have lots to tell, as you usually do. "Love, Malka."

She quickly signed her letter and placed it an envelope to be mailed. It was good for her to take a mini-break, to put pen to paper, whenever she had a free moment, to enjoy the magical way words merged into something coherent.

Rising from her chair, Malka stretched her tired muscles. She was sincerely grateful for her busy, bustling household, and constantly searched to find the humor nestled within the cracks and crevices of her hectic daily schedule. She considered it necessary to share those with an "adult" friend, whether it was on the telephone or through letter-writing. It gave her fresh spurts of energy to continue with her workload, and was an entertaining way to clear her mind of all her whirling thoughts.

The world had already embraced the new day when Malka opened her eyes. She was surprised to see the shafts of morning light already shimmering between the slats of the Venetian blinds. It had been a long night. Lovingly, she stared into the crib. The baby, who had suffered a bout of teething pain, was peacefully asleep now.

Today was a big day. Unexpectedly, their family had won a weekend getaway to a kosher hotel up north. Since the children were all home due to school vacation, she had decided to begin the vacation Thursday morning and incorporate the scenic train ride as part of the trip. True, this meant a more roundabout route and a longer journey, but she felt buoyed by visions of her children's exhilaration throughout this special trip. She wasn't deterred from undertaking this project, even though Menashe would only be joining them at the hotel late that night, due to his work responsibilities.

Malka strained her ears, trying to grasp a hint of what the older children had been up to, since no little heads had snuggled into her arms this morning.

The sound of little feet traipsing purposefully around the house reached her. A door slammed shut somewhere.

"Ssh … you'll wake up Mommy," she heard Elimelech fiercely whispering.

Malka sank her drowsy head back onto her pillow. So the children were in their "best children" mode. She was only mildly surprised. The children were excited about the great day. She allowed the feeling of contentment to wash over her for a moment as her mind once again reviewed the day's exciting agenda.

The train from Tel Aviv departs every hour. In order to make the 11:20 train, we have to be on the Tel Aviv-bound bus by 10:00. She glanced at the wristwatch on her nightstand. It was 8:00. *I had better get going.*

Leah Simons arrived at the central bus station and checked her watch. She still had a half-hour before the bus would pull into the station. Good. She liked to be early; to get her bearings, orient her thoughts, and remain calm. The very thought of rushing to the bus or huffing and puffing into an appointment horrified Leah. She assiduously expended effort to avoid chaotic scenarios.

Leah sat placidly, glancing through the newspaper she held. Turning to the last page, she reached for her pen and began filling in the blanks of the crossword puzzle. The ringing of her cell phone disrupted her favorite pastime. Leah checked the incoming number in her typical measured manner before answering the call.

"Hello, Annie," she said into the phone. "I am at the bus terminal now. Yes, I will be there in time for your train's arrival. Don't worry. All right. Bye."

While Leah carefully replaced her phone in its proper compartment in her bag, her thoughts were on Annie, who had recently arrived in *Eretz Yisrael* from Vladivostok, Russia. How bewildered this distant cousin of hers seemed to be in her unfamiliar surroundings! Leah tried to help as much as she could, and Annie indeed depended heavily on her.

The previous night, Annie had traveled to Nahariya, a city in the north, to visit an elderly aunt. Now she was heading back home, and Leah was due to meet her midway, in the Tel Aviv train station. Together the two of them would proceed to the embassy in Tel Aviv to arrange some documents that Annie still needed for her immigration process.

Eventually the bus arrived. Leah gracefully swung her shoulder bag over her arm, ascended the bus steps, and found a seat. Sitting ramrod-straight, she gazed at the line of passengers still making their way onto the bus and seeking their preferred seats.

Arriving at the bus terminal, Malka attempted to get her bearings amidst the bustling throng. Each of her boys, wearing a crisp checked shirt and sporting a navy sunhat, was pulling a small carry-on bag on wheels. Their sparkling eyes darted in every direction, trying to take in all the sights and sounds of this new and unfamiliar environment, while ten-year-old Shira somehow assumed responsibility for the two-year-old. The boys, easily distracted by one spectacle or another, often stepped out of line, and Malka didn't know on which to focus. Awash in a sea of humanity, she nevertheless needed to usher her small team on to the escalator — stroller, bags and all — purchase bus tickets, and learn the exact location of the bus to Tel Aviv.

Finally, the little family was comfortably ensconced in the tall plush seats on the bus. Sruli, next to Shira, was leaning back contentedly, his little feet dangling back and forth. Shimmy and Ari sat at the edge of their seats, taking care not to miss a single action, as their eyes cautiously followed every movement of the driver. Malka breathed a sigh of relief and smiled down to Sura'le, who sat perched on her lap. Sura'le was busily gurgling and chattering to their neighbor. Malka looked up into the smiling face of the middle-aged woman sitting beside her and greeted her politely.

Actions Speak Louder ... 129

Leah smiled down at the charming baby who was trying to pull the ruby ring from her finger. She observed the mother of the child gently removing the tiny hand from her ring and returned the greeting of the smiling young woman before returning to her crossword puzzle.

From time to time, Leah glanced up from her puzzle to watch the little family surrounding the young mother.

"Your children are so well-behaved," she remarked, pointing in the children's direction. Malka followed her gaze. Her children were completely engrossed in scrutinizing the various cars and trucks speeding past them on the highway. The sight of their shining faces bolstered her decision to make this family excursion on her own. She began to relax, leaning her head against the back of her seat, reviewing the morning's events.

She suddenly realized that she was still grasping the return bus tickets in her hand and rummaged in her bag to retrieve her wallet. Her hand returned from the interior of her bag, empty. Surprised, Malka thought back to the last time she had seen the wallet.

It was at the ticket counter when I received the change from the clerk, she remembered clearly. *What did I do with it after that? We had about five minutes to reach the bus, and I rushed the children to the right area.* She suddenly remembered stashing the wallet in the hood of the stroller. She had no way to confirm this now, however. The stroller was safely tucked in the baggage compartment underneath the bus.

Her heart plummeted. What if it was not there? How could she pay for the train tickets? She could just picture herself standing with her family in the sweltering streets of Tel Aviv, completely stranded. She imagined herself approaching a total stranger and asking for help. *No!* she screamed inwardly. She could never bring herself to stretch out her hands to a stranger. *Please, Hashem, help me,* she silently prayed fervently. *You are the only One Who can help me now.*

Anguished thoughts spiraled and swirled on top of each other, in an endless trail. Desperately she tried to relax her overwhelming feelings, tried to sort through the maze of her emotions. Her thoughts vacillated between guilt, fear, and anger. *Why didn't I make sure to put the wallet in my bag where it belongs instead of stashing it in the hood of the stroller? Why was I so reckless?*

She imagined a burly-looking man in shorts, gleefully laughing somewhere, clasping *her* wallet in *his* hand. *How could someone have done that to me? Couldn't he see that I was alone with five children? How callous!* She pictured him delighting with the three hundred shekels she had so carefully inserted in the wallet this morning. The scenes her anxious mind conjured up were so vivid and real; she followed her imaginary villain to the trashcan, where he discarded all her children's medical cards with derision. *Why is this happening to me? What message does Hashem want to send me with this?* Her chest felt tight and her hands clammy. It was hard to sit still.

Again, her baby lunged for her neighbor's hands. This time she went for the antique bracelet that graced the woman's wrist. The woman glanced up and Malka couldn't contain her nervewracking thoughts any longer.

"I left my wallet in the stroller! It is underneath the bus," she blurted out to the complete stranger.

The woman looked at her blankly, without saying a single word. After a moment, she was back at her puzzle. Malka's heart sank. She felt suffocated in her narrow seat, but there was nowhere to go. Shock and disappointment engulfed her. To have revealed her pain to a stranger, only to have it ignored, was too much for her. The stony silence of the woman sitting next to her heightened her frustration and made her feel so alone in her dilemma. Didn't this woman have a heart?

From the corner of her eye, Malka glared at the woman. She appeared to be in her mid-sixties. Heavy, old-fashioned rings adorned her long, slender fingers and a expensive pen was poised delicately in her hand. Her well-groomed but outmoded black *sheitel* evoked memories of Malka's mother, who had styled her *sheitel* that way twenty years earlier.

Malka's thoughts drifted back to her childhood home. Visions of old Mrs. Weissberg crowded her memories and she felt her tears dangerously close to the surface. How many times had her mother sat next to the unfortunate woman, pouring out her tales of woe? How patiently had her mother listened to the same stories again and again, always responding with kind and soothing words to ease Mrs. Weissberg's pain?

The present reality, however, etched painfully sharp lines in Malka's forehead and she stared at her neighbor incredulously. *Didn't she ever hear about chessed? Wasn't she even aware of the pain she inflicted with such callous indifference?* Perhaps not. Twenty long minutes had passed in complete silence. Malka engrossed in her memories; the woman writing away. *A typical Sabra*, thought Malka with indignation.

Just then, from out of the blue, the woman turned to her, "You were the last one to get on the bus. No one will have access to your wallet," she said.

Malka relaxed her taut posture and attempted to rein in her resentful thoughts. "Thanks for the encouragement," she whispered, "Hashem will help." Her memories of home had transported her to her caring parents. She could see her father as he sat at the table, bent over his well-worn *Chovos Halevavos*, reviewing *Shaar HaBitachon* yet again. She needed to place herself in the loving and caring Hands of her Father in Heaven, she resolved. Somewhat appeased, she began to imagine herself jumping off the bus, just reaching out to the stroller hood and reclaiming her wallet. How happy she would be if it were so. *Just a little bit longer*, she told herself, willing the bus to accelerate its pace; *it will be okay.*

At long last, the bus pulled into the train station in Tel Aviv. Instantly, without a word, her neighbor gathered her belongings and regally descended from the bus. Malka hastily assembled her brood and followed suit, rushing toward the baggage compartment. Malka practically crawled inside and searched every nook and cranny of its cavernous interior.

There was no sign of her wallet.

Backing out of the dark, silent interior of the baggage compartment, Malka stood blinking in the sunlight. She hadn't the slightest inkling of how to proceed from here. One thing was certain: she did not have a shekel to her name and no means at all with which to pay for the train to take them to the hotel. How she wished she could just indulge in a good hearty cry! How wonderful it would be to release her pent-up emotions!

Suddenly, she noticed two women rushing toward her, though she could not quite make out who they were. As the figures came closer, she recognized one of them. That frosty woman, who had sat next to her for the duration of the trip, was waving to her anxiously! Astonished, Malka stared in amazement.

Coming closer with a few graceful strides, the woman surprisingly inquired, "Where are you headed?"

"I was on the way to Maalot," Malka answered, fiddling with the straps on her bag. "But now, I am not sure."

"You do not have any money on you, do you?" the woman tossed the question at her.

Malka shook her head. By now, she was afraid that she would burst into tears if she attemted to speak.

"How much money did you have in your wallet?"

Malka swallowed hard. "Three hundred shekels," she answered in a barely audible tone.

Without another word, the woman who had sat near her and who had hardly exchanged a word with her throughout the entire trip, the woman who had sat upright and aloof, opened her wallet and withdrew three crisp hundred-shekel bills, pushing them into Malka's trembling hand.

"Th ... thank you." Malka could hardly get the words out. "Thank you so much." She was overwhelmed by this unexpected gesture.

"Please tell me your name and give me your address so that I can repay you," Malka implored.

"My name is Leah Simons and this is my cousin Annie." Leah calmly gave Malka her address, writing it in a page neatly torn from the small spiral notebook she kept in her handbag. Leah was not quite finished yet. Taking hold of one of the larger carry-on bags, she urged the children to follow her as she led the way toward the required platform. Her companion did the same.

The little group proceeded to walk toward the platform. At the far end of the walkway, Malka noticed a vast stretch of stairs descending toward the platform. Her eyes opened wide in alarm. She did not know how long the two women planned to accompany her. Surely, they had other things to do. How in the world would she navigate that endless decline with her stroller, bags, and children in tow?

She glanced at Leah, who continued on her way with total serenity, heading straight towards those threatening, endless stairs without any sign of slackening her pace. At the top of the stairs, she simply lifted the suitcase in one hand and held out her other hand to help Malka with her stroller. The children followed obligingly.

Leah did not cease her steady gait even at the platform. Instead, she walked confidently up to a young soldier who was waiting for the train.

"You, young man, be so kind and help them up on the train when it arrives," she stated. Her very bearing commanded respect and the soldier nodded readily.

Satisfied, Leah wished them a safe trip. Only then did she turn to leave, collecting her cousin with a glance and walking away without looking back.

For a long time, Malka stared after her receding back. The words of the Mishnah in *Pirkei Avos* (1:15) echoed in her mind, "*Emor me'at veasei harbei* — say little but do much."

A typical Sabra indeed: tough and resilient on the outside, but sweet, soft, and nourishing on the inside. She couldn't wait to write her next letter to her friend Mindy.

LAST-MINUTE CHANGES

Zahava strode purposefully down the corridor and headed toward Room 4523. White-uniformed personnel passed her along the way. The odors of the hospital, redolent with antiseptic, assailed her senses as she quietly contemplated the right words with which to bring some cheer to Ruth, her neighbor, who had recently been admitted to the oncology department. From afar, she suddenly spotted an orderly wheeling a patient out of Room 4523 and she quickened her pace.

"What happened, Ruth?" Zahava anxiously inquired as she came closer and saw Ruth lying on the gurney.

"Oh, hi, Zahava," Ruth replied weakly. "They just need to do some more tests."

"I see, um ..." Zahava gulped, searching for the right words to say. "Perhaps .... Do you think I should accompany you?"

"Oh, no. I'll be back soon," she said, a tired smile briefly spread over the patient's wan face as she waved good-bye.

Weighing her options, Zahava was determined to linger in the hospital and wait for her neighbor to return. It wasn't that she didn't have anything better to do that morning. On the contrary, Zahava was actively engaged in numerous community projects that entailed an untold number of responsibilities.

Every moment was precious to Zahava, and she swiftly conjured up the various possibilities with which to fill this unforeseen empty slot in her busy day. She paced the quiet hallway, absorbed in thought. Suddenly, a pitiful sight caught her attention and abruptly interrupted her rumination. *Room 4529* read the plaque on the door. A frighteningly pale face was framed by the white hospital pillow. The sick woman lay completely motionless and seemed utterly alone and forlorn. On a sudden impulse, Zahava entered the room. The patient didn't stir. She seemed to be a typical secular Israeli woman in her mid-forties, nearly comatose and apparently, Zahava surmised, heavily sedated. Here was the ideal opportunity to accomplish an additional act of *chessed* and appropriately fill the unexpected delay.

Pulling up a chair next to the woman, Zahava sat down and began to talk. She commenced her monologue by briefly introducing herself. To all intents and purposes, she appeared to be talking to herself, yet Zahava remained unperturbed; she felt certain that the woman's *neshamah* craved for, and indeed heard, every word.

Delicately, with genuine caring and warmth, Zahava took the woman's emaciated hands and gently poured water over them while reciting the *berachah* of *netillas yadaim*.

Her respect and love for every *Yiddishe neshamah* was evident in every subtle movement. Zahava tenderly placed the woman's right hand on her eyes as "they" said *Shema Yisrael* "together." Then, in a soft voice, Zahava proceeded to relate stories of *tzaddikim* and great men who had suffered immeasurable *yissurim* during their lifetime. Zahava told her about G-d and then lovingly asked her, "Do you know that there is a G-d?"

Suddenly the patient's eyes fluttered open. She stared at Zahava for an awesome moment before silently closing them once again.

Close to ten minutes passed in this manner, when unexpectedly, a shadow suddenly crossed the room. Zahava looked up at the tall, dark figure of the man who stood staring at her from the threshold. "Are you her husband?" she asked.

"Yes, I am," he swiftly responded. Finding no purpose in remaining any longer, Zahava silently left the room.

As she made her way back toward Room 4523, Zahava was surprised to hear hurried footfalls rushing after her. "*Geveret, geveret,*" the woman's husband called as he beckoned to her. She retraced her steps, whereupon the man promptly began asking her one question after another. With patience born of experience, and to the best of her ability, Zahava attempted to answer his queries on the subject of Judaism.

In the midst of this impromptu *kiruv* encounter, a danger alert suddenly struck Zahava; distressing alarm signals vibrated within her, spreading their shock waves throughout her very essence. With sudden, devastating disbelief, Zahava grasped the irony of the situation: the man standing before her, eagerly asking her questions — the sick woman's husband — was actually an Arab!

For a moment, the tiled floor on which she stood began to revolve around her with dizzying speed. Tremors of shock and disbelief shook her. The entire time she had spent in Room 4529, she had been talking to an Arab woman! The thought was frightening. Abruptly, she ended the conversation and, turning on her heels, she fled to a quiet corner of the corridor and attempted to sense the solid ground beneath her feet. Breathing heavily, she waited anxiously for her neighbor to return to her room. Zahava longed to run home.

Zahava stumbled through her doorway and collapsed onto her worn sofa. Questions ... millions of questions danced around her brain, refusing to grant her any respite. Again and again, the identical questions repeated themselves, plaguing her, mocking her, and depriving her of peace of mind. She pondered the meaning of it all. Achingly, and with a broken heart, she mulled over the devastating event. *How could this have happened? What does Hashem want from me? What message is He sending me? What am I supposed to do now? What does this all mean?*

Finally, with trembling fingers, she dialed the phone number of Harav Schechter *Shlita*. Her voice barely above a whisper, she hesitantly asked to come over and discuss an urgent matter.

"Actually, I must travel to Bnei Brak immediately. However," the Rav graciously offered, "as soon as I return, I will call you and you are most welcome to come at that time."

Still somewhat in a trance, Zahava replaced the phone in its cradle and glanced at her watch. It was 11:00 at night. She would meet with the Rav, she resolved, even if it meant waiting up till 1:00 in the morning.

Hardly a minute had ticked by when the shrill sound of the telephone startled her. Her nerves still on edge, she cautiously answered the phone, "Hello?"

It was the Rav on the line. "My trip to Bnei Brak was canceled, so you can come now."

In a moment, Zahava flew down the steps, hailed a taxi, and was driven to the home of the esteemed Rav.

Patiently, displaying genuine interest, the Rav listened as she proceeded to relate the day's events in vivid detail. Those questions that had plagued her throughout the day finally found their release in the relaxing confines of the Rav's warm home and caring presence.

When at last she ended her account, she felt as though a large boulder had rolled off her chest. Instinctively she took a deep breath and filled her lungs with the pure, *sefarim*-scented air. She felt refreshed, her shoulders relaxed, and she eagerly awaited the Rav's reply.

It was not long in coming.

"First of all, concerning the fact that you spoke to her about Hashem, they too believe in G-d," he said. Zahava remained silent, her fingers tracing the delicate pattern of the lace tablecloth.

"Besides, do you know how many of our girls are unfortunately there … among them?"

What? Were her ears deceiving her? Jewish girls … among them? Zahava's head jerked up involuntarily. A dark shadow had covered the Rav's countenance and he said nothing more. Zahava quietly thanked him and left, her head spinning anew.

The week passed uneventfully. Zahava's heartbeat returned to normal, as did her hectic routine. Shortly thereafter, Zahava again found herself at the very same department in the hospital, this time to visit someone else. Naturally, she set off to find her mysterious "friend" to learn how she was doing. However, the bed in Room 4529 was now occupied by a white-haired elderly woman. Zahava hurried to the nurse's station, where she inquired as to the condition of the previous patient. She discovered that the woman had been transferred to hospice care.

"Please, can you do me a favor?" Zahava implored the nurse on duty, "The woman who was in Room 4529 last week — can you tell me, was she Jewish?"

"I'll try to find out for you," the nurse replied, noting Zahava's intense desire to know. Zahava, as a regular in the hospital corridors, had long since established an excellent relationship with the nurses on the floor. Now this relationship served her well. The nurse rifled through her files and carefully scanned the forms.

"Oh, here I see something … interesting," the nurse mused. "It seems that her original name, Leah, was changed. The new name is Lyla."

A flash of recognition, like a red bulb, lit up in Zahava's brain. When she had entered the room that first time, she had indeed seen the identifying placard with the name "Lyla" clearly imprinted. Nevertheless, in her eagerness to perform a mitzvah, she had completely disregarded the fact that this woman might be a non-Jew.

How wondrous are the ways of Hashem, thought Zahava. *Who knows? Had my mind registered the name, I would not have washed her hands. I certainly would not have recited the Shema with her! So, this precious neshamah, on the brink of death, right before returning to its Creator, will merit to depart from this world having perfomed a vital mitzvah.*

Zahava felt blessed.

THE WORLD TO COME FROM A SINGLE DAF

Morty Shweibel strode briskly down Orchard Street, past the scores of peddlers hawking their wares from potato sacks and pushcarts in a cacophony of sales pitches. Vendors displaying everything from housewares to live, squirming fish, meat products, and fresh fruits and vegetables lined the streets for blocks on end. But Morty focused straight ahead, keeping up a steady gait. Deftly maneuvering his way past the savvy shoppers, he nimbly sidestepped a dropped pickle that was swiftly rolling away from the irate apron-clad seller and continued purposefully ahead.

Having disembarked from the subway that had brought him home from yeshivah across town, young Shweibel eagerly anticipated the warm welcome he would receive at home, as he did each day. He looked forward to his father's warm praise and his mother's tasty lunch. The trolley car would have saved him this lengthy trek from the subway platform to his home, but he could not afford the fare. Morty shifted slightly under the load of his backpack as his thoughts drifted to his dear father.

Growing up in the Lower East Side of Manhattan, Ralph Shweibel knew only poverty and struggle. At the age of ten, his formal education ended and he went to work at odd jobs to help supplement the meager earnings of his impoverished family. From then on, he tried to teach himself whenever an opportunity presented itself. Books from the public library and worn, frayed dictionaries that he managed to borrow were his teachers.

Working as a presser in a garment factory was heavy, exhausting work for a kid, but it strengthened his muscles and built his strength. When young hooligans from the nearby Irish community would descend on the Jewish neighborhood, as they frequently did, and fights were inevitable, Ralph never batted an eyelash. Flexing his muscles, he would lunge at the attackers and wrestle with them with mighty courage, fortified by the knowledge that he was defending his Jewish identity, of which he was proud.

Eventually Ralph used his natural boxing talents to become a professional boxer. This was the golden age of American Jewish boxing, a sport which had always been popular among the very poor. As a result of the rampant poverty and lack of formal education of the times, boxing was one of the few ways to make a living without an education. Ralph Shweibel rapidly became well-known among sports fans, who often bet clamorously on the outcome of the matches in which he participated.

Ralph Shweibel was proud of his heritage. He was proud to be a Jew. Painfully aware of his own lack of religious education, he strongly desired to provide for his son that which he himself did not have. Yeshivahs closer to home provided little more than Hebrew-afternoon programs for public-high-school students. This did not satisfy Ralph's educational requirements for his son. Only the best yeshivah and the best teacher would do for his only son, born to him in the twilight of his years.

Morty felt a surge of pride and admiration for his father, who had inculcated in him such a love for Torah, in contrast to most

American Jewish fathers of the period, who had tossed away their *Yiddishkeit* due to the pressures of making a living and the lures of American society. While so many aspired to raise their children with the desire to pursue American dreams, Morty's father had aspired to raise him with the desire to pursue Torah and Jewish values.

Turning onto Delancey Street, Morty spotted their fourth-floor window in one of the crowded tenement houses. He leaped up the stairs, taking them two at a time, and was soon turning his key in the lock.

His elderly father shuffled over and embraced him warmly, and his mother pecked him lovingly on the cheek, "Our yeshivah *bochur*," she exclaimed with satisfaction, as if this had been his first day of school. "Did you learn a lot of Gemara?" His parents beamed with pride. The three of them entered the tiny, sparsely-appointed kitchen, where his mother served them coffee, bread, and wholesome vegetable soup.

After a short nap, Morty sat at the kitchen table, swaying over his Gemara and reciting the words aloud in a sing-song manner. He understood how much pleasure his learning brought to his parents. Indeed, the stirring melody tugged at Ralph's heart. With misty eyes he observed his son, who seemed rapt in a world of supreme joy and bliss. It was a world Ralph longed to enter, but one to which he lacked the key.

Each day, when the identical scene would be reenacted, and the melodious Torah learning permeated their simple dwelling, Ralph would look on in a mixture of happiness and pain. As time went by, the sparkle in his eyes dimmed, the wrinkles on his face seemed to become more pronounced, and his back appeared slightly more stooped, replacing the figure of the erstwhile strapping, stalwart boxer of years gone by. The light that shone from the Gemara starkly contrasted with the dark shades of anguish that he felt because of his illiteracy. The gaping hole, the agonizing inability to become immersed in those holy words, troubled his soul and gave him no peace.

"Teach me," he implored his son one day as he tried in vain to make sense of the passage to which his son's finger was pointing. "Give me a part of this. Teach me Torah!"

Morty lifted his face and gazed into his father's eyes, which sadly reflected his intense yearning. *He wants so much to learn,* Morty thought. *But what should I do? How can I teach him Gemara when he does not even know the aleph beis?*

"Let's learn together," his father persisted, interrupting his son's thoughts.

Morty sighed. "Oh, Dad," he said compassionately. "It's not something that can be taught in one breath. This isn't for you." Noticing his father's crestfallen look, he quickly added, "Don't worry about it, Dad. Hashem loves you, too. He knows what is in your heart. He knows all the thoughts and desires of man, and that counts most. Hashem sees your *mesiras nefesh* for Torah, and for that you will get your reward."

It was not the reward that Ralph was after, however, and his son's words did little to assuage his desperate longing to learn Torah.

"Teach me just one page!" Ralph didn't give up so quickly. "That is all I ask of you, my son, one page."

"Dad, one page of Gemara is not like one page in a book; you must understand that."

Ralph Shweibel was not one to give up so quickly, and this time, too, he did not capitulate. He pleaded and entreated, presenting fresh arguments each time until he succeeded in overcoming his son's hesitation.

"But you must know that this is not something that can be achieved on one foot. We have to start from the very beginning," Morty informed his father.

Ralph had no problem with that. With the zeal and wide-eyed eagerness of a young child, Ralph absorbed himself in the age-old new studies. Slowly and patiently, the elderly man learned the letters of the *aleph beis*, the right-to-left reading, and the standard phonetics. It was not easy. At his age, his memory was not as sharp as it had been, and the new concepts proved to be quite a challenge.

Still, Ralph struggled over the *aleph beis* and worked ambitiously towards improved reading fluency — letter by letter and word after word. Soon he had mastered the letters and was reading with confidence. Ralph felt overwhelmed by his personal triumph. It was time to go on. He set about studying Chumash and then *Rashi*. The *Rashi* letters perplexed him at first and presented a new challenge. But with firm tenacity, he persevered and mastered them as well.

Morty patiently and steadfastly kept up the study partnership with his father as they studied the Chumash and then the Mishnah — and finally they began their first page of Gemara.

To Ralph, the days seemed to whiz by, each day carrying its own challenges and fresh new successes. Ralph, who thrived with this new mission, seemed to grow younger. There was a youthful spirit in his step and his back seemed to have straightened out. His eyes sparkled with tremendous satisfaction and *joie de vivre*. After all these years, his life held purpose and true meaning. Each day he waited enthusiastically for his son to come home from yeshivah and then, together, they would delve into the holy words of the Torah.

Summer turned to winter and winter blossomed into spring. When the year was over, Ralph, at long last, mastered his very first page of Gemara. His excitement and ecstasy at this incredible milestone were palpable. He hugged and embraced his son for helping him achieve this high point in his life.

"Let's make a party," the elderly man suggested with simple, youthful innocence.

Morty felt swept up in his father's supreme joy. But a party?

"Don't you make parties?" his father wanted to know, seeing the doubt in Morty's face.

"Sure, we make parties. It's called a *siyum*, Dad, not a party."

"Then a *siyum* it shall be."

"But a party — a *siyum* — is normally reserved for finishing an entire *masechta*. Not a single page."

"Never mind that. I want to have a party or a *siyum* or whatever you want to call it. This is a tremendous *simchah* for me, and I want to celebrate this achievement with a party, er ... a *siyum*. I would like to praise Hashem for His great kindness in leading a poor, illiterate boy so far."

Morty, more than anyone else, understood his father's struggle: his victory in an almost insurmountable endeavor. After all, his father had climbed a towering mountain and now felt as though he were standing at the peak. But a *siyum* for one *daf*? Nonetheless, realizing that his father's heart was set on having a *siyum*, Morty resolved to approach HaRav Moshe Feinstein and request his sagacious advice.

Rav Moshe Feinstein listened attentively to the young man's inquiry. The Rav encouraged him and advised him that, although ordinarily a *siyum* was celebrated after the completion of an entire *masechta*, in light of the unique circumstances, it was appropriate to make a *siyum* for the completion of the one page his father had labored over.

In parting, the venerable sage also assured the young Shweibel that he, the *Gaon* himself, would be there to attend the momentous occasion. Morty felt much strengthened by this, knowing full well that the Rav's illustrious attendance would add a significant dimension to the *simchah*.

The lofty atmosphere in the shul was tangible and people shook their heads in wonder. A *siyum* for one *blatt* Gemara! Yet HaRav Moshe Feinstein himself had deemed the occasion important enough to attend; a factor which seemed to permeate all those who attended with great spiritual excitement. Many

Torah scholars were there in honor of the luminous dignitary who graced the event.

His eyes alight with an angelic glow, Ralph Shweibel scanned the room. He was filled with emotion, his face radiant. The extraordinary *simchah* he felt at this auspicious moment accompanied him throughout the evening.

Rabbi Segal commenced the program with heartwarming opening remarks, praising the honoree of the *siyum* for his tremendous respect and appreciation for Torah. "Let me tell you a story," his voice reverberated across the room.

"A young woman rushed into the study of the *Taz*, Rabbi Dovid Ben Shmuel Halevi [author of the *Turei Zahav*]," he began. "Her heartrending cries echoed throughout the house. 'Rebbe! Rebbe! My son is dying. The doctors have given up all hope. Please help me.'

"The *Taz* looked at the unfortunate woman with compassion but shrugged, 'Am I Hashem? What can I do? There is nothing I can do!'

"The woman was inconsolable. Bitter tears coursed down her cheeks. She stood before the venerable sage and cried and cried. Suddenly she exclaimed, 'Let the Rebbe use the *zechus* of his Torah and the Torah of his students from even a single day. I am sure that the merit of that Torah will bring salvation!'

"'Then you have prevailed,' replied the sage. 'Your son will be saved!'"

The speaker looked around at his spellbound audience. Ralph Shweibel sat enraptured as he listened to the skilled orator, and Morty's eyes glittered with understanding. Rabbi Segal stroked his beard and continued his narrative.

"The students of the holy *Taz* were perplexed. They raised two questions: 'If the Rebbi indeed had the ability to help, why did he abruptly dismiss her plea? Moreover, didn't the Sage already know that the Torah possesses that tremendous ability? Did he need a simple woman to tell him that …?"

Rabbi Segal paused, allowing his words to sink in. The audience waited expectantly.

"'This simple woman grasped the tremendous value of Torah! That,' the holy *Taz* emphasized, 'was what brought the salvation!'

"The heightened appreciation that our honorable Mr. Shweibel has for Torah is well known! How awesome! Who can measure the value of the single *daf* that he has mastered?" Rabbi Segal's impassioned words resonated with clarity and meaning.

More speakers rose to the podium, weaving profound expositions on various teachings of *Chazal*. The powerful words lodged themselves within hearts and minds, greatly uplifting all those who attended. It was an evening they would not easily forget.

The morning after the momentous *siyum*, the report spread like fire and stunned all the attendees of the previous night's *siyum*. The news shook the community! Eyes bulged from their sockets and mouths hung open in shock. Crowds of people congregated around the posters plastered onto the walls and poles throughout the neighborhood, studying the words that announced the funeral of Ralph Shweibel.

Throngs of grieving people came to accompany the elderly man on his final journey. Harav Moshe Feinstein himself attended the funeral, and his followers, aching for words of consolation, longing to find meaning in this man's sudden death, wove their way closer to their leader and guide. Rav Moshe's holy words were not long in coming.

"It is written, '*Yesh koneh olamo beshaa achas*, One can acquire an entire world [the World to Come] in a single hour.' In the same way it can be said, '*Yesh koneh olamo bedaf achas*, One can acquire an entire world with a single *daf* of Gemara!'"

How awesome is the merit of those who study Torah! Who can measure the value of a single *blatt* Gemara?

LIBERATED MEN

*I*n a time and place where the meaning of freedom faded into a distant past, where one's right to live was determined by those who hadn't the slightest inkling of living right, there were men — no, giants — who clung tenaciously to the source of all freedom — the Torah and the mitzvos. While unchained men remained prisoners of the mind, the imprisoned Jews were free to choose. And choose they did.

When I asked my grandfather to tell me his story of the Holocaust, I braced myself for the cloud that would inevitably cross his features and dull his eyes as he would reach back in time and dredge up painful memories. I was in for a surprise. My grandfather's worn face lit up, and I stared at the smile wrinkles around his eyes. As I listened, spellbound, to his memories of *that* time, understanding slowly dawned. His tale wasn't one in which he told about the horrors, painful as they were. He didn't dwell on the blow he received to his head that almost killed him, so close to liberation. No, there wasn't a trace of anger or bitterness of anguish in his words. Instead, he related to me, speaking slowly, as though savoring it again, the story of each precious mitzvah that he managed to keep.

Yechezkel straightened his back, wiped the perspiration from his brow, and placed the clumsy sledgehammer at his side. He looked around at the large expanse of woodland and endless strips of railroad tracks, and suddenly he felt so alone. Alone in a vast, frightening world.

Munkatabur.[1] Military. These were new words, necessitating new survival instincts. Yechezkel's forced-labor unit was stationed in the forest to construct railroads for the army, constantly under the watchful eye of the commandant.

Accustomed to the sheltered, tranquil life inside the yeshivah walls, Yechezkel found himself thrust suddenly into a world gone mad. Bewildered and alone, he struggled to maintain a foothold on the rocky terrain of a foreign planet, a frightening, unpredictable existence.

Where are Mama and Papa now? Has Papa received the letter I mailed last week and the one from the week before? Painstakingly, lovingly, Yechezkel penned a letter to his father, week after arduous week. How those letters had relieved him, ridding his heart of the painful yearning within. But why hadn't he received any letters from Papa? Surely Papa would have responded, as he always did, with soothing words of encouragement and subtle reminders to strengthen his trust and faith in their Father in Heaven.

Presently, the crunch of footsteps on dry twigs reached his ears. Looking up, Yechezkel saw the familiar figure of Nachum, his fellow laborer, briskly weaving his way toward him through the tall, imposing trees.

"Come see what I've got," Nachum shouted, holding out a quivering hand.

---

1. In Hungary, forced-labor battalions called *Munkatabur* were established in 1940 under the command of Hungarian military officers. Every able-bodied Jew was conscripted to slave in war-related construction work under brutal conditions. Without adequate shelter and food, and subject to extreme cold, thousands of these Jewish forced laborers died before the German occupation of Hungary in March 1944.

A few quick strides and Yechezkel's eyes grew wide as he beheld a most exotic treasure resting on his friend's outstretched palm.

"A tomato?" Yechezkel was incredulous. "How in the world did you get hold of a tomato?"

Yechezkel allowed happiness to wash over him. Hashem was so good to him. It wasn't just the tomato of today. Yesterday a farmer had agreed to sell them a few drops of real milk, and the week before that the mountain had benevolently allowed a thin trickle of water to form a stream between its rocks. He and his fellow prisoners had taken turns dipping into the shallow water, exultant in performing the ritual immersion in a kosher *mikvah*.

Succos was suddenly upon the group of forlorn slave laborers. They sat wearily — a lethargic group of young men — reminiscing about Succos back home, as they waited impassively for their ration of watery soup to be distributed.

"I will never forget the smile of my brother, Chaim'ke, when we hung up his very own succah decoration," Nachum said, staring into the distance.

"You have no idea how enticing the smells of my mother's challos were," Gedalia chimed in. "I cannot forget the lavish meal she prepared. It was a meal fit for a king."

Nachum stood up abruptly, brushing off some twigs. "We can't have the lavish meal," he said. "We will not be able to sit around the Yom Tov table with our families. But," his voice rose a decibel, "we can have a succah!"

No one moved. Gedalia smiled grimly. For a moment, he wondered if Nachum had succumbed to hallucinations, retreating into a fantasy world. He had seen this happen to others, especially when the hunger pangs had grown too powerful to bear.

Yechezkel, though, felt a glimmer of hope within his pained heart. Maybe it was possible. They had been fortunate before, he had to admit.

Momentarily immobilized by a flash of memory, Yechezkel thought back to *Erev Rosh Hashanah*.

By some miracle, his group had been successful in securing the kommandant's authorization to recite their holy prayers on the day of Rosh Hashanah. Some of them had succeeded in stealing into a nearby ghetto. In the haunting stillness of the ghetto, they had discovered a precious few machzorim, and, much to their joy, a genuine shofar! How they had rejoiced.

But soon enough, it had appeared that their plans would have to fall by the wayside ....

The glorious sun rose in its resplendent, imperturbable majesty on the morning of Rosh Hashanah — a stark contrast to the new group of inmates pummeled out of the cargo train with the help of the bludgeons and rifle butts of their Nazi guards. The news they brought with them spread in quick whispers: Germany had occupied Hungary.

Suddenly, Yechezkel heard malicious laughter ripping through the crowd. Seeking the source of the guffaws, Yechezkel's heart constricted in pain. Standing before them, in his shiny boots and be-medaled uniform, the SS officer introduced himself as the replacement for their former Hungarian taskmaster. He had arrived with the consignment of inmates.

"You want to pray?" He sneered at them, his eyes burning with hatred and scorn. "What do you think this is, a synagogue? I will show you what kind of synagogue this is. All of you — go bring your hammers and sledges. Schnell!"

Now, sitting on the damp earth, Yechezkel again felt the cold fingers of disappointment that had clutched at his chest. To work on this holy day? They had come so close to observing the holiday with a trace of proper respect, only to have it slip away at the last moment.

But they had encouraged each other to go on, drawing strength from their bottomless well of faith. If this was the will of *HaKadosh Baruch Hu*, they would serve Him this way, too. They would find purpose and significance through chanting the sacred words of the prayers even while their backs hunched over the railroad line they were forced to extend.

As Yechezkel toiled under the scrutiny of the SS guard, his lips whispered the holy words of the Rosh Hashanah prayers. Suddenly, unbelievably, he heard the stunning sound of bombers droning overhead. The loudspeaker crackled to life. "Attention! All workers must spread out into the fields immediately!!"

Among the tall reeds and trees, Yechezkel and his friends were left alone. Alone with Hashem. They managed to stay together as a group as they wandered and prayed.

A trembling finger pointed to the distance. "See those geese paddling in the pond? They are free, free to bask in the warmth of the sun, free to swim about, free to do as they please. And we, we breathe in the confined air of ...."

"All that water!" Yechezkel interrupted. "We can perform the mitzvah of tashlich." With joy in their hearts, they scrambled down the hill to toss their sins into the water. The pain and anguish of their living nightmare faded for the moment. Even as he walked through the Valley of Death, Yechezkel could feel Hashem's presence.

Yechezkel, deep in thought, was oblivious to Nachum's entreaties to come and build a succah. His mind now transported him back to the recent eve of Yom Kippur, the holiest day of the year.

The small group that had gathered together for the Kol Nidrei Prayers stood waiting with trepidation for the services to begin. R' Moshe, the oldest of the group, had been chosen to lead the services. But he stood rooted to the ground, staring at a single page of his prayer book. Tears were streaming down his withered face. No one stirred.

After some minutes, Yechezkel looked up and sent a searching glance over R' Moshe's shoulder, — to catch a glimpse of the latter's focal point. The Priestly Benediction with which parents bless their children leaped off the page, and tears stung Yechezkel's eyes. He understood now why R' Moshe was crying.

R' Moshe's wife and children had been murdered by the Nazi war machine. Now an aching heart cried for the children who would no longer be blessed by a loving father, and cried for a wife who no longer stood by his side.

But most of all, a pained heart cried for himself — bitter, heart-wrenching cries of a lone survivor. Yechezkel cried along with him while eyes moist with tears looked on.

At last R' Moshe tore himself away from his thoughts. His eyes scanned the group of boys surrounding him. "I have no children of my own to bless this year," he said in a choked voice. "Would you allow me to bless you, my boys, instead?"

Yechezkel shifted from one leg to the other, surreptitiously peeking at the others from the corner of his eye. The air was thick with emotion. David's face had drained of all color; his chin quivered. Nachum was dabbing at tears with the corner of his sleeve, and Gedalya, his face ashen, was swaying back and forth with a low moan. One by one, the boys stepped forward and bowed their heads dutifully under R' Moshe's trembling hand.

The small group remained standing for some time, each one absorbed in silent memories of home. Then R' Moshe began the Ma'ariv prayers and the boys joined him in pouring out their hearts and souls to their Father in Heaven. In the ditch of despair and depravity, in a world gone mad with mercilessness and malice, his group of boys found solace in the holy words of prayer.

"Come! I will show you how to build a succah," Nachum said, stamping his feet. Yechezkel allowed himself to become caught up in Nachum's excitement. So did the others. With a new sparkle in their sad eyes, they indeed fashioned a makeshift succah between two abandoned traincars, using some twigs, a discarded plank as a platform, and plenty of determination.

"No decorations on our succah this year, huh?" Gedalia said with a hint of a smile.

"That's right, no paper chains, no pictures of rabbis smiling down at us," Nachum rejoined, "but it is a succah nonetheless!"

"True. So what if there is only room for four? We'll take turns!" Gedalia responded.

As each one took his turn to embrace and to be embraced by the warmth of this precious mitzvah, forgotten was their constant hunger; their painful escort of unceasing suffering lay vanquished for a little while.

Shemini Atzeres found them on the move again. Marching briskly in the cool night over hills and valleys, bridges and rivers, the group of boys arrived, at last, at a quaint, old train station. There, they collapsed on the cold, hard earth, awaiting further orders.

Yechezkel sat listlessly; he felt sure that his feet wouldn't take him another step. Suddenly he noticed Nachum crawling in his direction. He was hauling a small wooden box behind him. What was inside? And where had he found it here, in the middle of nowhere?

"See this box?" Nachum spoke in an undertone. "I carried this with me throughout our entire journey. Even though my feet are swollen and blistered and my hands are almost numb, I had to bring this along."

"How in the world did you manage that?" Yechezkel was incredulous.

"How I managed?" Nachum asked with a tired smile.

"They didn't take it away from you?" he whispered. "What's inside? Jewels? Bread?"

Nachum reverently placed the mysterious box on Yechezkel's lap. "Go on, have a look yourself," Nachum urged.

Yechezkel opened the box. Tears sprang to his eyes; they glistened in the white light of the moon. Inside the box lay something that far exceeded his most wistful dreams.

It was a small *Sefer Torah*.

In a single quick movement, Yechezkel bolted upright. Nachum slowly hobbled to his side.

"*Hakafos*!" Yechezkel exclaimed. "How could we forget?"

Under the deep velvety sky, the shimmering stars twinkled, gleaming down at the weary sufferers, hands clasped in unity as they danced around the priceless *Sefer Torah*. All through the night they danced and sang. They danced with the freedom of liberated men, unfettered by the snide remarks of their non-religious peers, and unimpeded by their bone-tired exhaustion.

The Torah and mitzvos, linked with their unfaltering faith in Hashem, carried them above the shackles of anguish and torment.

They were free men.

Not free from their tormentors, but free to serve their Creator.

THE VALUE OF A MITZVAH

Moshe walked swiftly through the narrow streets of Jerusalem's Shaarei Chessed neighborhood, weaving his way under the timeless arches and twisting alleyways framed by stone walls reflecting the golden hues of the sun. Its sights and sounds were mesmerizing. Its cobblestones were worn smooth by the generations of people who had walked upon them. A worn Gemara nestled under Moshe's arm while his mind delved into the profundities of a difficult *sugya*.

Suddenly he spotted the familiar figure of R' Betzalel the *Milchiger*, as the milkman was affectionately called. Moshe lengthened his stride, eager to engage the milkman in a Torah discussion.

R' Betzalel Goldstein, the impoverished milkman with eyes that sparkled with intelligence and a dignified demeanor that characterized his piety and saintliness, earned his meager sustenance by delivering milk to the poor families of Jerusalem.

Since iceboxes couldn't keep the milk fresh for long, the milkman was a welcome figure in the streets of Shaarei Chessed. Kerchiefed woman would line up in front of his galvanized steel buckets, carrying pots and jars of every sort, into which he would pour the wholesome milk.

Even the putrid odor issuing from his hat didn't restrain the good women of Jerusalem from collecting their precious supply of milk for their families.

However, the smell greatly perturbed Leibel, one of the residents of Jerusalem who was able to see through the facade of simplicity the milkman sought to portray, and he sought to rectify the matter. This unassuming man, Leibel realized, was nothing less than an eminent, albeit humble, Torah scholar. Leibel felt that it was a lack of respect to allow a pious Jew of such caliber to wear an old, worn-out, malodorous hat. Thus, although money in Jerusalem was scarce, R' Betzalel came to have a new hat, purchased by Leibel.

The next day, to Leibel's utter dismay, R' Betzalel's brand-new hat emitted a repugnant odor. Respectfully, he drew the milkman's attention to this phenomenon.

"What happened? I bought you a new hat. Why does it smell so ... so not fresh?"

The milkman smiled and placed a gentle hand on Leibel's shoulder. "Thank you for your kindness. I much appreciate the new hat you have bought for me. But you see, when I deliver the milk, it is the women who come out to do business with me. I'm concerned, I don't want them to befriend me. So I took my new hat and dipped it into the herring brine from the barrel at the herring merchant's shop, so that anyone who comes near me will be repulsed and stay away. That way, the women won't come too close to me."

It is said that before Rabbi Bengis assumed the position of the *rosh av beis din (ravad)*, Second Chief Rabbi of Jerusalem, he nearly declined the offer when he met the milkman. "If this is the *milkman* of the Holy City of Jerusalem, I do not know how I could be the Rav of a city with such citizens." And when Rav Aharon Kotler came to *Eretz Yisrael* for a visit, he drove to Shaarei

Chessed on a special mission, just to lay eyes on the legendary milkman and speak with him in learning.

As Moshe's footsteps brought him closer to the milkman, he noticed that R' Betzalel's countenance was a picture of ecstasy; his weatherbeaten face wreathed in smiles, his feet seemingly leaping in the air with elation.

"Good afternoon, R' Betzalel," Moshe greeted him, somewhat puzzled.

"Ah, R' Moshe, come and look!" the milkman exclaimed. "Look what I have found!" A small bundle of cash was clutched between his fingers.

Moshe knew the milkman's dire financial situation well; he barely subsisted on the profits from the milk he sold. His daily menu consisted of a dry piece of bread with milk. If times were good, he might also have an onion. Moshe's heart rejoiced at R' Betzalel's unexpected windfall. Surely this money would be enough to provide his simple needs for at least a few years.

"I have a question which needs some investigation," R' Betzalel declared, gesturing with his free hand. "According to the *halachos* of *hashavas aveidah* [returning lost objects], when someone returns a thousand dollars that he found, is that considered one mitzvah or is every cent that he returns considered its own mitzvah?"

A wide grin spread over on R' Betzalel's face. "Moshe," he said in a confidential tone, as though entrusting him with a secret, "I have ten proofs to verify that each *grush* is a separate mitzvah! I am so very happy," R' Betzalel's clear voice rang out. "I am gaining thousands of mitzvos!" Before Moshe's astonished eyes, the milkman literally danced a jig right there on the street.

"Do you understand, Moshe?" he sang. "This is a gift! A gift from the *Ribbono Shel Olam*. He thought of me! He sent it my way."

By now Moshe had recovered his wits. The milkman's joy notwithstanding, Moshe was sure he was not about to give up on food and basic provisions for a number of years.

"R' Betzalel," he turned to the milkman hesitantly, almost fearfully, "who says you are obligated to return the money? Maybe it does not have the *simanim* [marks or symbols required by *halachah* through which a lost object can be identified and claimed by the one who lost it]. Maybe you have no obligation in *hashavas aveidah*?"

Instead of being pleased, though, R' Betzalel's smile disappeared, his dancing came to an abrupt standstill, and he lapsed into dejected silence.

Moshe gazed at the milkman's crestfallen face. The eyes that had shone with joy a moment ago now mirrored only deep sadness. R' Betzalel, Moshe realized, was shattered. When the milkman spoke, his voice was almost a whisper.

"I had calculated the thousands of mitzvos I would obtain, and now you are telling me there is no mitzvah here?" he asked disconsolately. "I would never keep the money!"

"Why not?"

"Because ... because it's not mine; I have to give it back. But now you are telling me that it does not have a *siman* and therefore the mitzvah is exempt from being fulfilled and there is no mitzvah?!"

"What is so terrible? Why can't you keep it? What's wrong? Maybe the person has given up hope and you are allowed to keep it."

"What am I going to do with it? What do I need it for? I have, *baruch Hashem*, bread to eat and salt water in which to dip it."

"R' Betzalel, today butter is not considered a luxury. So you will have some butter on your bread. What is so terrible about that?"

"Why do I need butter?" R' Betzalel was adamant. "So the worms should have more to eat after they put me in my grave?"

The Value of a Mitzvah

Moshe realized that argument was useless. The most articulate of speeches would not convince the milkman to keep the money. Anxious to restore the milkman's good cheer, he steered the conversation in another direction.

Stroking his beard, he said, "Perhaps there *is* a mark that can be a sufficient form of identification. Maybe there can indeed be a mitzvah of *hashavas aveidah* here."

R' Betzalel's unhappiness immediately melted, and a radiant smile of joy lit his face. He embraced Moshe. "*Baruch Hashem!*" he said, with obvious pleasure. "A mitzvah of *hashavas aveidah* is a diamond worth more than money can buy!"

Moshe grinned. How could he have erred by thinking of depriving the milkman of his *simchah shel mitzvah*! To this righteous milkman, the money itself paled in comparison. The man standing before him was living in a different realm; a world where the reality of a higher purpose existed.

"Moshe," R' Betzalel smiled broadly, "This is yet another proof that this mitzvah encompasses a thousand mitzvos!"

Some people are rich, some are poor. Some are ambitious, some are lazy. Some people recognize a good business deal, some are oblivious. Betzalel *Milchiger*, Jerusalem's beloved milkman, could perceive the diamond within each mitzvah.

I'M GOING ON VACATION

The crisp morning breeze cooled her as she hurried toward the bus stop. The melodies of the various birds singing to their Creator punctuated the quiet stillness of the morning hours.

Rochel inhaled deeply. The oxygen that flowed into her lungs was a gift, compensation for the hectic dawn hours of rushing around the house in order to be able to catch the 6:45 a.m. train to Manhattan.

Chaim too, seemed to appreciate the pristine ambience of the morning hours. Sucking contentedly on his thumb, he peered out at the world from the cozy vantage point of his stroller. Perhaps he somehow sensed that it was he who necessitated this bi-weekly trip. After all, his three other siblings had remained at home. Soon, however, his peaceful demeanor would drastically alter; when the doctor would treat him, the pain would prove to be too much for this otherwise tranquil nine-month old.

As his mother proceeded to lug the stroller up the stairs leading to the train platform, Chaim remained blissfully unaware of the intense pain to come. Gurgling happily, he smiled charmingly at the stranger who offered his mother a helping hand.

Rochel took a seat and closed her eyes, her hands wrapped securely around Chaim's waist. These trips were not easy for her.

However, as the train chugged its way along the tracks, Rochel did not complain. She silently thanked Hashem that her son's medical problem could be corrected, and asked Him to further help her manage to undertake these trips.

For a moment, she thought of her husband, Asher, and she wondered. *Am I seeking to emulate Rochel, the wife of Akiva? Or have I crossed the line to utter foolishness by declining my husband's offer to take the day off from kollel and replace me on this mission?* She considered all the consequences. Her young children, who would be home before her return, would be sent to the various homes of her kind friends. Later, she would arrive home exhausted, both from the trip and the cries of her baby, to a houseful of little children who needed a mother. She thought of her sincere desire to build a Torah home. She squared her shoulders. No, she would not let those exasperating ideas impinge on her innermost desire, she resolved.

There was something else, though, that niggled somewhere in a corner of her brain. She felt a tinge of resentment about something else. Ironically, seated between throngs of people heading for work, she felt alone, yet she cherished the private solitude the train ride offered, a solitude that provided an opportunity to clear the cobwebs of undesired feelings and thoughts from her heart and mind.

It was the older boys, she knew now. It had started with only one, but the number had steadily increased until there were four. They had been a young couple back then, the happy parents of their first child, when they were approached by a member of their community. Would it be possible for them to welcome Yossi, a boy of 15, into their home? Young, energetic, and idealistic, they eagerly acquiesced, happily undertaking this special mitzvah. The boy, an orphan hailing from an out-of-town suburb, wished to learn in New York at a well-known yeshivah. He needed a warm home and a caring heart to tend to his physical and emotional well-being.

Almost naturally, Rochel and Asher accepted their new role as parents to the unfortunate boy. When Yossi was expelled from yeshivah, Asher made sure to get him back in. On mornings when Yossi refused to get out of bed, Rochel lovingly spoke to him until he agreed to confide in her the troubles of his day and the conflicts he had with his friends.

Patiently, with warmth, they taught him to behave. With incredible tact they taught him to enter the home calmly, until his habit of storming into the house became a thing of the past. They even taught him to say "Thank you."

With time, three more teenage boys joined their family, even as their own family rapidly expanded. Both very giving people, Asher and Rochel invested tremendous time, devotion, and effort into this project, yet reaped from it an equal amount of satisfaction and pleasure.

Rochel thought about all this now as her baby slept peacefully on her lap. It wasn't the boys who bothered her now. It was her own thoughts that nibbled at her peace of mind. The bi-weekly trips to Manhattan were taking their toll on her. She felt exhausted and found it increasingly harder to serve the boys three times a day. *I do not have to do this,* she thought. *But if I do it, I should not grumble inside about it. I am angry, I am cross, yet I want to do this right!!*

As the train headed toward Manhattan, her mind moved toward finding a solution. She sorely wanted to do this mitzvah with her whole heart. She contemplated her choices. One alternative was to send them all away. After all, her family had grown, along with the obligations she had toward them. But how could she do it to these poor boys? Another solution was to keep giving as before and silently stew in resentment.

Suddenly her face brightened. A third, far more preferable option, struck her like a bolt of lightning. She would simply ask them for help. The instant relief she felt at this resolution washed over her like a wave and remained with her for the rest of her arduous day.

When Rochel returned home with Chaim, she found the little ones waiting for her, all snuggled peacefully under their blankets. Asher had collected them from the various neighbors to whom they had gone after school. Rochel showered them with all the attention and warmth they had missed throughout the day. Boo-boos had been bandaged and tears wiped smoothly away by their mother's gentle hands. Rochel felt sure that she merited an extra dose of *siyatta diShmaya*, perhaps as a reward for her *hachnasas orchim*, when it came to handling her children.

She entered the kitchen where the older boys were already sitting around the table, waiting for their dinner. With experienced hands, she quickly served them the supper she had prepared the day before.

When the sounds of forks scraping against the plates and the tinkling of glasses had abated, Rochel presented her plan.

"Tomorrow I am going on vacation," she announced.

Simultaneously, four pairs of bewildered eyes looked up at her. A moment of silence ensued. Then, an explosion of questions erupted as they all stood in amazement.

"Vacation?"

"Asher too?"

"Where are you going?"

"But tomorrow is Friday!"

Rochel regarded the foursome with a touch of amusement. "I am not going anywhere!" she exclaimed.

Their faces flooded with obvious relief and their features relaxed. Shragi and Yossi sat down again. Rochel plunged ahead.

"I am going on vacation tomorrow right here in this house," she said. "I am going to divide the work between the four of you.

"Yossi, you will clean the *fleishig* side. That means the dishes, the stove, and the countertop. Menachem, you will mop the kitchen floor; Shragi will make the potato kugel; and ...."

"I don't know how to make a kugel," Shragi protested.

"If you make the kugel, there will be kugel," Rochel patiently replied. "And if you will not, there won't be kugel. I am not doing it."

Rochel looked at Tzvi and for a moment she hesitated. Tzvi was a *chassan*. A genuine *masmid*, he learned every spare minute of his day. How could she do this to him? He would not even know how to perform a household task. Outside of his Gemara, nothing existed to him. Still, she could not single him out from the group. Her eyes scanned the kitchen.

"Tzvi, you will do the *milchig* side," she said. That did not usually involve too much work.

The boys quickly recovered from their initial surprise. Their eyes reflected the enthusiasm they felt towards this arrangement. They actually welcomed the ability to contribute to the home and were grateful for the opportunity.

That Friday the boys took over; the kitchen became their domain. Rochel heard their animated discussion as they cleaned, clattered, and scrubbed. She had decided that she would not stand over them; she would allow them to work at their own pace. When she went into the kitchen to fetch a towel, she noticed that Tzvi was diligently washing the dishes with only his bare hands and cold water. "Tzvi," she said gently, "we use soap for washing dishes."

"Ah," he said and reached for the soap. Rochel watched as he continued washing the dishes with his hands, albeit using the soap.

"There is a scrubber in the sink that will help with the washing," she said. "And you can use warm water."

She watched as his eyes surveyed the sink. Lifting the baby-bottle brush, he carried on with his task. Moving toward him, she reached into the sink and handed him the right scrubber. Then, reminding herself that she was not their *mashgiach*, she walked out of the kitchen.

Soon the fragrant aroma of the kugel baking in the oven spread through the apartment. The sound of moving chairs and running water was no longer heard. Rochel entered the kitchen. She was met by four happy young men. As they looked around the kitchen inspecting their own work, a deep sense of satisfaction lingered in the room.

Then came the biggest surprise of all.

"Thank you so much," Yossi called out.

"Yeah, thanks a lot." It was Shragi. "Can I make a kugel again next week?"

"It was really great," Menachem joined in. "It feels good to do something around here for a change."

Tzvi modestly averted his gaze and quietly said, "Thank you for teaching me. I am getting married soon and now I will be able to help my wife."

Rochel's eyes shifted from the shiny floor to the sparkling faces. A warm glow spread throughout her heart and thrust fresh energy into every fiber of her being. She knew then that this would be a moment that would be imprinted in her memory forever.

WHEN MORE IS LESS

*C*hani was a super-organized mother of three young children. Fiercely devoted to her offspring and very affectionate, she still managed to run an immaculate household, working more with willpower and energy than actual physical strength. She felt it imperative to stick to her impeccable standards; the bottle of window cleaner was almost a natural extension of her hand. The mirrors, the windows, the doorknobs were her silent witnesses, staring inertly at the sight of her frenzied rushing from one task to another.

In the early morning hours, Chani could be seen swaying over her worn *siddur* before the rest of her brood would need her. Her meals were always balanced and nutritious, and she never skimped on ironing even the slightest crease out of her family's clothing. Even the ribbons tied around each set of linen were proof that this kind of perfection existed in a real home. A peek into her linen closet — or into any other closet, for that matter — was a veritable delight for the eyes. The symmetry of everything in her house was perfect, right down to the evenly spaced hangers in the closets.

Chani shrugged off any compliments to her housekeeping ability.

"It is really no big deal," she would say. And she meant it seriously.

"Everyone has their talents and capabilities. Mine are energy and strong willpower. I simply have lots of energy and willpower, and they belong to the One Who gave each of us our own unique traits."

Work never fazed her. To the contrary, it energized her — the mere thought of what needed to be done sent waves of energy surging through her.

That is why Pesach was her favorite time of the year. She scrubbed and scoured, and scrubbed some more. Not only was she in full harmony with what she liked to do best, but it was a mitzvah, too!

Then came the year that she contracted hepatitis. No one relishes being sick, but to Chani this development was particularly devastating. She detested any signs of weakness in herself.

She suffered tremendously, but not from the physical pain. Her terrible agony was rather due to an intense feeling of helplessness and frustration at her incapacitation. Understandably, Chani's distress was magnified ten-fold since it was happening right before Pesach.

Shimon, Chani's husband, gently comforted her with soothing words and kind injunctions of what Chani herself had been known to say.

"Strength comes from the *Ribbono Shel Olam*," he said, "and ultimately we are in His control."

Besides boosting her morale, Shimon undertook a major part of the workload Chani usually shouldered, delegating lighter chores to the little ones.

Gradually Chani submitted to her lack of control and focused on happily accepting the will of *HaKadosh Baruch Hu*. She did whatever she was able to and spent lots of time reading storybooks, making up songs, and playing games with her children. Slowly, she learned to relax and relinquish to others the frenetic pace of her daily routine.

She found solace and pleasure in an unexpected benefit of the episode. Her children were learning to be increasingly more self-sufficient and responsible, as well as to care for each other with tenderness and devotion. They were also becoming accustomed to finding solutions to their problems as a natural adjunct to Mommy's not being available all the time.

Erev Pesach approached quickly, and Chani could no longer rest. There was just no way she could sit and do nothing for the seder. Despite feeling weak she rose above her limitations and threw herself into last-minute preparations.

Finally, when every last corner was sparkling clean and every piece of silver cutlery was laid on the resplendent table, she allowed herself to collapse into bed, completely overcome by exhaustion.

When Shimon arrived home from shul, he found the little ones tucked into bed and his wife in a deep slumber. Suddenly he felt completely overwhelmed by the responsibilities he had been juggling over the previous few weeks. Exhaustion washed over him, and he felt a strong need to refresh himself with a short nap before starting the seder. *Just for half-an-hour, then I will wake Chani for the seder.*

The hours passed in complete silence as the family slept. Time dutifully performed its own task as night gave way to dawn ... and still they slept.

Then, as the birds began to stir and the world embraced the new day, Shimon's eyes suddenly fluttered open. At first, although he sensed something was wrong, he couldn't quite grasp what it was. As his fogged mind cleared and the hard fact hit him like a spurt of icy water, his heart sank, and he felt cold all over. He wished he were still dreaming.

His heavy pacing woke his wife, who looked around in utter bewilderment.

"What's going on?" she whispered. Sucking in a huge gulp of air, she suddenly sat up in total panic.

"What happened to our seder? Is the night really over? Can this be happening to us?" The questions tumbled out like water gushing from a broken dam.

Shimon stared at her hopelessly, his eyes mirroring the distress she felt.

"I'm going to the Rav," he said finally. In a flash, he was out the door, leaving Chani alone with her agonizing thoughts.

It wasn't long before the little ones' special morning voices began drifting into her room as they delighted in welcoming the new day.

Chani could not face them yet. Anguished thoughts battered endlessy at her mind. She tried to sort through the maze of her emotions. Her heartstrings vacillated between a deep feeling of emptiness over a missed seder, acute regret at the loss of so precious a mitzvah, and overwhelming guilt feelings at having allowed this to happen.

How she wished she could turn back the clock. *Can it really be that our seder night is gone forever?*

Shimon returned. His anguished expression had changed to one of calm acceptance. Chani felt her spirits lifting somewhat.

The Rav had listened calmly and intently as Shimon had poured out his unfortunate tale. Instead of the condemnation or rebuke Shimon had anticipated, only nonjudgmental, kind words of understanding had been forthcoming.

"All of us can on occasions display signs of weakness and imperfection," the Rav had remarked. "We are only human. *Sheva yipol tzaddik, vekam* — the *tzaddik* falls seven times, but has the courage to get up again each time. To err is human, but to stoop down and pick up the pieces — that sometimes takes tremendous resolve."

Somewhat comforted, Chani felt herself gradually releasing her grip on her remorse as Shimon repeated the words of the Rav.

She felt an immense sense of relief as she realized that her strong need to be nothing less than perfect at all times was really a weakness.

Suddenly, she became aware of a new strength — the strength to face her human limitations. That is indeed the perfect way Hashem created us — with our strengths and our limitations. We are not complete; we each have our faults and flaws, and by accepting our vulnerabilities and inadequacies humbly, we really grow. If we can relinquish our perceived control over our limitations, we can then gain an increased ability to focus on how to overcome those deficiencies. We can strive for true improvement and try to gain genuine inner perfection, which is a lifetime adventure.

It is precisely our imperfections and our ability to choose right from wrong — and sometimes make mistakes in the process — that make us the perfect beings that Hashem created in His perfect world.

And so that night, the second night of Pesach, Shimon and Chani celebrated the seder with enthusiasm. It took effort to focus on what they had gained rather than to dwell on what was lost.

It wasn't easy to dispose of the pangs of regret and guilt still fresh in their minds. But they did it, with open hearts and minds and sincere, deeply felt acceptance.

THE GIFT

Ahuvi sat on her pink ruffled bedspread, staring into space. The bright sunlight shining into her room through the window cast a dreamy appearance on the enchanting nook she called her own. She always retreated to her special corner when she needed to think things through.

But the hurt in her heart gave her no respite. Rina had not called her or spoken to her for the last three months.

Unlike the other students at Bais Penina, upon finishing elementary school, Ahuvi had been the only one to switch schools for high school. She had entered Bais Penina High School the year before because the elementary school she had attended didn't have a high school. Bais Penina, on the other hand, consisted of an elementary school and a high school, which the student body would join as a matter of course. Geography, too, was a factor. Ahuvi's family had moved into the neighborhood just that previous summer. New to the school and the locale, Ahuvi had greatly appreciated Rina's kindness in showing her the ropes in her new surroundings.

She liked Rina and was eager to create a closer friendship with her, especially since their mothers were friends of long standing, going back to their own school days.

Truth be told, it was always Ahuvi who made any attempts to establish a relationship. Rina always waited for Ahuvi to approach her and initiate any conversation or activity. Ahuvi's outgoing nature soon had her spreading her wings and enjoying friendships with other girls. She quickly became a popular and well-liked student and had many friends. Countless amicable conversations made their way between her telephone and those of the other girls.

Rina, on the other hand, was of a rather taciturn nature and seemed to find it harder to express herself in conversation. Her reticence did not earn her the popularity that Ahuvi mastered in such short time. Rina longed to be the center of ebullient conversation, surrounded by laughter and ardent listening faces. She wanted to be like Ahuvi. She would have given anything to walk home from school every day in the company of so many happy companions. Yet somehow she always seemed to be shrinking at the sidelines. Her mother, too, felt the loneliness of her daughter. It pained her to see how the phone hardly ever rang for the teenager. She was well aware of Rina's lack of friends and sometimes made some vague remarks regarding that in her frequent conversations with Rochelle, Ahuvi's mother. Still, she believed that this was something her daughter needed to work out for herself, albeit with her full support.

Quite frequently Ahuvi would call and fill Rina's lonely heart with friendly chatter and happy words. Ahuvi wasn't one to forget a good deed done for her and was forever grateful for Rina's befriending her in those early days. Yet Rina would invariably get the feeling that this was done out of charity rather than because of authentic good feelings.

This unfortunate belief, though, was due mainly to Rina's own feeling of inferiority rather than to factual substance. The reality was that Ahuvi truly liked Rina, who occupied a very special place in her heart. She admired her special, soft-spoken nature and strong logical understanding of everything around her. Rina always seemed well-balanced and was not easily swayed by outer influences to go against what was right. Unlike Ahuvi's intense emotional response to everything that happened, Rina would always remain calm and composed and, most importantly, logical. She always worked out an event or problem using her mind rather than her heart, and Ahuvi therefore greatly respected Rina's judgement about the various issues that came up in their lives, especially because Rina was never impulsive and never acted out of a sense of urgency, as Ahuvi did. This characteristic, more than anything else, was what Ahuvi strove to learn and desired to emulate.

Yet so many times when Ahuvi would call, she would be rewarded by a lecture from Rina. Rina would point out one of her wrongdoings, moralize about it, criticize her for it, and give her a piece of her mind. Interestingly enough, Ahuvi appreciated this angle of talk and always found an element of truth in Rina's words. Many times she saw it as a welcome change to the praises sung to her by her other friends.

Sitting in the special corner in her bedroom, her thoughts turned to the last conversation she had had with Rina. Her forehead puckered as she tried to focus on that memory with utmost concentration. She desired to find a way to figure out Rina's enigmatic behavior. But most of all, she hated to have an "enemy."

She remembered the conversation clearly. It was Ahuvi who had called to enjoy a friendly chat with her classmate. This time, though, the rebuke she had received had been entirely out of line, she thought, and a bit sharper than usual.

"What makes you think you're so great that you can do whatever you want? Anything you want to do is always right for you! But of course, that's your right, your privilege!" Rina had said in an icy tone, voice oozing with unconcealed sarcasm. Then

Rina had launched into a particularly vicious attack, dissecting every part of Ahuvi's personality.

Shocked by the onslaught but eager to avoid confrontation, Ahuvi had tactfully steered the conversation to calmer spheres, asking Rina about her ideas for the latest project they had been assigned in class and about her upcoming shopping plans. As soon as possible, Ahuvi gracefully ended the conversation and hung up the phone.

That had been three months ago, and Rina had not looked her way since. But Ahuvi was very uncomfortable about the situation.

The next day Ahuvi turned to her homeroom teacher for advice.

Mrs. Leidereich was a respected teacher. Tall and imposing, she gave the impression of a woman who knows where she's headed in life. At the same time she possessed a wonderful heart of gold; she was a truly caring mentor for those who sought her guidance. Her *Yahadut* lessons were enriched with powerful stories and practical pointers on how to apply the lofty lessons taught in the classroom to real-life situations. More than anything else, Mrs. Leidereich had a very positive influence on her students.

As soon as Mrs. Leidereich stepped out of their classroom, Ahuvi followed, and by hurrying a bit managed to catch up with her teacher.

"Mrs. Leidereich, is it possible to have a word with you?"

The pair walked side by side through the corridor and then came to a quiet spot where Ahuvi bared her heart to Mrs. Leidereich.

Mrs. Leidereich carefully listened to everything Ahuvi said, asking questions here and there where she needed clarification. Ahuvi, very conscious about forbidden speech, had first questioned the teacher, asking whether she was allowed to talk about another student. Since the talking was for a constructive purpose, Mrs. Leidereich said it was permissible, but still, no names were mentioned.

Ahuvi felt her teacher's genuine understanding and the sincere empathy emanating from her warm eyes. This gave her the courage to open up and talk. Ahuvi marveled at the way Mrs. Leidereich seemed to put everything else aside, giving her student her full attention and concentration, and focusing entirely on the issue at hand. They stood for some time in this private corner. Ahuvi related her numerous attempts at bridging the gap that had emerged between her and Rina, and of how nothing seemed to help. She felt herself reliving all her pent-up emotions caused by a misplaced guilty conscience and festering turmoil.

"It almost appears to me that this is what the girl wants from me — constant friendly overtures on my part — just so that she may have the pleasure of casting it away. For her part, she never comes toward me. What am I supposed to do now?"

"Let's think of it as a club membership," Mrs. Leidereich said at last. "*We* are the ones in charge of our membership, and we should decide who gets to belong and who does not. Sometimes it is good for us to revoke a membership or perhaps suspend a membership for some time, and then renegotiate the relationship.

"Now, that's not to say that you confront your friend and tell her, 'Listen, my dear, I am revoking your membership.' Not at all, that's not the way it works. We still retain our friendly terms, we greet each other, and we may walk home together and talk about this and that, and keep up an amiable relationship.

"So what do I mean by 'revoking a membership'? It is something that takes place in one little neat department of your own mind.

"We want friends who help us grow, who help us bring out the best in us, our inner values and principles that sometimes lie dormant somewhere inside. When we are criticized too often, we become too paralyzed to bring those values to the fore and let them shine. Nobody likes to feel hurt and put down, so in an effort to protect ourselves from hurt feelings, we become overly occupied with creating barriers and cover-ups to mask our vulnerabilities and weaknesses from our pseudo-friends and even from ourselves.

"A true friend is someone who allows you to be yourself, to free yourself from the fetters of perfectionism and strong outer facades. Our own unique greatness emerges and we feel special, which all of us really are, each in our own way. Only then, from this higher altitude and eagle-eye perspective, can we allow ourselves to peek at our deficiencies and failures. With the help of a caring friend, we acquire the courage to face our weaknesses, and we gain the desire to strive for true inner improvement. That is because we are secure in the knowledge that *though I am not perfect and at times I may stumble, my friend will be at my side, believing in me, lauding me on, and celebrating my successes together with me.* Only then can one truly grow and blossom.

"It seems to me that by constantly re-approaching your friend after all her attempts to push you away, you are actually handing her the authority to rule over you and the relationship. Leave her alone. She seems to need you so that she can, somehow, fill her own need for power and control, or perhaps in order to feel good about herself in a kind of seesaw effect. That is, 'If you are the one down, then by virtue of that alone, I am the one up.' Try to see if she will come toward you for a change, especially since you did nothing to hurt her feelings. I have a feeling that she *won't* come toward you, so do not become despondent. Good luck, Ahuvi."

Ahuvi had much to think about over the next few days. According to Mrs. Leidereich, Ahuvi did not have to do anything at all — she was fine. She could just sit back, relax, and forget about Rina.

Still, she did want to find a way to make peace. She hated the fact that there existed someone who might feel hurt by her in some way. For days she mulled over her teacher's advice and her diverse feelings on the matter, until finally she arrived at a conclusion. Ahuvi came to a firm resolve to prove to Rina that she, on her

The Gift

part, harbored no ill feelings. She would buy her friend a birthday gift and mail it to her. It would be a gesture that would say, "I still care about you." This act would surely give Rina an opening to approach her. Ahuvi would take it from there, and decide about the membership after that.

Ahuvi spent days thinking about the perfect gift. Finally she decided on a silver necklace with the words *Someone Special* engraved on the pendant. She wrapped it in a creative display, laboring diligently over the design. To her it was a labor of love and joy. She felt confident and happy. It felt great to rise above the limitations of what might be considered proper and take a step beyond that to try and bring sunshine into someone's life. In her mind, she carried on many conversations with Rina, anticipating her call and their restored harmony. It did not matter to Ahuvi that there would probably never again develop a rich and fulfilling relationship between the two. That was not the point. It was more a silent pact of forgiveness that Ahuvi was after at this juncture. She wanted to make it crystal clear that, on her part, she felt no misgivings or anger toward Rina. She did not mention a word about her plans to her other friends. She knew they felt it unnecessary and even demeaning on her part, but she didn't care and felt she wanted to rise above those attitudes.

The gift was hand-delivered by Leah, Ahuvi's younger sister, and the waiting game began. But the call did not come that day; neither did it come the day after. Ahuvi struggled with her emotions as they vacillated between anger and feelings of utter foolishness. At the end of the week, Rina phoned. In a stilted voice, she formally stated her thanks for the gift and the wonderful way it was packaged. They spoke for a few minutes and then ended the conversation on a smooth note.

There were no shouts of "wow," no ringing bells extolling her virtuous act, and no round of applause, but Ahuvi felt great. She felt uplifted, carried above the realm of petty grievances and revenge. She felt whole, knowing that she had acted on what she felt was the right thing to do.

She knew the feeling of, "Who is strong?" Ben Zoma says, "He who subdues his personal inclination, as it is said: 'He who is slow to anger is better than a conqueror of a city'" (*Mishlei* 16:32).

GUARDIAN ANGELS

The curtains are drawn to reveal a fantastic scene — a palace complete with a royal throne and majestic decor — all built entirely from Lego bricks. The puppet show has begun.

Motty, crouching underneath the desk, peeks out from behind the couch cushions concealing him from the view of his audience, consisting of Naftali, Yehoshua, and Tova, his siblings. Encouraged by his success, judging by the wide-eyed audience he was "seeing without being seen," his voice takes on an increased dramatic dimension and he continues his performance, spinning a beautiful tale enacted with the help of his puppet actors and Lego props. His audience sits enthralled, as they generally do when presented with Motty's agenda of entertainment. Truth be told, it doesn't always match his mother's idea of fun, although this time she becomes equally enraptured.

Unlike the time, not too long ago, when the house was unexpectedly and completely swallowed up in darkness!

A serene silence had descended upon the house as the children were relaxing contentedly in bed, snuggled cozily under their warm fuzzy blankets, after having said *Krias Shema* and after having been kissed good night. While everyone else was slowly drifting into dreamland, Motty's young mind was busy thinking about all the important matters of life and all the hidden secrets of the universe that needed to be sorted out in his little head. His spinning mind was busy churning up some delightful ideas with which to experiment.

Unable to vanquish his tingling feeling of excitement, he slipped out from underneath his covers, ran to the hefty air conditioner stored in the corner of the hallway, and shoved it with all his might to the nearest outlet. He already knew from an earlier attempt that the plug didn't fit into the wall socket. But this time he had a super idea.

Silently, he grabbed a transformer from where he had seen his mother plug in her mixer when she needed to make up for the lack of voltage between her American machine and Israeli electrical power. With skilled hands and silent movements, he deftly forged the connection between the two plugs and then stuck the attachment plug into the outlet. A stunning blackness was the shocking result!

Trembling in fear, he catapulted straight back into his bed, willing his wildly pumping heart to slow down, but the thumping continued within his ribcage long after the blown fuse was turned back on.

The next day the incident was all but forgotten. Perhaps he needed to make room in his mind to completely concentrate on his new project ....

"Mommy, can I have that little black box ... the one that your camera film comes in?" He brightly asked one day, his face a picture of innocence, shining with happy anticipation.

"Sure you can have it, darling," Sheina responded naively. Preoccupied with a thousand other demands, Sheina took a new film cassette from its little black box and delivered the box straight into the outstretched hand of her eager son without further ado. After all, why would she think he might need the little container for anything other than to store one of his collections?

Why indeed?

How about a newfound collection comprised of a murky liquid substance? The kind that won't simply rinse off with water … or soap … or even good old-fashioned scrubbing. Ink! Homemade ink, produced most conveniently through the process of squeezing the tubes of liquid inside pens and markers! The first chance Sheina had to check on him (in order to discern the reason for the lack of the familiar sounds of falling objects that he couldn't reach but pulled down from higher shelves with the hooked handle of an umbrella), she found him dipping feather into ink, painstakingly writing tiny letters on her best stationery — his subsitute parchment. That was his stint at *Sofres*, though the moment he got bored and before Sheina had a chance to offer her sage advice, she found him pouring the excess of his paraphernalia — including the "quill" — down the drain in the bathroom, necessitating a visit from the trusty plumber. Not a very uncommon experience, especially when one is curious to see what happens when the dollhouse baby gets a bath in the toilet, or an entire box of tissues is banished down a drain.

At age 7, one is still far too young to be a *sofer*.

One would think that at that tender age, a child would be too young to comprehend the depth of pain and the intensity of anguish resulting from a terrorist act. Perhaps. But the profound pain and paralyzing fear that Motty experienced after the suicide explosion on the Number 2 Bus held the intensity of that of an old man. Yet the tools to handle the enormity of the traumatic situation were still sorely lacking.

Though far away from the vicinity of the attack, and despite not knowing any of the victims personally, Motty himself became a victim of the stories he heard in *cheder* from his all-knowing young contemporaries. He was acutely troubled and thoroughly distressed on a deep level during the day and was without respite at night, when nightmares came to haunt him, jolting him out of his bed and propelling him like a missile into Sheina's.

Sheina had long conversations with her son. They spent a lot of time talking together. They talked about Hashem Who protects and guards us all, talked about the facts and figures; i.e., the number of bus lines and buses making their rounds every day and the thousands of people continuing their routes. They recited chapters in *Tehillim* together, and they even experimented with various *segulas* (spiritual remedies).

Motty would continue to sit on the ledge of the barred windowsill, tears streaming down his cheeks as his heart hammered in fear, waiting to catch a glimpse of his father returning from work via bus!

One afternoon, Sheina sat with Motty, drawing and coloring pictures together. As they spoke about the pictures, Sheina was struck by the profundity of his feelings. "This picture," Motty said, taking all the crayons in his collection in a tight grip and fiercely swirling them around on the page, "is how much it hurts when I remember about the bomb."

"Where does it hurt you?" Sheina questioned him.

"Over here," he said pointing to his chest, "in my heart."

"Why does it hurt?"

"Because those children have no fathers anymore ... or mothers ... or children!"

Sheina stared at him. She was stunned.

Each morning before leaving to *cheder*, Motty pleaded with his mother to repeat after him, to "promise me there won't be a bomb today."

"I promise," Sheina would say, silently praying, beseeching Hashem in her heart, "*im yirtzeh Hashem,* there will not be a bomb today."

"On the bus."

"On the bus."

"And nowhere else."

"And nowhere else."

Only then would he allow himself to relax his tense features, and a faint smile would appear on his lips. Only then would he gather the courage to leave the house to catch his van, leaving Sheina staring after his receding back, wondering what the day would bring. *Who knows if today will be the day when another sadistic suicide bomber will break the child's trust in his mother, who is supposed to know it all and who is supposed to possess the capacity to protect him from danger?* Sheina wondered. She knew that she did not fit that Divine role and instituted a change.

From then on, before Motty left for *cheder*, Sheina would say a *passuk* from *Tehillim* 91, and her son would repeat after her. *Ki malachav yetzaveh loch lishmarcha bechol derachecha* — He will charge His angels concerning you, to protect you in all your ways; it became their daily ritual.

The metamorphosis that occurred in Motty was immediate and complete. He became transformed. No longer did he sit by the window each evening, and gone were the nightmares. The pictures he drew became colorful and lively, and the stories he told were happy ones. When he came home from school with the familiar rip in his pants, Sheina knew she had her Motty back.

The days and weeks passed quickly. There was no time for their daily formal departure. In a hop, skip, and jump, he was out the door, *tzitzis* flying in the air, a perpetual smile glued to his face. Motty trembled in mock fear, not from the thought of bombs, fires, and missing children, but from the culpability of felonies like Sheina's broken eyeglasses, a jammed stereo, and crashing light bulbs.

Then one day Sheina received an exquisite gift.

The family was all seated around the dinner table, chatting about their day, with Sheina making a conscious effort to allow each child a fair chance to express the events in his or her day.

It was Naftali who was in the midst of relating, in the most dramatic form he could muster, a detailed description of the frightening dream he had had the night before.

"I was so scared," Naftali said, shuddering visibly at the memory.

Suddenly, and completely unexpectedly, a confident voice rang out.

"Naftali, do you know what you should do when you have a scary dream?" Motty said kindly in his older-brother tone, gesturing theatrically with his hand to create a melodramatic effect.

"Say, *Ki malachav* ..." he paused slightly to add significance to his words, "*yetzaveh loch lishmarcha bechol derachecha*!" he ended with a flourish.

Glancing up at his mother for approval, their dancing eyes locked for a blessed moment of supreme joy.

SETTLING ACCOUNTS

"Things cannot go on like this anymore, Feige. We must find another tenant."

Tenant? For a moment Feige didn't quite comprehend what her husband was talking about. The two were walking down the long hospital corridor toward the neonatal ward, where their precious baby was waiting for them. What did a tenant have to do with the beeping monitors, the smell of medicine, the numerous medical personnel milling about?

But she was familiar with Shmuel's style of dealing with the stress of the moment. As if on cue, whenever the jitters hit him, he would whiz off to the land of logic, his comforting escape zone.

"It is not like we didn't give him a chance," Shmuel continued matter-of-factly, as though he had been sitting relaxed in a comfortable armchair, one leg crossed over the other. "It's time to take things more seriously and find someone who can pay the rent."

The rent. That's what he meant. Already she was straining to catch sight of her baby's isolette, though they were not yet inside the ward. "Yes, we have to pay the rent," she said, somewhat distractedly.

Shmuel cleared his throat. "Feige, *we* don't have to pay the rent," he said. "But we must find someone who will."

Understanding suddenly dawned. She swallowed hard. "You're not thinking of evicting Itche!" she said.

Her husband didn't reply. He silenced his cell phone as they both entered the intensive care unit.

Jenna, the nurse, waved to them and Feige hurried over, anxiety etched on her face. Shmuel's even pace didn't change, his face a determined mask of indifference.

There was much more to see today, and Feige's face glowed as she peered into the isolette. For so long little Shiffy had been bandaged up to her nose, from which a thin feeding tube had spiraled out, converging with an intravenous port that had jutted out of her tiny arm, and her face had been hidden by the ventilator tube. Now, only the identifying bracelet graced her right foot.

"She is free at last, Jenna." Feige said, valiantly reining in some of her ecstasy. "We are taking her home today?" she half-stated, half-questioned, never for a moment taking her gaze from her baby.

Can it be? She remembered now how many times she had come rushing to the hospital, ready to sweep the baby into her arms and head straight for the exit, only to be told, "Mrs. Rothbart, Shiffy had a brady incident during the night. We have to keep her under observation for another twenty-four hours." Bradycardia. She dreaded that word. Yet eating and breathing and swallowing all at once seemed to overtax the premature baby, who had simply stopped breathing. Time and again they had left with empty arms and devastation in their hearts.

"She is doing very well," Jenna said, waving a stack of forms. "After these are completed, you will be on your way, ma'am."

Feige instinctively bent down to retrieve her baby. Shmuel, standing at her side, with his arms behind his back, nodded his head politely.

Back on the expressway, as the infant lay quietly in her carseat, Feige stared into her baby's black eyes; she had so much to be thankful for. Coming home at last — how rich the new baby made her feel. Visions of poor Itche staggering up their front path in his torn shoes rose before her. Everything about him conveyed a sense of sadness — his slight limp as he walked, his rumpled jacket, and the perpetual tightness around his mouth and jaw.

"Oh, hello, Mrs. Rothbart," Itche would call out every time he saw her. His words were always the same, as though he had been repeating them from a written script. "I have been meaning to come by. You see, I don't have the money just now. Don't think I forgot about it. You should know it is on my mind every day." And then, as he would lift his hands heavenward in his habitual gesture, he would add, "*Hashem yaazor* — Hashem will help."

She sighed. Shmuel turned his heads sideways, keeping his hands firmly on the steering wheel. "What is it?"

"I was just thinking about Itche. For some reason, I feel so sad for him. The poor man never hurt a fly. Such a gentle soul, always smiling, always hopeful. I am sure it can't be easy for him, living the way he does. Do you know how painful loneliness can be? The reason he divorced his wife was because he wanted to lead a Torah life and she wasn't ready. He came here to try to earn an honest living and …" she sighed, "he is just not making it."

"I know it would be a real *chessed* to keep him," Shmuel hurried to explain, "but you have to understand, the new baby will need a lot of therapy, the last installment for our bungalow is due next week, and don't forget the bill for Elisheva's braces. Feige, we simply need the money."

Feige allowed her head to fall back on the seat. She felt tired.

"You cannot possible throw him out on the street like a discarded cigarette," she told Shmuel with closed eyes.

"We have been through this so many times, Feige. We converted our basement into a studio apartment for rent, not for the fun of it, but because we need the money. Do you realize that besides a litany of excuses each month, he hasn't paid his rent for six months?

"Someone has got to pay the bills," Shmuel added in a low tone. "And that someone happens to be me."

"But where will he go? He doesn't know a soul in this country aside from us. We can't do it, Shmuel."

Maybe I should have forgone our summer vacation in the Catskills this year, she ruminated. It was hard enough traveling to the hospital in the city, and if the added expense demanded that Itche be evicted, it was hardly worth it. Yet Shmuel had argued that the children needed to escape from the crowded streets and the sweltering heat of the city. He had insisted that the trips to the hospital, halfway between the city and the country, wouldn't be a hassle at all. Today they had returned to the city and hurried to the hospital, with their boxed belongings simply stowed in the house, ready to be unpacked.

"Shmuel, Hashem knows what our needs are," she said softly. "He will surely help us, you'll see."

But her husband brushed her off. "Woman's talk," he said. "There is a reality, you understand? The reality is that I have a mortgage to pay. The reality is that we have to repair the leak in the roof. The reality is that …."

Feige didn't hear more. Reality? How did precluding Hashem from the picture define reality? But she knew better than to voice her thoughts. It was Shmuel who carried the burden, after all, though she knew without a doubt that Hashem was taking care of them. The miracle of her tiny baby did not allow her to forget. Still, knowing Shmuel, she was certain that he would never throw anyone out on the street. So what was the point of exciting him any further with her talk? Besides, the car lulled her into dreamland and she drifted in and out of sleep for the duration of the trip.

With her eyes still half-closed, she watched her husband maneuver his white Volvo into the tight parking space in front of their home. The baby, cradled in her arm, slept on even as she stepped out onto the concrete sidewalk. As she walked up the few steps to her house, she noted the water dripping from her neighbor's air conditioner, the polluted city sky, and the dense humidity that hung in the air like a heavy curtain.

She sensed it as soon as she entered the door; the reeking stench drifting up from below nearly suffocated her. Shmuel, whose sense of smell was almost nonexistent, nonchalantly went about his business. He poured himself a glass of cold ginger ale, listened to his messages on the answering machine, and returned a few phone calls.

Feige hastened to place the baby into her crib and then darted down the stairs and knocked on the door. There was no answer — and Itche did not own a telephone. Running back up, she jogged her memory for her neighbor's phone number.

"Hi, this is Feige Rothbart speaking. May I speak to your mother, please?"

"She is not home right now, but this is Leah. Are you home from the country already, Mrs. Rothbart? Mazel tov on your new baby."

"Thank you, Leah. When will your mother be home?"

"I'm not sure, but if it's urgent, can I help you with something?"

"Yes, it is very urgent. Would you happen to have any information about our tenant, Itche?"

"Yes, yes, I do know. Actually, he gave me a message to tell you when you come home. It's a good thing you reminded me. He said to tell you not to throw out any of his stuff, that he is coming back. He …."

"Not to throw out his stuff? That he's coming back? What do you mean? Where is he?"

"I don't know. I think — Israel. Yes, Israel. He said his mother was very ill and that he had to go take care of her. But he said he is coming back and that you shouldn't get rid of his belongings. Why, is there something wrong, Mrs. Rothbart?"

"Okay, thank you so much, Leah. I really have to go now."

Feige replaced the receiver, grabbed the spare key she kept in the kitchen cupboard, and hurried down the stairs again.

She flipped on the switch, flooding the room with light. A startled rat scurried past. Then another big one darted for cover under the low bed at the far side of the room. Feige stood rooted to the spot, stifling a scream. She did not know where to step, what to expect, or the source of that terrible odor. Her eyes swept over the stark furnishings of the room. Dark coffee stains circled a chipped mug that sat on the countertop. A broken broom leaned against the wall next to an old, faded jacket that hung from a nail haphazardly knocked into the wall. She looked at the single chair beside the table, which was covered by a threadbare tablecloth on which some moldy bits of bread lay scattered about. An open carton of cottage cheese, green by now, stared up at her.

Feige mustered the nerve to follow the smell to its source. It was the fridge. Apparently, Itche had unplugged the fridge in order to save on electricity before he left. In the freezer she found a decaying tray of raw meat that had leaked all around. The fridge revealed a moldy cucumber, spoiled milk, and an open package of yogurt that was oozing from the container. Slamming the fridge closed, Feige leaned against the door and cried, tears streaming down her careworn face. She was already exhausted by the trip home, dreading the dozens of unpacked boxes, and now she had this maddening mess with which to deal.

Wearily, she dragged herself up the stairs and collapsed onto the sofa. Minutes had ticked by when Shmuel, poking his head into the living room, found her staring into space and instantly surmised that something was wrong.

"The baby ...?" Shmuel hurried toward the crib.

"The baby is fine, Shmuel." Her fingers shot to her lips, in an effort to stop their quivering. "Shmuel, you can't imagine what's going on downstairs. Moldy cheese; rats took over the place. Who knows how long he has been gone?"

Ever the practical one, Shmuel promptly grabbed the telephone directory from his desk and proceeded to look for an exterminator. "What's the problem? We will hire Maria to get the place clean and next week we'll take in a new tenant. That's all there is to it. What was it you said before? Hashem takes care of us. Don't you see? Thank Hashem for the wisdom of women"

Despite her misery, Feige couldn't keep back her smile. She couldn't figure him out. One minute it was "woman's talk"; the next minute it was "wisdom of women."

"Oh, no, hold it. Not so fast," she said. Briefly she related to him her conversation with Leah, the neighbor's eldest daughter.

"So, you see, we have to keep the place for him."

Shmuel was quiet for some time, pondering this information. Then he dialed the number of an exterminator. As he waited for someone to come on the line, he said to her, "I will try to track Itche down and set the facts straight, and we'll take it from there."

But they couldn't find him. They tried every contact they could think of, any link that would lead them to the vanished man. Itche was nowhere to be found. Days turned into weeks and then months. The apartment downstairs sparkled once again, the older children went back to school, little Shiffy learned to smile. Finally Shmuel went to see his Rav.

Rabbi Weiss listened to all the details as Shmuel told him about Itche. In light of the circumstances, he ruled that in this situation they were allowed to give away Itche's meager belongings *lesheim mitzvah*, for a worthy cause.

Years flew by. Shmuel and Feige never heard from Itche again. Once in a while they would talk about him, reminisce about the simple purity he had exuded. But he had literally disappeared without a trace.

The Rothbarts moved to Israel and only rarely did Feige think about that dreadful moment when she had found rats roaming around her basement.

It was the day of Shiffy's twentieth birthday. Feige was busy in her Jerusalem kitchen, creaming a three-tiered cake in honor of the event, when she received a phone call from a woman who identified herself as Dafne.

"Shalom, Mrs. Rothbart." The soft voice coming over the phone spoke in a heavy Israeli accent. Despite the friendliness in the voice, Feige could not place it.

"Do I know you?" she asked, continuing to wield her spatula.

"You don't. But I know *you*."

Feige set down the spatula. "I'm not sure I understand what you are saying."

Dafne laughed uncomfortably. "*Al tidagi* [Don't worry]. I will explain myself. Do you remember you had a tenant in America some, maybe, twenty years back?"

"Itche!"

"Yes, yes. I am pleased. I see you know what I am talking about."

Suddenly the kitchen Feige was standing in faded away. In its place Feige saw another kitchen. The table covered with a threadbare tablecloth. An open carton of green cottage cheese lying forlorn amidst some moldy bits of bread. The tray of decaying raw meat in the freezer, dried-out drippings all around it. It all came back to her now, her tired muscles, the excitement of bringing little Shiffy home at last. It was hard to believe that twenty years had already gone by. And yet, here she was preparing a birthday cake for that erstwhile little baby.

"Itche died this week. He was very sick man, *Hashem yishmareinu* [Hashem should protect us]. Itche used be my husband, *at yodat* [do you know]? But I wanted to wear pants. I could not cover my hair. It was very difficult for me. But he was a nice man. Very! And now he went to *Shamayim* [Heaven].

"But one thing is a very big problem. Itche always talked about the *chov* [debt]. Every day, maybe. He said, 'When I will have money, I will pay back the *chov*.' *Kol hazman* [all the time]."

Feige's voice failed her. With her cordless phone in her hand, she left the kitchen and headed for the recliner. Her legs were shaking. She needed to sit down.

"Hello? You are still there, yes?" Dafne wanted to know.

"Um. Hmm. Yes," was all she managed to say.

"*Tov.* I want to come to you in your house. I must to pay the rent money for him. I don't want *chas vechallilah* that he have a *chov* in *Shamayim*. When is good time that I can come to you?"

Feige gulped. This woman wanted to pay back the rent that Itche couldn't pay all those long years ago? Could it be?

"I don't know the exact amount. You tell me and I will bring it to you tomorrow. I will come with a bus from Tel Aviv. Is nine o'clock in the morning a good time for you?"

Gathering her wits, Feige managed to reply, "*Baruch Dayan ha'emes.* Yes. Itche was a very special person. Thank you, Dafne. I will look up the amount in our records and I will get back to you."

True to her word, Dafne arrived at nine o'clock on the dot with payment for a year's worth of rent, so that Itche, the gentle man who had been her husband so many years ago, should not have a debt in *Shamayim*.

Who can measure the value of a Jewish soul?

THE SUCCAH THAT REMAINED STANDING

When I enter the succah at my parent's home each year, my gaze silently traverses the long walls in search of one beloved picture. The picture, a painting of a lulav and esrog, so real one can almost reach out and feel the esrog's bumpy texture, is essentially a souvenir. Once, long ago, it was fashioned with love by a little boy. It had been painted on plain white fabric that concealed a brick wall. Thirty-five years later, the picture hangs in the succah of my father — who was once that little boy — as a precious memento of days gone by.

The painting has a story to tell. It is the story of a happy and loving family who sat around a worn table within their makeshift succah, content and at peace with the little that they owned. It is my aunt who offers to narrate the charming tale for me.

"Every year," she nostalgically begins, "on *Erev Succos*, my father would traipse down the old rickety staircase to the damp cellar that reeked of the petroleum-filled heating tank, to inspect our forlorn succah. We children would scamper after him, our excitement barely suppressed, each vying to have the first glimpse of our succah. The succah was a solitary door comprised of a hodgepodge of wooden strips and affectionately dubbed 'the succah.'

"My father, who was no friend of the hammer or the nails, would carefully scrutinize 'the succah.' He'd check for loose nails or splintered pieces of wood that needed restoration, and then would lovingly proceed to patch up the door.

"After the nails were all in place, Father would painstakingly and meticulously attach the door to the old wooden fence on one side and the stone wall on the other side. Another stone structure projecting from the house at the far end completed our humble succah, and the family felt blessed.

"Sometimes, I would dream of having a 'real' succah, a glorious and impressive succah; one that would more closely resemble those of my neighbors and friends. As Father banged and hammered, I would stand at the side, wistfully designing my dream succah. *Maybe this year*, I would wish in my heart, *our* succah *would truly be exquisite.*

"The next-door neighbors had a 'real' succah; a magnificent, ready-bought structure. How I envied them that succah! To me, 'store-bought' qualified as 'real.'

"'The Meyer's succah is s-t-u-n-n-i-n-g! They also have blinking lights! They really do!' I announced to no one in particular.

"My mother eyed me lovingly, 'Yes,' she said, 'they really have a nice succah, my dear. It is so wonderful that they have a nice succah.' Her face sparkled with the genuine elation she felt at the neighbor's pleasure. 'We have a beautiful succah too,' she emphasized.

"It was a beautiful succah indeed. Its grandeur was its simplicity. It was a succah that spoke of determination and whispered of devotion. That was the soul of our succah. Every corner of it exuded warmth and sincerity. It was a succah produced to the best of our ability and we weren't ashamed of it. When my friends came around for the master viewing at night, my heart would pulsate with pride at our family-produced masterpiece.

"One memorable year, my father offered me a dollar. My brother, Moshe, and I ran as fast as our legs would carry us to procure a precious piece of green carpet with which we adorned the floor of the succah. After that, I managed to wheedle a nickel from my mother. I hurried to R' Chaim, the merchant down the block, to obtain another ornament to beautify the walls. When my brother drew the lulav and esrog on that white sheet, I was convinced that there was nothing nicer in the whole world. I can still feel the excitement that surged through my veins when his artistic gift was completed.

"I helped my father bang nails into the old table and bench that threatened to fall apart with the slightest movement. Then I scrubbed them clean with a vitality born of desperation, until they gleamed. My father lovingly washed each piece of bamboo for the *s'chach* before he spread the stalks over the succah. My sister polished the old cutlery until it looked like new. Mother was kept busy handing nails and other paraphernalia through the window of our apartment, all in the midst of her own cooking and stirring the steaming pots.

"One year, on the first night of Succos, strong gusts of wind blustered all around us as we huddled around the table, trembling as much from the cold as from the apprehension we felt. Would our cherished succah withstand the storm? Would the precarious wooden fence, the wall at the left side, survive the powerful gales of wind?

"My father, oblivious to our uneasiness, eyes shut, fist tightly clenched, recited the Kiddush with intense devotion. Mother served the tasty food — spiced with that unique Yom Tov flavor — through the window. Still, the wind did not abate. Ripping and roaring mightily, it proceeded to tear down one neighboring succah after another. The sadness all around us was palpable as our neighbors looked on in shock, completely immobilized. All their ready-bought succahs I had envied so succumbed to the formidable windstorm.

"Our charming little succah remained standing that night. The wind could not blow away a succah that was built with love and enthusiasm. The strength of the family's closeness and loyalty held the fort.

"Years later, when my father grew older, his sons, who in the past had helped him, had moved away. The wooden fence bent out of shape, and so we reluctantly exchanged our tired and worn succah for one that was bought — and starkly impersonal. Although my mother had framed the section of the white sheet that held your father's masterpiece so that it could be a part of the new succah, I felt overwhelmed by sadness as I stepped into the pristine succah that year. The dream of my youth had become a reality; the external shell of our new succah was magnificent indeed, but gone was the tangible joy of loving cooperation in working toward a common goal. The intrinsic vitality of dedication and *mesiras nefesh* was no longer a part of the succah walls."

ALONE WITH HASHEM

Ilana Iskovitch clutched her Gucci handbag as she sat in the restaurant casually looking out the window, observing the women in fur coats flitting through the mall. As for her, she had finished traipsing through the outdoor shopping complex for the day.

While she waited for her order to be served, she pictured the stunning bangle studded with yellow diamonds that lay securely inside her pocketbook, and she mentally congratulated herself on her keen shopping abilities. Only last month she had seen the bangle at 40 million rubles, and now that the price had been slashed to 20 million rubles, she felt she had struck a grand deal.

The waitress placed her order of fresh black caviar in front of her. It was her favorite dish. The lumpfish roe — at two thousand rubles — lay perched neatly inside the hollow atop a globe of crushed ice, and was served with a mother-of-pearl spoon that prevented the tiny black eggs from oxidizing and losing their original flavor. Ilana loved the exquisitely delicate taste of the caviar.

Her cell phone buzzed. Nodding politely at the waitress, Ilana answered the call.

"No. NO!" she shouted into the phone. "It cannot be. Not my Alexei!"

All eyes turned to stare at the woman who had dared to create a disturbance in their elegant café, but Ilana didn't notice them. The room swam before her. Her knuckles quickly turning white, her fingers grasped the tasseled edges of the tablecloth as if her life depended on it.

"And Katya?" she panted, her heart beating rapidly. "Where is she?"

Scraping her chair back noisily, she grabbed her shopping bags and fled, abandoning her luxurious dish to the curious speculation of the other diners. Looking neither to her right nor to her left, Ilana kept running, her feet pounding the pavement. An old woman who, with the aid of a cane, was making her way down the street, stopped her slow gait to look back and stare. Ilana darted right on, stopping short of the honking traffic. As a bus zoomed by, blasting her with air, she stepped out into the intersection. A car swerved just in time to avoid her! Still, she did not slow her pace and continued running at a fast clip, rushing to get to Alexei's school.

The high-pitched voice of Anya, her children's devoted nanny, chased after her. *He's gone. He's gone.* Ilana willed the voice to stop or she would go mad. But the voice persisted. *I went to school to pick him up, but he wasn't there. Police were there. They were taking the report from the headmaster. Alexei was kidnaped at around four o'clock this afternoon, they told me. That was an hour ago, five minutes after dismissal.* The words circled in her brain, tightened her chest, quickened her pulse. And again the refrain, *he's gone, he's gone, he's gone, he's ....*

It couldn't be true. Ilana didn't believe this nonsense. She was going to find him, by any means. Maybe he was locked in the washroom, or maybe he was too engrossed in play to hear the school bell ringing. All kinds of things could have occurred. But surely no one had taken her Alexei away today. Soon she would find him squatting on the floor in the kindergarten, merrily building a tower of blocks. He would look up and break into a wide grin when he'd see her. He would jump up and wrap himself around her and she would hug him to her heart ....

Her husband's BMW, parked at a peculiar angle in front of the school, reminded her with a start that she had left her own gleaming Mercedes in the parking lot of the shopping mall. She noticed the family chauffeur sitting idly at the wheel, his window rolled down. Surely her husband, Vladimir, would be coming toward her now, swinging Alexei playfully in his hefty arms. They would get into the car and speed away to the safety of their own home, far from horrifying kidnaping stories. Her mind simply refused to accept the report she had heard from Anya.

But there in the schoolyard was her husband, empty-handed, eyes raw with fear, pacing back and forth like a wounded animal. Anya, close at his heels and working hard to follow Vladimir's zigzagging stride, carried on an endless monologue, repeating the same words over and over again. Upon noticing Katya's little hand clasped inside Anya's, heart-shaped face smudged with tears, her chin quivering, Ilana waved and shouted, "Katya, Katya!"

A police officer approached her, swinging his baton up and down. "The school is off-limits right now, Madame."

"Where is Alexei? I want to see him."

The officer scratched his forehead. "You are Madame Iskovitch, the mother of Alexei, right? Well, look here, I suggest you take your husband and the little kid here home." He shrugged. "We will call you with any further developments."

Ilana didn't respond to his advice. "Where is Alexei? I want to see him," she repeated.

"There has been an abduction, Madame," the officer growled and raising his voice menacingly, added, "Now get moving, do you hear me?"

Dimitri, the chauffeur, apparently heard the officer, because he immediately emerged from the BMW. "Come with me, Madame Ilana. Let's go for a drive," he urged.

Alone With Hashem

For a moment the battle between panic and logic raged within Ilana. *Calm down, relax, you can't fall apart now,* she ordered herself. *Vladimir can't, Anya won't. You must remain strong to hold the fort.* Gradually, her face took on a staunch expression as reason triumphed. After a moment, the idea of taking a drive actually appealed to her. *Perhaps we will find him yet, lost and crying at a street corner,* she ruminated as she got into the car. Vladimir, completely bewildered, took her cue, and robotically followed suit.

In the dimness of twilight, the small party scrutinized the streets, peering anxiously through the windshield at the quiet roads and boulevards as they cruised slowly along, watching for any suspicious movements. From afar they noticed a lone, motionless figure. Dimitri stamped down hard on the gas pedal; the car responded by speeding forth. As they came closer they passed a blanket-covered homeless man who sat leaning against a wall, half asleep.

Up ahead, they could distinguish the silhouette of someone else. Dimitri zoomed forward. The figure of a woman balancing a heavy water bucket on a wooden yoke came into view. The woman, who obviously had no running water, was making her way precariously along the slippery path to her tumbledown apartment. *How lucky she is,* thought Ilana, *bringing home water for her children's baths — children who are safe at home tonight.*

Dimitri turned onto the main boulevard. On either side, huge mansions stood on spacious grounds; Ferraris and Maseratis were parked in the driveways. Here and there they spotted a private helicopter on a front lawn. The gaping chasm between the rich and poor — proof of an economy that had not been working since the collapse of the Soviet Union — stared them in the face. In the distance they noticed an accordion player standing at the street corner, forced to sing for his supper.

The car veered to the right and coasted through another avenue. Dilapidated shacks dotted this street, some sloping dangerously, others without roofs or glass in the windows. A babushka puttered outside to close the rickety gate of her small yard, frightening off a few cats that were ferreting through the refuse lying beside the steps. At the sound of their car approaching, she lifted her face and grimaced at them. Another shadow came into view and the BMW raced forward. Vladimir moved closer to the windshield to have a better look.

An elderly drunkard wobbled on.

Aside from the ticking of the clock as the hours marched on, absolute silence reigned inside the car. Katya fell asleep, her blond tresses spread over Anya's lap. Ilana bit her lip; the child's schedule was out of kilter — something she detested — but that was not important now.

Suddenly, the jarring sound of Vladimir's mobile phone jolted their already tangled nerves. Anya awoke and began to cry.

"*Da*," Vladimir said. Ilana noticed that her husband's voice suddenly seemed to be that of someone thirty years his senior.

At first only a static drone echoed through the telephone line. Then finally, a muffled voice came on. "We got your kid," the anonymous caller stated. An involuntary gasp escaped Vladimir's throat.

The static noise returned for a moment before crackling back to life again. "He is in good condition."

Vladimir leaned forward. "Where is he?" he asked. "What do you want?"

"You want him, ha?" The booming voice reverberated in the car. Vladimir gripped the phone fearfully; everyone else held their breaths, the tension in the car palpable. "The day after tomorrow, bring 70 million rubles to the Mazdory train station. We're giving you time to get the money — in cash, of course. Once there, you will find a man wearing sunglasses and a black sheepskin hat. He will be holding an attaché case. When I get word that you have handed over the money to him, you will get your kid back."

"I want to speak to my son first," Vladimir said weakly.

"Listen, man, you don't get to dictate any terms to me. I am in charge now. All your money is stolen from the people," the voice became fierce. "You, the oligarchs, and the bourgeoisie, you took everything away from us. We, the Russian citizens, must now take it back. Do as I say and you will have the kid back; you got me?"

The phone went dead.

Dimitri slammed his fist on the steering wheel. Vladimir leaned back, staring vacantly ahead, his fingers absentmindedly toying with his phone. Ilana's heart hammred wildly, her whole body trembled, and the sounds of Anya's exaggerated sobbing grated on her nerves.

Two days later, the money exchanged hands — quietly, without complaint — there was no point in aggravating the thugs further. One never knew how they would retaliate. Alexei returned, but ordinary life didn't. The trauma of the kidnapping left its insidious damage; it deeply affected their quality of life. For Ilana and the children, the perpetual fear that accompanied them wherever they went robbed them of peace of mind. Vladimir turned to alcohol in his effort to lift the depression that had pulled down around him, like invisible window shades.

"I live in a gilded cage," Ilana confided to Margareta, her massage therapist, one evening.

"Why so much sighing? What pleasures does Madame lack?" Margareta replied, indicating the vast living room with a sweeping gesture. "Madame has an indoor swimming pool, a bowling alley, a ballroom, a kitchen, and even an indoor ice rink! There is no need for such sadness."

"What is it all worth, Margareta? A marble mantelpiece with a mirror above it, but all I see is the reflection of a sad woman staring back at me. Ankle-deep carpeting that is supposed to impart coziness, yet I feel not the slightest security or contentment. I have no life! I cower behind high walls, hulking bodyguards, and security cameras.

"I must get away from here. I have begged Vladimir to allow

us to go and live in Israel. There we can live freely. We can learn about our Jewish roots. We can fill our lives with meaning. But Vladimir refuses to hear me. He says he won't think about leaving his business, his colleagues. He says I must be out of my mind for wanting to leave our mansion, our wealth, and go live in a poor country."

"And you don't agree with him?"

Ilana sighed.

"Margareta, don't you understand me? A house that is filled with gold and silver but is empty of meaning, empty of freedom, is not a home."

"The master is different since … since … Alexei," Margareta attempted to change the subject.

"Yes, he is. He is very depressed. You see how listless he is most of the time. When he is not drinking, his depression lifts, only to give way to those frightening bouts of rage."

"He is angry only because he is trying to gain back some of the control in his life that he feels he has lost," Margareta whispered.

Gradually Vladimir was turning into a melancholy man, given to unpredictable outbursts of rage. He returned home from work later and later. Once or twice he would even staggered into the house in the wee hours of the morning, reeking of alcohol, leaning heavily on Dimitri's sturdy shoulder.

Then, one night as she was sleeplessly tossing and turning in bed, Ilana came to a bold decision. Since that fateful day that Alexei had been kidnapped, she realized, she had nothing left. Her husband no longer took interest in her; she had no husband, no freedom, no purpose — just raw, icy fear. She was ready to leave. She had nothing to lose. In the early hours of dawn, she packed just a few of her belongings, gently woke her two children, ordered a cab, and quietly headed to the airport.

Eretz Yisrael. She remembered her grandmother talking about the land where the sun was always shining. Yes, she was a Jew, though she honestly had no idea what that meant. It didn't matter. In Israel she would find out — and perhaps find a way to fill the throbbing void that had descended on her heart.

Ilana stepped into the elevator, straightened her hair in the mirror, and finally gave in to the racing thoughts that she had forced herself to repress all morning. So here she was, a woman who, a mere few weeks before, had presided over a large staff of her own maids and servants, chefs and gardeners, bodyguards and chauffeurs. She had left all her material treasures, her beautiful jewelry, in Moscow, and now she was about to become a cleaning woman in some unfamiliar home. No, she did not regret her decision, though she knew that it would take time to acclimate to a culture and standard of living so far removed from the life she once knew.

Ilana admitted to herself that there was a spring to her step these days. She felt happier, content. No longer did she have to look over her shoulder every time she stepped out of her house. Katya and Alexei seemed to adjust happily to their new school, a school geared for Russian *olim*. She smiled as she pictured Larrisa, the sweet girl Katya had befriended so soon. An overall feeling of contentment had settled over the family of three. *Too bad Vladimir did not want to come along,* she thought. *There is so much healing in this country.*

But right now, standing poised, ready to knock on the door of the Klein's apartment, she felt tense. *What if I don't know how to work hard? Maybe this woman would rather employ someone experienced? How will I manage this?* But then the words of Shulamit Brody, the woman she had met at Ulpan and who had referred her to this address, came back to her. "*Geveret* Klein is a very nice lady; you will like working for her. Don't worry, she will teach you how to do everything."

Ilana took a deep breath and timidly rapped at the brown door. Her knock was answered by a young child. A woman in a pretty housedress and neatly combed wig quickly appeared at the door and greeted her warmly.

"You must be Ilana?"

Ilana nodded.

"*Shalom*, do come in. Welcome to my home. Shulamit Brody called me last night to tell me all about you. She said such nice things." Complimented by the encouraging comment, Ilana's nervous apprehension dissipated.

Mrs. Tirtzah Klein took her on a tour of the small apartment, showing Ilana the ropes of her new job. Ilana felt an aura of kindness and warmth envelop her. As Mrs. Klein proceeded into the kitchen, the light streaming through the window and the fragrance of something baking in the oven added to the relaxed ambiance.

"It is Thursday today, so we have lots of peeling to do." Mrs. Klein handed her new employee a washing cup with which to wash her hands. Perplexed, Ilana fixed questioning eyes on her employer.

"Every morning, when a person wakes up, it is like he has become a new person," Mrs. Klein explained as she began peeling some of the vegetables that were heaped on the countertop. "So we wash our hands to begin the service of Hashem again, especially before handling food." *Plus, one mitzvah leads to another. Your neshamah will get the taste and beg you for more.* But she didn't say that aloud.

Ilana nodded, and, though she wasn't sure she understood, she did as she was told.

"You see, it is the same as the *Kohen* who washed his hands before his service." Mrs. Klein put down the potato she had been peeling to pass Ilana a towel. "Here is another peeler; we'll do this together."

Ilana took the peeler and tried to follow Mrs. Klein's deft movements as the vegetable peels seemed to fly into the garbage pail.

"I don't think I know who Mr. Kohen is." Ilana's brows were knitted. "Who is he?"

"The *Kohen* was the one who did the service in the Temple."

"Temple? What is that?"

With patience born of much experience, Mrs. Klein related all about the *Beis HaMikdash* and the service of the *kohanim* and *leviim*. Ilana listened in rapt attention, lapping up the words like a thirsty wanderer returning from the dry desert. Mrs. Klein had a way of keeping her audience captivated.

"You know, Mrs. Klein," Ilana said suddenly, "last week I took my children to the park. There were some kids there, with side curls just like the pictures my Bubba used to show me. But those children weren't nice. They taunted us saying, '*goy, goy*,' pointing fingers at us, and running off, giggling. In Russia, I am a Jew; here, I am a *goy*. I'm surprised. Jewish kids, why do they do this?'

Mrs. Klein clucked her tongue. "That must have been a trying experience for you."

Ilana looked down at her fingers. "Jewish people shouldn't do that."

"Children need to be taught. Even Jewish children," responded Mrs. Klein.

"But Jewish kids are supposed to be different. Better."

"You're right, Ilana. And the Jewish people have many laws on how to treat others with kindness and respect. The Torah is perfect. But that does not mean that Jewish kids are perfect. Children need to be instructed and guided in the right way. It can take time until they learn."

Ilana reached for another carrot. "I want my children to learn Torah. But I think that first I must learn. Mrs. Klein, can you teach me Torah?"

The time passed pleasantly for Ilana and soon her first day of work was over.

It did not take long for Mrs. Klein to realize that although Ilana listened mesmerized, hanging onto each word with wide eyes, she was not yet ready to take active steps toward changing her life. A way of life becomes embedded in the fabric of a person's being and it is not easy to achieve a complete metamorphosis and become a new person.

Mrs. Klein, however, didn't despair. With genuine love in her heart, she continued answering the myriad questions that Ilana threw at her. She taught her about Shabbos, about keeping a kosher home, and about various other mitzvos. Deep in her heart, Mrs. Klein felt that, like the water slowly carving a hole in the stone that Rebbe Akiva observed, the timeless truth of Torah would gradually seep into Ilana's heart, to make a difference in the life of a pure *Yiddishe neshamah*.

Through the years that followed, Ilana became a cherished member of the family. When the family celebrated a bris, an engagement, a wedding, Ilana was always there at Mrs. Klein's side, helping her with all the many tasks that had to be done.

"Chany, please take the *Birkas Hamazon* booklets to the hall," Mrs. Klein instructed her daughter as she opened the oven door to check on the potato kugel for the *Shabbos sheva brachos*. In a little while, the out-of-town guests would be arriving at the homes of the various hostesses with whom she had set them up. She would send over a platter of cake and piping hot kugel to welcome them. The phone was balanced on her shoulder as she waited for the catering company to answer her question about some last-minute changes.

She glanced up at the kitchen clock while she waited, mentally reviewing the past week. Ilana had seemed tense, she realized.

The manager came back on the line and confirmed her order. She ended the call and proceeded to check her to-do list. There were so many odds and ends that needed her attention. While setting set up the ironing board to iron the younger girls' *sheva brachos* dresses, her thoughts turned to the conversation she had had with Ilana on the preceding Monday. They had been at the wedding hall, waiting for guests to arrive.

"We have a doctor's appointment tomorrow," Ilana had said. "I don't know what is happening with Katya. All of a sudden she is having these fainting spells."

"What do you mean?" Tirtzah had looked at her in alarm.

"Once again, this morning Katya had a sudden, blinding headache and then suddenly fainted. We rushed to the emergency room, but the doctor told us that it was probably from dehydration. He said she should go home and drink more."

"That's all he said?"

"Yes. But Mrs. Klein, this is the third time this happened. I don't know what to do; I'm scared. I made an appointment with Doctor Leiser, our pediatrician."

Mrs. Klein hadn't heard from Ilana since then. Now it was twelve o'clock on Friday afternoon, and still no sign of Ilana. *Where could she be? Perhaps I should have called her on Tuesday.* But the morning after her daughter's wedding had been a hectic day, and she planned to catch up with Ilana on Friday morning, when Ilana was due to help with the *Erev Shabbos* chores. She felt a chill in the air. A gust of wind whistled through the open window, like the harbinger of bad news. Mrs. Klein shivered and closed the window. *It looks like I'll be washing the floors today myself,* she thought.

Just then the phone rang. Mrs. Klein rushed to answer the call.

"Hello?"

The sound of sobbing was all she heard. After a moment, Ilana's ragged voice spoke, "Mrs. Klein? I … I'm so sorry … I cannot come to you today. I know it's the *sheva brachos* but …"

"Ilana, don't worry about that. What's wrong?"

"Everything. Everything is wrong, Mrs. Klein." The sobbing grew into heart-wrenching cries.

Mrs. Klein's insides twisted into a tight ball. She wanted to say something, anything, but her breath caught in her throat.

"I'm sorry, Mrs. Klein, I don't want to ruin your happy occasion. I am hanging up now. Good bye."

"Wait, Ilana. Where are you?"

"I'm in the Children's Hospital," she paused, "in the oncology ward. *Shabbat Shalom.*"

For a long time, Mrs. Klein just stared at the phone. She had grown so close to her cleaning woman. There was something about her — a certain nobility of spirit — that was endearing. Surely she needed someone to be at her side. A woman all alone undergoing such a frightening experience needed a caring presence.

Hastily, she scribbled a note to her married daughter, who would be walking in any minute to help with the preparation for the *Shabbos sheva brachos*. She proceeded to arrange some kugel and cake on a plate and hurried downstairs. A taxi sped by. Tirtzah flagged him down, entered the car, and instructed the driver to head to the hospital.

She found Ilana easily enough, sitting hunched over in the lounge, arms dangling at her sides, her face ashen. Ilana's face visibly brightened upon seeing Mrs. Klein. Sitting down beside her, Tirtzah took Ilana's hand.

"Come, let's talk. I'm sure this is too heavy a load to carry on your own."

Ilana nodded. It was very difficult to struggle with all her fears on her own. She felt relieved to have a listening ear, especially that of Mrs. Klein, the woman she so admired.

"You know the doctor's appointment we had on Tuesday, right?" she began. "The doctor sent us for a CT scan immediately." Without warning, the tears began to spill as she remembered. Quickly, she controlled herself, unwilling to make a scene.

The laboratory technician had handed her the results and sent her right back to Doctor Leiser. His waiting room was filled to capacity, but he had ushered her into the office as soon as she had arrived.

Ilana sat at the edge of her chair, anxiously reading the doctor's expression as he studied the results, and was quick to notice the cloud that crossed his face. Then the doctor looked up at Ilana and put all the facts out on the table in his simple, straightforward manner.

"She has something there."

"What do you mean 'something'?" Ilana asked.

"Your daughter has a growth in her brain. How extensive it is, an MRI will reveal. But your daughter requires immediate medical attention. She will need radiation to diminish the size of the growth and then surgery to remove it. I am afraid this is very serious, Mrs. Iskovitch."

He paused. Ilana shrank back in fear.

"To cure your daughter, well, it is a complicated procedure involving a neurosurgeon, and ..." the doctor broke off, fixing his gaze on a spot on the wall. "Let's first do the MRI scan. I will speak to the technician myself and schedule an appointment for you on Sunday. I'll be there as well."

Ilana sat rooted to the spot, the blood rushing from her head. She knew about such surgeries. Not six years had passed since her niece, her sister's daughter, had received the identical diagnosis. Ilana clearly remembered the pain, the exhaustive radiation treatments, the paralyzing fear. Her niece, Olga, had never recovered, though. The surgery had given her back her life, but she remained an invalid, mentally unstable.

Through a haze she heard the doctor talking. "Your daughter needs to be admitted to the hospital immediately for some preliminary tests, and, of course, she needs to be kept under observation."

Ilana still didn't move. A cold sweat bathed her body. She envisioned the new life that lay before her: A life filled with doctors, nurses, injections, IV lines, the oncology ward, treatments, and long, lonely nights of fear and despair.

"So here I am," she said to Mrs. Klein, "alone in the world, facing the frightening prognosis that will be revealed in the next forty-eight hours."

She sat blinking rapidly, trying to hold back the tears that were threatening to cascade down her face again.

Mrs. Klein embraced her, "Ilana," she said, "it's okay to cry."

Ilana brushed the comment away. Leaning slightly forward, she whispered, "Mrs. Klein, do you remember what I told you about Olga, my niece?"

"The one who came out of surgery with serious complications?"

"Yes, my niece, Olga. What if …" Ilana broke off. The thought was too horrifying to contemplate.

"Everything will turn out fine, you'll see. Look to Hashem, Ilana." She embraced Ilana and gazed deep into her tortured eyes. "I know these are very difficult times for you. But try not to despair. Pray. Remember that it is not the doctor who heals; Hashem heals. He is the Healer of all healers. And you know, Shabbos is a *shemirah* [protection]. It is *shomer* [protects] all those who keep her; that is what it says in the holy books."

Suddenly, from somewhere deep in her heart, Ilana cried out, "G-d, if You heal Katya and she comes out of this ordeal alive and healthy, in body and mind, I promise You … I promise You that I will … I will keep Shabbos. Yes, I will become *Shomer Shabbos* if You heal her. Please help me."

Tirtzah Klein stared wide-eyed. *She is bartering with HaKadosh Baruch Hu? Who are we to negotiate with Him?* The idea was completely foreign to her. In fact, she seemed to recall that from a *halachic* viewpoint it was forbidden to do so. *It is best to place our total trust in Him and know that even if a sword is resting on our neck, His help can come in the blink of an eye. Sometimes, He brings us tribulations just so that He can hear us cry out to Him, "Abba, help me." But to barter with Hashem ….* She kept her thoughts to herself, though. Her heart was filled with compassion for the anguished, desperate mother.

Tirtzah leaned forward. "Shabbos itself heals. That is what is written in the Torah. Hashem is our loving Father. He loves you and cares for you more than you can imagine."

The hours moving steadily on. Finally, Mrs. Klein turned to Ilana apologetically, "The *kallah* is waiting for me .... I had better run home."

Ilana walked her to the exit.

"On such a hectic day, you came to be with me. I ... I don't have the words to thank you enough," she said gratefully.

"There's no need to, Ilana. Just remember you are not alone. Hashem is always with you. All of us will be praying for you. Have a good Shabbos."

Sunday morning arrived. Ilana lost track of how many hours she had been awake. Her face was drawn, with large circles under her eyes.

"It will be all right," Katya whispered to her mother as an orderly wheeled her into the lab.

All through the MRI procedure, Ilana sent her prayers aloft. She paced back and forth like a caged animal, first in the lounge, then through the long corridor, until she collapsed into an armchair in the waiting room, too nervous to sit still and too exhausted to continue walking.

She sat, resting her head in her hands. Visions of a different life flitted across her mind. The anxiety and fear she had lived with in Russia came back to her with a vengeance. Only this time it was Katya's life in the balance. She wondered where Vladimir was now, what his reaction would be at a time like this. She shrugged. More alcohol, perhaps. She thought of Dimitri, her spacious mansion, her Mercedes, her life of wealth that was but a faded dream.

I gave up everything. For what? To come to the Jewish land, to breathe freely without fear, to find meaning and purpose in my life. Am I living my life any differently?. Up until the nightmare of this week she had lived freely. But was she really free? She wasn't strolling through the shopping malls all day. She didn't have the budget for that. But her life was certainly filled with more meaning here. That was clear.

Again, she got up and resumed her pacing. The door opened and the doctor came into the room. An involuntary spasm played over his face. "Mrs. Iskovitch?"

Ilana tensed, staring at Dr. Leiser in alarm.

"Mrs. Iskovitch, do you believe in miracles?"

Ilana rose from her chair, confused.

"What do you mean, Dr. Leiser?"

"We did the MRI and we don't find a speck of the growth. Nothing." He shook his head in disbelief. "Absolutely nothing."

Ilana's jaw dropped. She wanted to speak but failed. She stared at the doctor, at the nurse, and then at the doctor again. And then astonishment gave way to a broad smile.

"Thank you, Hashem," she breathed softly.

A PROMISE KEPT

"And remember, I'm here for you always, anytime. You can just pick up the phone and call me," Chaya Lowinger says with tears blinding her eyes, before replacing the phone in the cradle.

A sigh of searing pain escapes her.

Pessy looks up at her. Understanding is evident in her kind eyes. To the staff of the Bonei Olam office, pain is no stranger. Founded by a group of individuals who had experienced the hardships of childlessness themselves, this organization seeks to relieve couples of the financial, emotional, and physical stresses resulting from infertility. Yet these kind individuals do so much more.

"My heart goes out to her," Chaya confesses to Pessy. "She wants to know if she's doing something wrong." The words of this particular caller are still throbbing in Chaya's mind. *My sisters, my younger brothers, they all have families of three, four children.* The woman had spoken amid heartbreaking sobs. *It is horrible feeling so envious, but my heart bleeds every time I am together with them. Am I undeserving of this blessing? What should I do? How can I merit to hold just one child in my arms?*

"She said she does not talk to anyone," Chaya was speaking quietly, as though to herself. "It is too difficult for her to open up. I am glad she feels that we understand her."

Pessy nods as she turns to the pile of letters waiting on her desk. Words need not be spoken, in this office. How can one describe the anguish, the turmoil, the confusion of a woman experiencing childlessness? And the endless questions — those heart-wrenching questions of an anxious mind, groping in the darkness, searching for an answer.

There are also those questions that remain unasked, hovering silently in the air, because there are no answers. Yet Chaya's patient voice of comfort never wavers. When darkness, despair, and despondency rob the sufferer of a reason to go on, Chaya seeks every avenue of possibility to offer hope that will overcome the hurt.

A contemplative mood reigns in the office as Chaya tackles the myriad tasks waiting for her attention, and Pessy places the various letters into their respective files. Insurance agencies, utilities, doctor referrals, papers and more papers; and recently some checks were arriving too, due to a fundraising mailing they had done.

The staff members view their work as a battle of strength over sorrow, hope conquering heartbreak, and faith to prevail against shattered dreams. In this office, giving up is not an option, words such as "can't" and "impossible" are not part of their lexicon. No stone is left unturned. Every possibility is pursued until tiny sprouts of hope begin to take root in the heart of the caller.

R' Shlomo Bochner, one of the founders of this organization, has developed a strong and dedicated network of doctors and fertility centers across the world, enabling Bonei Olam to offer unsurpassed medical and financial assistance to all applicants. R' Bochner never says "no," and he never turns anyone away.

Indeed, so many worthy individuals have taken up the cause, arranging fundraising events across the globe, from Brooklyn to Bnei Brak, Johannesburg to Jerusalem, and everywhere in between. Jewish hearts have been inspired to give, regardless of the size of their pockets. Nevertheless, the costs are staggering.

The checks were slowly piling up on her desk. Five-dollar checks, ten-dollar checks, twenty-dollar checks. Occasionally a check of $100 appeared and sometimes a check of $180 also made its way into the pile. Every penny counted. Every dollar would assist in covering their formidable expenses.

Pessy picked up another envelope and slit it open. A certified check made out to Bonei Olam slid out. Pessy stared. Her jaw dropped. Without a word, the ecstatic woman shot up from her seat, ran over to Chaya's desk and shoved the check under her nose.

Chaya squinted. Suddenly her eyes almost bulged from their sockets. It was a check for $10,000. "When ... where ... who is this from?" she asked.

Pessy scrutinized the front and back of the check. There was no name on it. "I have no clue," she replied. "Who could it be? Who would send a check without a name?"

"Let me see," Chaya took the check. As a certified check, it wasn't drawn on an individual's checking account, but was issued directly from the bank.

"This is so strange," she said. "$10,000 out of the clear blue?"

"You think it is because of the mailing we did?"

"But why isn't there a name on it? Didn't they want a tax deduction?"

"Perhaps Mr. Bochner knows something about this," Pessy said, still searching for a sign.

"How would Mr. Bochner know anything if there is no name? Anyway, Mr. Bochner is out of the country now." It was *aseres yemei teshuvah*, and Shlomo Bochner had gone abroad to spend the *Yomin Noraim* with his Rebbe.

"I guess we will wait until he comes back from *Eretz Yisrael*," Pessy said, swiveling her chair back into place at her desk.

"Here is something," Chaya said, pointing to a number that was scrawled at the side of the check. "I see it has a phone number on it! At least we have a lead. When he comes back, Mr. Bochner can phone this number and see what this is all about."

When R' Shlomo returned, he was indeed surprised to see the check. He did not recall talking to someone about a check of this amount. He wasted no time in dialing the phone number that had been written on the check.

"Hello, this is Shlomo Bochner from Bonei Olam."

"Yes," the thick-accented voice that answered the phone hinted to a rather elderly man. "How may I help you?"

"We received your check in the mail. Thank you very much. *Tizku lemitzvos*."

"It was my pleasure." The voice did indeed seemed pleased.

"I was wondering, what is it about?"

"What it is about? This is a check. I do not understand what you are asking me."

"Yes, but there was no name on the check."

"Ah, why would I need my name on the check? This is a donation. I am not looking for honor, for great awards, you know. I just want to give, that's all."

"Thank you, Mr. ... What did you say your name was?"

"I didn't. It is really not important, what my name is. The main thing is that you should have lots of *berachah vehatzlachah*. The name is not important."

Shlomo's curiosity was piqued.

"Okay, the name is not important," he agreed. "And again, thank you very much for your generous contribution. But tell me, sir, what is the reason that you sent us such a large donation?"

"This is my *hakaras hatov* to Hashem!" The elderly man said, his tone rising an octave, his joy obvious. "You know what? Let me tell you a story."

Like an angry eagle, World War II spread its wings over the Jewish communities. The inhabitants of the once-vibrant towns and *shtetls* — which until recently had bustled with life — sat huddled together within the walls of the ghettos; some of them hurrying through quiet alleyways and feverishly planning escape, others trembling in fear. All of them dreading the frightful actions called *Judenaussiedlung*, during which the Gestapo would round up men, women, even children, and dump them into waiting trucks like piles of rags.

As Gershon would lie in bed at night, with eyes open, unable to sleep due to hunger and fear, he would listen to his brother, Shimon, lying beside him, groaning in his sleep. He would listen to the quiet murmurings of his parents and he would feel his heartbeat thumping in his throat. Lately, people were disappearing from the streets, with only a handful returning, badly beaten, broken and bent by pain and humiliation. One sad incident followed another and terrible rumors spread throughout the ghetto.

Mornings were no better, as everybody moved around the crowded apartment as though walking on eggshells. The other families crammed into their tiny apartment were busy preparing hideouts underneath the stairwell, in the attic, and in closets. Some had even attempted to escape to the nearby forests, but were barred by soldiers and policemen stationed all around the city.

Fear lurked in every corner; deportation was imminent. An *aktion* had taken place in the nearby town. A cloud of worry had enveloped Mama, who had a premonition that the family would be separated. Her tired eyes, set deep within her worried face, seemed to recede even more with each passing day.

Then came the terrible day. Gershon was standing near the window, peering out at the street through a slit in the curtain. Shimon was peeking over his shoulder. Outside, all appeared deceptively normal. Not a word was exchanged between the two brothers, but the silence hung heavily in the air.

Suddenly Mama approached them. Gershon felt her light touch on his shoulder, and out of the corner of his eyes, he noticed Mama lovingly patting Shimon's head. Shimon's large, saddened eyes stared up at her. Slowly he turned to face his mother.

Mama opened her mouth to speak, then shook her head and shut her lips. She tried again. "Gershon, Shimon," she whispered, sobs choking her voice. She paused for a moment to pull herself together. "I want you to realize that it is very likely that we will be separated from each other," she said and then lifted her hands in the air. "Maybe even forever."

Gershon couldn't hear it. Something inside urged him to turn on his heels and flee. With all his being he wanted to run from these terrible words. But he did not run. There *was* nowhere to run from the awful truth. Gershon remained frozen in place. With his eyes, he begged Mama to say it wasn't so, to say that the danger would pass. Life would soon return to the way it was, and once again he would be standing at the door, *sefer* in one hand, the lunch packed by Mama in the other. And Mama would wish him a day full of *berachah* and *hatzlachah*.

But Mama didn't seem to share his mental picture. Standing calmly in her usual regal manner, she continued, "My dear children, when the Gestapo come and get us, I do not know what will be. One thing I ask of you. Please take care of each other."

Gershon stood erect, not daring to utter a single word lest the dam restraining his oceans of tears break. Shimon couldn't look at Mama. His chin quivered and there was a noticeable tremor in his hands. But Mama, her gentle blue eyes reflecting so much sorrow, did not break down.

"Gershon," she whispered, "if you manage to find a *shtikel broit* [a piece of bread], share it with Shimon." Gershon nodded solemnly.

Mama turned to Shimon, "And Shimon, if you come across a *bissele vasser* [a little water], remember that Gershon is also thirsty."

Mama paused. She turned her eyes heavenward, whispering a prayer supplicating Hashem to grant her children life. Gershon swallowed hard.

"Take care of each other, my dear children," Mama repeated. "Wherever you go, wherever you hide, take care of each other. This is what I ask of you. Do whatever you can, but do not separate!"

Things happened so suddenly afterwards. The Gestapo stormed their apartment and chased them from their home and into the waiting trucks.

Gershon and Shimon held on to each other as they endured the worst of human cruelty. They never forgot their mother's parting words, and, indeed, they managed to stay together and to care for each other through the inferno of Treblinka and the evils of Bergen-Belsen.

Then they arrived at Auschwitz.

Mengele, may his name be blotted out, stood at the platform in his impeccable uniform and shiny boots, casually swinging his finger to the right and to the left. A stoical clerk would stamp a six-pointed star on the forehead of each person assigned to "Life." Those fated for the gas chambers were not stamped.

The long line of suffering prisoners trudged slowly forward. Broken, beaten, and humiliated, but with a powerful desire to live, Gershon dragged his brother along. His heart pumped wildly. His dear brother Shimon, so scrawny and sickly, appeared half-dead. He could hardly hold himself up. Would Shimon make it past the discerning gaze of this Angel of Death?

In a moment, Gershon's doubts vanished as the Nazi *Haman* nonchalantly flicked his finger to the left … and then, before he could even think, it was his turn.

His mind numb, Gershon did not quite grasp that he had been slated to the right — to life. Like a shadow, he languidly followed his brother to the left side, before an SS guard shoved him to the right and his forehead was brutally stamped with that telltale red mark that separated him from his brother.

Tears welled up inside him, blocking his vision. He had promised his mother. They had been through so much together, caring for each others' wounds, splitting their morsels of food, and — miraculously — they had never been separated. How could he break his promise now?

A plan began to take shape in Gershon's mind — a dubious, daring plan, but a plan nonetheless — built on unquenchable hope, inspired by a long-ago promise.

With a prayer in his soul and heart pummeling his chest, Gershon hurried over to where his brother was standing. Fervently he kissed his brother's forehead. And then he kissed it again. Shimon stared blankly, apathetically, as his brother showered him with sloppy kisses. Gershon *appeared* to be unaware of anything else going on around him. Like a man possessed, he kissed and kissed.

But from the corner of his eye, Gershon remained on the lookout. When he was sure that the Nazis weren't watching, he quickly pressed his forehead, with the red mark granting him the right to live, against Shimon's forehead. Satisfied, he backed up to inspect his handiwork. A red stamp now appeared on his brother's wet forehead. Wasting no time, he dragged his brother to the right, and not a moment too soon.

"Both of us survived the war, Mr. Bochner; we were spared. No one else from our entire town survived."

He fell into a reflective silence. Shlomo Bochner, mesmerized by the story, remained motionless in his seat.

"Many years have passed since then. My brother is gone and I am already an old man. But I have no children.

"I sent you the money because I owe a debt of gratitude to Hashem. I survived the war. I survived together with my brother! I want to help a couple who does not have children. I want a couple to experience the joy of having children.

"I did not put my name on the check because that is not important. The reason I am telling you the story is so you should have *chizuk* to continue your beautiful work. Hashem gives the strength to go on. Just remember — there is a Master of the world."

A ROSE AMONG THE THORNS

The following story illustrates the strength of the Jewish people. It is a story of remarkable heroism in the face of utter insanity. "Like the rose maintaining its beauty among the thorns, so is my faithful Beloved among the nations" (*Shir HaShirim* 2:2).

I am grateful to the Kaliver Rebbetzin for sharing her story with me.

In the time of our greatest sorrow, deep inside the bowels of the earth, where the Nazis, *yemach shemam*, forced us to dig anti-tank ditches in the path of the advancing Red Army, we cried out, "*MiMaamakim Karasicha Hashem*" ("From the depths I call to you …") (*Tehillim* 130).

The earth was frozen over. The Germans would throw a grenade to break the surface and force us, young women and girls, to dig two and three meters deep into the ground. Every Shabbos morning, two girls would stand vigil to warn us when the SS guards would approach. We didn't want to work on the holy Shabbos. We sang *zemiros*, we swapped stories of *tzaddikim*, we drew strength from one another.

I remember one Friday night during a death march. I was sitting with my two nieces on a thin pile of straw, resting from the backbreaking labor in a barn at the roadside. And as the sun dipped below the horizon I suddenly remembered that it was Shabbos.

"Let's daven," I urged, "in honor of Shabbos."

Some other girls came to join us and we sat and sang *Kabbalas Shabbos* and *Lecha dodi*. We felt mesmerized by the words. They reminded us of bygone days, and we allowed ourselves to become enveloped in the sweet memories that those words evoked.

Suddenly, the *Blockelteste,* who had been sitting in her room behind the wall we shared, burst upon our small group huddled together in song and delivered a vicious slap to my face. Before I could get my bearings, another violent blow landed on my other cheek.

"You are still praying?" she asked. Her face was crimson, contorted with fury, her eyes bloodshot.

A sudden Jewish pride arose within me like a pillar of smoke rising from a chimney.

"Yes," I answered her calmly but in a firm voice, "we are still praying."

Her lips were trembling with rage. She gritted her teeth, planted her hand on her hip and snarled angrily, "You still think that you will get out of here?"

There was absolute silence in the room. No one moved. When did anybody ever challenge the *Blockelteste*? At that moment, time seemed to stand still. My eyes took in the frozen, terror-stricken faces of my friends, and I arose from my crouched position. I had more to say.

"With Hashem's help," my voice emerged with a strength I didn't know I possessed, "we will get out of here."

The *Blockelteste* opened her mouth to speak. Then she stopped. Her arms went limp, her shoulders sagged. Then, without another word, she turned on her heel and left.

It was the middle of January. World War II was drawing to a close, although it would be months before Germany surrendered. I was now holding on to my last vestiges of strength. The British and American armies were approaching the concentration camps from the west; the Russian troops were advancing from the east. The Germans were frazzled. Truth and justice were closing in on them and they felt trapped. They didn't want us, the witnesses of the horrific atrocities they had perpetrated, to be around to tell the story.

So they devised a new form of cruelty: the infamous death march. We were a group of six thousand women and girls driven out through the gates of Auschwitz, Poland. Weak, ill, broken in body and spirit; survivors of brutality, forced labor, illness, and starvation. Now the Nazis were yanking us, like dogs tied to chains, to Bergen-Belsen, Germany.

The roads were icy. We wore only the thin-striped prisoners' garb. We shivered in the cold, like laundry flapping in the wind. But the SS men harried us at gunpoint, unrelentingly, without granting us even a morsel of bread.

It was one o'clock in the morning when the Germans finally stopped the grueling march; not because they cared about us, but because they themselves were exhausted and wanted to rest. Under the open skies, shivering, on the ice-covered ground, we allowed blessed sleep to soothe our starving bodies until morning dawned. Then, without any prelude or preamble, they roused us from our slumber and drove us on, as we stumbled on our weakened legs, bleary-eyed and ever hungry, with nothing else but the powerful will to live.

Even the animals were more fortunate than we. They received food — food that in our eyes was fit for kings. They received warm shelter, although, admittedly, sometimes we would be lucky enough to spend the night with them in a stable or a pigsty. For six agonizing weeks we were driven mercilessly. The guards walked on one side of the unpaved road, while we trudged on the other side.

I remember when we arrived at an abandoned concentration camp. Some of the girls prowled in the kitchen and found a treasure worth more than precious diamonds: potatoes cooked in their peels. Euphoria traveled like wildfire, hunger cried out in anticipation, and many managed to swoop down upon those potatoes before the Germans arrived and barred the rest of us from entering the kitchen.

I can vividly recall the two potatoes I managed to procure that night. I was so proud. This time it would be I who had succeeded in bringing some food to my two nieces, instead of the other way around. Suddenly, out of nowhere, two large hands appeared and snatched them right out of my grip. That night, it was sleep, once again, that helped me overcome my hunger pangs.

The next morning we were on the move again. The shoes that I had brought from home had long since become tattered and had been discarded. With the wooden clogs the Germans had provided us, it was impossible to walk in the snow. So with nothing but woolen socks on my feet, I marched along the snowy roads.

Alongside me walked my sister Rivkale's two daughters. Surale was eighteen — only a year younger than I — and Chayale, seventeen. We were famished, frostbitten, and close to despair.

I could not walk anymore.

The frosty Polish winter, the terrible cold, the exhausting six-week march, were too much to bear. I felt that I simply could not place one foot in front of the other. All I wanted to do was to sit down and give up.

Gradually, I started lagging behind my nieces. Soon I was far behind the suffering column that was steadily moving farther along.

Eventually, I sat down on a stone, forlorn and alone, in a frightening world. Even fear could no longer prod me on. Aside for some handfuls of snow, I had not eaten for days.

Suddenly, from the distance, I could make out two figures

pressing their way back through the masses of inmates moving forward. As they came into view, I noticed that they were my own two nieces, desperately attempting to emerge from the rows of skeletal people.

"Auntie," Surale panted as she reached me. "You must not stay here."

"Please let me be."

"No! No!" she pleaded. "You must come with us."

"My dear nieces, I am so sorry, I just cannot go on."

"But they will shoot you," Chayale cried, her charcoal eyes burning with fear. "Please don't do this to us."

I stared at them blankly. I didn't know from where to draw the strength to continue.

Chayale crouched low. "A miracle occurred," she whispered into my ear. "It was a gendarme himself who told me to run and get you. He said to us, 'Your sister remained sitting on a rock. If you do not get her now, I will shoot.'"

They didn't dally too long. They weren't going to let my apathy delay them. Surale took hold of one arm, Chayale grasped my other arm, and they literally dragged me along.

After hundreds of kilometers, the SS men finally packed us into open wagons. These wagons were originally designed for cattle. We were squeezed together like sardines, one human pressing against the other. There was not an inch of space between us.

Quite unexpectedly, the SS guards tossed to each of us what seemed to be a black brick. Upon closer inspection, I realized that it was a small piece of bread, black and hard. I savored each crumb. The taste was heavenly, and I could never know when this would happen again.

Suddenly one woman declared, "Make room for me!"

From her appearance and the way she spoke, it was clear to me that her mind could not take this abuse any longer. She had apparently gone mad.

"Make room for me," she insisted. "I must go to sleep."

Make room for her? Where? How? What did she mean? My mind raced, trying to make sense of what the woman was saying. Suddenly, she grabbed my hand and dug into it with her teeth. Then she bit the hand of the women crammed to my right. I reeled in pain and nearly fainted. I saw stars and my head began to spin from the agony. But the poor woman was oblivious to all. She simply lay down at our feet. Instinctively I jumped, terrified that my foot would be her next target. But there was nowhere to escape.

My hand swelled up to the size of a football. In this manner I continued the horrific journey. The wound turned black and red and there was nothing I could do. Two days later, the bitten woman to my right succumbed to blood poisoning and died. As for myself, I reckoned it was only a matter of a day or two. The pain was simply unbearable.

Five days later we arrived at Bergen-Belsen. I was still alive. This was toward the end of February 1945. After six harrowing weeks of marching, we had, unbelievably, reached our destination. Of the original six thousand inmates who had left Auschwitz, only four hundred girls entered the gates of Bergen-Belsen.

Even now, on our arrival, no one deemed it necessary to grant us a bit of food or a sip of water.

I lay on the muddy asphalt floor in a stupor. My red, swollen feet were frostbitten, numb, and bruised. My hand throbbed and ached. I was hanging on to a thin thread of life.

Suddenly the *Blockelteste* entered with a bucket filled with black coffee. A line of starving inmates formed. We each had a small metal cup attached to a thin rope tied around our waists, and it was this cup that we held in front of us, waiting with bated breath for it to be filled.

Somehow I managed to get myself in line. I stood listlessly. I did not have the stamina to count the people in front of me. The cup I held out vibrated in my hands. My turn came and I gazed at the life-sustaining liquid being poured into my cup. I felt so weak. I was tottering from the fever and intense pain. I placed the cup close to my quivering lips.

Suddenly the clouds parted in my befuddled brain and a flash of clarity occurred to me.

Ribbono shel olam, I thought, *what am I doing now? So, I will drink one more little bit of black coffee in my life! Is this all there is to it? This is the last thing I will do before I meet my Creator? Ribbono shel olam*, I cried silently, *Let me do one more mitzvah. Let me have the opportunity to sanctify Your name one last time.*

Like a shadow, I hobbled over to the open window. I tried to steady my quaking body. I placed the cup of coffee in my left hand and I washed my right hand, then I switched to wash my left hand.

Negel vasser. For long hadn't I washed *negel vasser? Father in Heaven, I want to arrive home to You as pure and untainted as You sent me down here.*

I stared at my empty cup. There was not a single drop of liquid left.

I cannot explain to you what happened next. Suddenly I felt life-giving energy surging through my pain-wracked body. I felt revitalized, I felt invigorated.

I knew right there, standing by the open window, blinking into my empty cup, that I had received a new lease on life. From that moment on, the swelling on my hand went down, the redness diminished. There was not a doctor in sight. Without water to wash the ugly gash, without antibiotics, without any ointment, my wound disappeared.

A small, barely visible scar remained. A silent testimony — a poignant reminder — that when a *Yid* is *moser nefesh* for a mitzvah that is beyond the realm of the natural, the reward that transpires is also in a manner that is *chutz miderech hateva*, beyond the realm of what is natural.

FLIGHT OR FIGHT

"What did you pack in here, rocks?" Ari Feldman asked his brother Shlomo, as he heaved a suitcase out of the trunk.

"You know the ladies, they think they cannot travel anywhere without folding and packing in the whole house. And I mean that literally."

Ari chuckled as he proceeded to haul out the next overstuffed piece of luggage.

Leah winked at Malka and rolled over a trolley on which to place their bags. Their husbands' banter was as familiar to them as their love for each other was compelling. Ari deftly piled one suitcase on top of the other, and the two Feldman brothers and their wives began making their way toward the check-in line.

The excitement in the air was palpable. It wasn't every day that they traveled to a niece's wedding. As the ladies exchanged stories about how they had farmed out their kids to various homes, the men squabbled goodnaturedly over their opinions of the situation in Israel. For although they were traveling from New York to Antwerp, a Jew's heart is always in its homeland.

"Y'all from Europe?" Ari and Shlomo spun around and found themselves looking straight into the round face of a cowboy.

"We happen to be from New York," Shlomo offered. By the look of his hat and boots, it seemed that the stranger would be more comfortable in the rodeo, riding broncos or roping calves, perhaps. A thick cigar jutted from the side of his mouth.

"We are traveling to Europe for a wedding tonight."

"Y'all from New York? I see. Big city." And then, "Y'all Jews?" His eyes widened. "I don't know nothing about Jews. These here are horns?" he asked pointing to their sidelocks.

"You want to touch it to see for yourself?" Ari asked. The man's eyes almost fell from their sockets. Just in time he caught the thick cigar that had almost dropped from his mouth. But he did indeed reach out his finger, ever so gingerly.

"Gee. It's hair. I could not understand why you would have horns. I don't know."

The queue before the check-in line began to move forward at a faster pace. The Feldmans were next in line. Shlomo shifted from one leg to the other. Waiting patiently wasn't one of his strong points.

"Next," came the laconic announcement of the clerk.

Suddenly Ari gasped. "I don't believe it!"

Three pairs of eyes stared at him.

"What happened?" Leah, his wife, asked.

"We are missing one suitcase!" Ari scanned the area in wonder.

"Are you serious?" Shlomo glanced at his watch.

"You're right, Ari. The gray paisley suitcase. Where is it?" Leah said, her voice rising in alarm.

"Gray paisley?" Shlomo shook his head. "I don't think I saw that one."

The eyes beneath the cowboy hat blinked. Jauntily, he sidled over to them. "Guys, I believe it is your turn," he nudged.

Ari looked at him with unseeing eyes. "I think we left it at home. We left it at home. It's right inside the front hall."

"Oh, no," Leah was almost in tears. "That's the one in which

Flight or Fight 235

I put my best shaitel. Wait … the wedding gift. It's also in there! What are we going to do now?"

Not one to lose his composure under any circumstance, Ari made some quick mental calculations. He knew his wife was a consummate born-and-bred "Boro Parker"; she would feel very uncomfortable without her attire being "just so." He also knew that her chic facade was a real reflection of her magnanimous personality. And with the euro as high as it was, it would cost him a pretty penny to replace the missing wedding gift.

He motioned to the cowboy to go ahead as he quickly conferred with his brother. "Don't worry about us, Shlomo. I will call my driver and send him to pick up the valise and bring it here to the airport. I know we don't have too much time, but there is still a slight chance that we could make the flight."

Shlomo and his wife checked in and proceeded to the gate, while Ari and Leah frantically waited for their missing luggage near the automatic doors.

An air of excitement reigns at airports. Masses of people come and go, and the sounds of high heels clicking, suitcase wheels rolling, and intermittent loudspeaker announcements all blend together in a cacophony of urgency as passengers rush to their assigned gates.

Shlomo, intent on keeping his rolling carry-on bag upright while following the arrows to Gate 16, was swept along in the rush of humanity. None too eager to travel without his brother and sister-in-law, he hoped against hope that somehow, someway, the driver would make it just in time.

Against the backdrop of clamor and commotions, the waiting area at the gate is a peaceful oasis. It is here that people finally sit back and relax before boarding commences. Shlomo, however, was far from relaxed. He stood, shifting from one leg to the other, before the large screen flashing departure times, anxiously studying the numbers as though they held the answer to whether or not his brother and sister-in-law would make the flight. "If you don't mind me asking," he suddenly heard a somewhat familiar voice, "I was wondering. That fellow you were with before, is he your brother? Y'all look like two peas in a pod. He's gone?"

"He'll be here soon," Shlomo replied, keeping his eyes focused on the screen. He was in no mood to make small talk. "I hope," he added.

The fellow shrugged goodnaturedly and sat down in a nearby chair, swinging one rather long leg over the other.

The minutes were piling up now. The clipped tones of the various announcements in every foreign language were beginning to grate on Shlomo's nerves. Finally, he broke his vigil next to the screen and slumped into a chair, too.

Once again the microphone crackled into life. "Attention all passengers: Passengers flying to Brussels on El Al flight 016 are requested to proceed to Gate 16. Boarding has now begun."

Shlomo and Malka joined the line as it meandered along, all the while throwing anxious glances over their shoulders, hoping against hope to catch sight of Ari running in their direction.

Once on board, all eyes turned to the screens showing a stewardess explain where the emergency exits were and where to stow the carry-on bags. Just when the caricatures of little people appeared to explain how to lock one's tray table, adjust one's seat position, and fasten one's seat belt, Shlomo's cell phone erupted in a happy jingle.

Leah willed the hammering in her throat to stop. *Control yourself*, she commanded herself. *Hashem runs the world. Whatever happens, happens.*

"There is another flight we can take," Ari, who had gone to look for an El Al agent and was now coming toward her, was saying rather loudly. "It is a bit of a roundabout way through

France, but if we miss this flight we can try …. He's here. He really is! Look at that!" Ari took off in a shot toward his driver, who was lugging the gray paisley suitcase and almost collided with an elderly couple.

Ari thanked the driver profusely and then alerted the El Al agent whom he had notified beforehand. The agent issued a few hurried orders into his handheld transceiver. Finally catalyzed into action, husband and wife darted through the terminal. Virtually vaulting over lounge chairs, they bounded toward the desk at the departure gate, all the while lugging their gray paisley suitcase.

"Yes?" a bored clerk looked at them quizzically.

Ari thrust his tickets in front of her nose, panting for breath.

"I'm afraid you missed the flight."

Leah's heart plummeted to the heels of her highly uncomfortable shoes. Blushing fiercely from the humiliation of missing a flight, she blinked away the tears that threatened just beneath the surface.

Ari remained entirely unperturbed. He reached for his cell phone. The unaware passersby would never suspect that here was a man who was experiencing a mini crisis of sorts. "Shlomo," he said calmly into his phone, "we are here at the gate, but they are not allowing us on."

"The final boarding call was announced ten minutes ago, sir."

"I am aware of that, ma'am. But as far as I know, an El Al agent radioed instructions about us."

"I understand. However, the aircraft will soon be backing away from the gate. The pilot is preparing to taxi down the runway. Traffic cannot be suspended, you know."

Hashem is with us, Hashem is here, Leah was repeating to herself over and over again. *Hashem does what's best for us, Hashem is with us.*

"Look, I really must make this flight. Is there anything you can do for us?"

The woman was beginning to show signs of impatience. She was tapping her foot and shaking her head.

Inside the plane, Shlomo's cell phone lay wedged between his shoulder and ear as he stowed his carry-on bag in the overhead bin. "We are so close to the airplane," his brother was saying, "only one door away, but yet so far. It looks like we will have to go through France. So have a safe flight, and we will see each other at the wedding, *im yirtzeh Hashem*."

Shlomo leaned back against his seat. He fidgeted this way and that, but he couldn't find a comfortable position. His brother was right there, just on the other side of the door. *Can't I do something?* his conscience prodded him. *What can I do? I can't make a ruckus here. Everyone will stare at me, with my big hat perched on my head and my long payos dangling by my cheeks.*

"I feel so bad for your brother," Malka was saying somewhere beyond the crescendo of inner voices arguing inside him.

"So do I," Shlomo murmured. The voices insisted that he take immediate action.

So do I, so do I, so do I. The words took on a life of their own as they spiraled in and out through the chambers of his heart. *So do I. I really feel bad.* He clung to those words as though sympathy would extricate him from the grip of the guilt that wouldn't relax its clutches.

"Good morning, ladies and gentlemen, welcome aboard El Al flight 016 flying to Brussels …."

What am I doing sitting on this plane while my brother is barred entry? The voices were unrelenting. *Do something,* they silently screamed, *anything.*

His head was beginning to spin. *How can I? I'll make a fool of myself. It can even be a chillul Hashem.*

Suddenly, Shlomo shot up from his seat.

"Where are you going?" his startled wife asked him.

"I'll be back in a minute," he replied vaguely.

I will do mine and Hashem will do the rest, he told himself as he made his way toward the cockpit with an air that said, *I know what I'm doing.*

"My brother is right outside waiting to get on the plane," he told the stunned co-pilot. "Can we let him in?"

The frozen smile on the officer's face disappeared. "Sir, the door has already been sealed. Passengers can no longer board Flight 016."

The flight attendant appeared from out of nowhere and began to take charge.

"Sir, the 'fasten-seat-belt' light is flashing," she said firmly but politely. "Please have a seat. A flight attendant will be with you shortly."

The co-pilot nodded vigorously, expressing his opposition to opening the door at this time.

Shlomo wasn't taken in by their brusque attempts to push him aside like a pesky child. He flashed the co-pilot his most endearing smile. "You are one-hundred percent right," he said. "I am completely on your side. But the guy outside, he is my brother. And the two of us have another brother in Belgium. We are flying to the wedding of his daughter. Maybe you can be so kind and allow him on board."

The business-class passengers, who were privy to this bizarre conversation, squirmed uncomfortably in their seats. Even the flight attendant was taken aback by the simple language of the heart.

The co-pilot eyed the bearded Chassidic guy standing plaintively before him. He was wearing a long frock coat and a round beaver felt hat. This wasn't a new sight; he had seen this look lots of times before. Yet this man's plea had touched him for a reason he could not quite fathom. The words, spoken from the heart with such warmth and caring, were laced with so much love that he found it hard to ignore them.

Shlomo held his breath for a moment and then forged ahead, "Sir, I am sure you don't normally do this. But if you open the door for my brother, I will appreciate it so very much. You don't know how much it would mean to me and my family."

The co-pilot found his tongue. "You know, I'm someone's brother too, and I am not sure I would have done this for him. But I am so awed by your sincerity that I will forgo regular procedure and open the door for your brother."

Shlomo extended his hand, the co-pilot followed suit. It was a warm, solid handshake. The door was duly opened. All passengers looked up as the door sealed once again behind the last two people to board the flight. The stewardess deftly stashed their gray paisley suitcase somewhere and showed them to their assigned seats. As the couple walked down the aisle to take their seats, all eyes upon them, Ari suddenly felt someone tugging at his sleeve.

"I have never before seen them opening the door after the last call," the cowboy they had met at the check-in counter said, grinning broadly. "I am just green with envy that you have a brother like that."

A MAGNETIC CHANGE OF HEART

As water reflects a face back to a face, so ones's heart is reflected back to him by another (Mishlei 27:19).

"Hi, there!" Tzippora threw out her greeting to no one in particular.

"What's up?" someone echoed in return.

"Oh, hello, I was sure I had missed the bus! It's late, isn't it?" It was a thin voice coming from a short, cute girl with dark skin.

"Yeah, I've been standing here for ages waiting for the bus to arrive," a broad-shouldered kid, rummaging in her overloaded duffel bag, gruffly stated.

"Here it comes!" one girl called out.

Indeed, there was the bus, lumbering around the corner. In a flurry of activity, the girls were soon comfortably ensconced in its seats, glancing out of the tinted windows at the passing scene of the sights and sounds of city life.

Gila leaned back in her seat, her eyelids closing involuntarily. All those sleepless nights of the past week were taking their toll on her. Her head leaning back, she thought about all the plans that she had been working on during the recent days and nights. As a first-time counselor, she had been so completely immersed in composing the songs and cheers for Bunk 5 that normal life had faded into oblivion and she had not had time for matters as trivial as sleep.

Now, against the background din of chattering girls, Gila sat pleasantly absorbed in her thoughts. It was good to just sit and think. She pictured the adorable faces of her campers. They would all be depending on her to give them an amazing experience this summer.

Several hours later, the cozy-looking suburban cottages dotting the lush green fields had replaced the tall city buildings, indicating that they were nearing their destination.

"See that gray line over there?" Gila said to her friend Devorah Leah, pointing to a dusky strip of color on the horizon. "That is where the city pollution ends and the pure country air begins."

The chartered bus rolled into the camp parking lot amidst hand-clapping and cheers of applause from the happy girls. Mrs. Rosenwasser, the camp director, and the two head counselors, Chava and Pery, warmly welcomed the exhilarated girls as they descended from the bus.

As Gila, blinking in the sunlight, stepped off the bus, Mrs. Rosenwasser, holding a clipboard at her side, approached her.

"How was the trip, Gila?" she asked, without really waiting for an answer. She was studying the clipboard she held.

"Oh, it was great," Gila replied as she glanced around, trying to get her bearings.

"Well, Gila, we have a slight problem here."

"A problem?" Gila's heart stopped.

"Yes," the director said, looking up. "You see, the number of girls in Bunk Five is insufficient to fill two separate bunks, as we had originally believed it would. The two groups have been merged into a single bunk, and, as a result, we have no need of so many counselors. We have chosen you, Gila, to serve as a … uh," Mrs. Rosenwasser adjusted her eyeglasses as she glanced at her clipboard again, "the counselor for special activities instead."

A Magnetic Change of Heart

Gila swallowed hard. "Special activity counselor …?" she hesitantly asked. "Wh… what is that?"

"Throughout the summer, there will be some days in which the head counselors will be doing something extra, something special. On those days, they will need special help for the extra work that is involved."

"And the other days?"

"Oh, it will work out fine, don't worry. For now, find your assigned room, unpack your belongings, and come join us in the dining room for lunch."

Gila stood rooted to the ground, stupidly staring ahead. Dreamlike, she watched Devora Leah and Chaya animatedly gesturing to each other. She saw the other girls, her friends, milling about as they scrambled for their suitcases and handbags, lugging them to their respective rooms. She felt removed, gazing at their movements, not one of them, but an onlooker from the sidelines.

How it hurt.

What would my mother have said? She desperately tried to grab hold of something, some anchor that would help her to take hold of herself.

"This challenge was meant for you," she almost heard her mother say. *I will explore the experience and I will use it to grow,* she thought. *I will live up to this challenge, b'ezras Hashem, I will not forfeit it.*

Valiantly, she strained to overcome the painful emotions filling her. She swallowed again and again.

After a long moment, she was part of the group again, throwing back her head in laughter at the joke someone made. As she mingled and chattered with the others, no one would have guessed what had transpired between Mrs. Rosenwasser and her.

After lunch she joined Sari and Nechama, her would-be partners, the counselors of Bunk 5. They discussed their plans for the next day, when the campers would be arriving. With aching pangs of regret, but with an outer facade of nonchalance, she taught them the bunk song she had labored over, and together they sang.

Later that evening, as she walked, head down, along the thick grass and inhaled the pure country air, she struggled with her emotions. It was hard to change her mindset so quickly. She had prepared for camp as a counselor, dreamed about camp as a counselor, and had arrived at camp as a counselor.

A familiar voice called to her from afar. She lifted her face, her hands shielding her eyes from the sun. Someone — she could not tell who, for the strong rays of the sun obscured the silhouette — was running toward her.

"Oh, there you are!" It was Devora Leah, completely out of breath, long beige skirt askew and long auburn tresses flapping against her shoulders as she ran. "Do you know how long I've been searching for you?" she panted.

Moving closer, Devora Leah took hold of Gila's shoulders and, looking her squarely in the face and in one breath, shot her friend a barrage of questions. "What is happening? Is something the matter? Are you homesick?"

Gila couldn't talk. Not yet. She had to think things through on her own first. "No, Devora Leah, not at all. Why? What makes you think so?" she responded nonchalantly, her face breaking into a wide grin.

Her friend fixed her with a confused stare. "Gila?"

"Yes?"

"Um, never mind." Devora Leah instinctively felt Gila needed some privacy and she didn't want to pry. "If you don't want to talk, I understand."

Ironically, it was just those words that helped Gila ease up. Devora Leah wasn't forcing her to speak, yet she made her feel, in no uncertain terms, that she was there for her. Yes, she did want to share her pain with her friend.

The twilight hues peeked between the tall treetops and the setting sun slowly faded below the horizon as two girls sat and talked. When Devora Leah finally left to join in the preparations with her own partners, Gila was feeling much relieved. Devora Leah had listened very carefully to everything she had said. After that, they pondered thoughts about the virtues of judging others favorably. Gila had determined with fresh resolve to give Mrs. Rosenwasser the benefit of the doubt. After all, the camp director surely had not meant to hurt her.

The sun dispatched its rays through the dusty windowpane, light sweeping over Gila's sleeping face as a contented smile played at her lips. A tiny bird hopped onto her windowsill and cocked its tiny head. "Good morning," she twittered to the world at large.

Gila's eyes fluttered wide open. Careful to avoid bumping her head on the upper bunk, she jumped out of her lower berth. She must not be late.

The early-morning serenity felt good. She traversed the short distance between her bunk and the lobby, where Rebbetzin Landers would be briefing the respective "Shiur Counselors" for their daily lessons.

Her thoughts drifted to that first night, some short weeks back. It soon became apparent how her own positive feelings toward Mrs. Rosenwasser, transmitted through her manner of interactions, were mirrored back to her. Like a magnet, her own altruism and good will attracted precisely the same response in Mrs. Rosenwasser's heart. The director was pleased and touched by Gila's positive attitude, which displayed no animosity or resentment.

As Gila was rushing through the camp lobby one particularly hectic day, Mrs. Rosenwasser had unexpectedly approached her.

"Gila," she said, in her usual soft-spoken manner. "We would like to offer you a job for the second part of the summer.

Ruchama, Bunk Five's Shiur Counselor, will be going home. We thought that you would be an appropriate candidate to fill the position. Would you consider it?"

"Would I consider it?" Gila didn't comprehend the question. "I would be extremely honored. I would be positively delighted. I would … I would jump for joy!"

And she literally did … straight into the arms of Devora Leah who, with a look of pride on her face, was rushing toward her to congratulate her.

THE REAL THING

Suzanne was a very deep and inquisitive child with a strong imagination. She attended Hebrew school, but didn't gain much educationally because at that time the system was not equipped to deal with her learning disability. Suzanne grew up very confused. Inside her home she found that her family was proud to be Jewish, but that Jewish pride didn't carry with it anything else. There were no rules to follow, no obligations to keep, and an almost imperceptible message of "keep it quiet on the outside" accompanied it all.

Suzanne's *neshamah* pined for the real thing. However, though she was looking for something real in life, she did not know what the "real thing" was. The child would spend hours staring into space, dwelling on the concept of life and death, an expression of her need to understand the world around her. Although these ideas were never mentioned in her home, her own thoughts made her extremely anxious and terribly insecure. Occasionally she would experience a panic attack during which she would scream and cry out, "I am having another worry!"

Her parents tried numerous ways to placate the terrified child.

"Calm down. What's wrong?"

"I don't know. Everything is so fake. Nothing is real. It's all so strange and I am so alone."

"It's okay. Don't think about such things."

But to Suzanne everything around her felt so temporary. She yearned for a way to soothe her overwhelming insecurity.

Twice Suzanne went to see a psychiatrist, once at age 6 and later at age 13. Doctor Carolyn was very nice and was well-intentioned, but she did not help in the slightest. *When those feelings come up, clench your fists, count to ten, and breathe.* Was that the best advice she could offer?

But though she clenched and counted, clenching and coutning did not address her real-life questions, and her panic attacks did not stop. However, with time she was able to suppress her anxiety and keep it inside and in control.

It was an ordinary day, like any other. Suzanne strolled along the streets, accompanied by her friend. Suddenly, a blue Chevrolet swerved out of nowhere, it seemed, and in a single, terrifying moment, hurtled straight into her friend. The impact of the collision flung the girl's body into the air, where it spun three times before smashing into the concrete.

Suzanne stood rooted to the ground in utter shock. She couldn't breathe. Suddenly an unbelievable sound surged up from somewhere deep within her and she shrieked as if possessed. It was a single word. There, among astonished onlookers, Suzanne, dressed in denim jeans and a short-sleeved shirt, screamed, pleadingly, desperately, the holy name of Hashem. Without knowing, she knew one thing. Inexplicably, at that moment, she knew without a shadow of a doubt, that only Hashem could help them. It was a moment of clarity; a moment when she felt utterly and helplessly dependent on Hashem. It was an incredible moment.

Where did Hashem's name come from at a time when she could not think straight? She did not know. Something inside her just took over. True, she was there, standing right at the scene, but she wasn't there, she wasn't in control. A sudden beam of light shone brightly, illuminating all her childhood fears. Nothing is real, that was confirmed. Only Hashem is real.

The Real Thing

And that day she learned that when one calls out to Him with sincerity, He hears. At the hospital the girls were told that, logically, no one could have remained alive after what had happened. It didn't make sense at all. Not a single bone was broken. Suzanne had called out to Him and He had responded to her call.

Suzanne was 14 when her parents started observing Shabbos, but she never thought that its rules applied to her as well. Her parents, freethinking and noninterventionists, refrained from applying pressure to her. Shabbos, to her, was a day like any other.

At 16, she left high school and for three years attended to a college where she was the only Jew. She discovered that most people were negative, false, bitter, and hypocritical. Again, life wasn't real. Everybody around her wore a mask. The world, it seemed to her, was out to impress and nothing else.

She had strong ideas of her own, though. Putting up pretenses was anathema to her; whatever she was, people would just have to accept her "as is" — and not everybody around her cared for her integrity. That is when she took upon herself a conscious commitment to live and seek a life of authenticity and positivism.

One day Suzanne received an offer she could not refuse. She was invited to work on board a cruise ship for an eight-month cruise. She was 19 years old, and her parents knew they didn't have much say in the way she chose to run her life. Still they tried, "Why don't you try and ask them if you can refrain from working on Shabbos?"

Their young daughter, however, failed to see the necessity of such a sacrifice.

Nevertheless, her mother proceeded to purchase candles. Then with the use of a simple kitchen knife, she painstakingly cut the long candles into short ones so that they would be easy to use and were enough to last for eight months. (Small candles were hard to find at that time.)

"One thing I ask of you," she implored her daughter. "Light two of these candles every Friday night."

Suzanne compromised. She lit the candles, yet she worked on Shabbos.

Her awareness of Hashem was a part of her being, as it is a part of every *Yiddishe neshamah*. Occasionally she would go up on the deck and speak to Him. Nevertheless, lacking the perspective that would come with time, her relationship with her Creator was a one-way relationship — one she remembered when she wanted something from Him.

On board the ship, Suzanne became friendly with another employee, Sarah, a very religious Christian girl from South Africa, and who invited her to attend Bible classes. One day Suzanne noticed that Sarah was counting and organizing her money.

"What are you doing?" Suzanne inquired.

"I am separating the money I earned."

"Why?"

Sarah looked up at her, the surprise evident in her wide eyes. "You should know! We got this from you Jews. I am taking a tithe; I am separating 10 percent of my earnings."

A stabbing pain shot through Suzanne. How ignorant she felt. *This Christian girl is telling me what I needed to do?* She felt so ashamed, so inadequate, so uneducated. At that moment she experienced a jolt of realization. She felt robbed of a Jewish education.

In truth, Hashem was calling to her — in so many different ways and with so many different messages — until finally she heard Him calling and actually got the message.

Upon returning from her cruise, she received a phone call, out of the blue. Ilana, whom she had never met before, was asking her to come work at The Jewish Learning Exchange. After her intensive work on the ship, the tranquility of an office job appealed to her, and she accepted.

It took one year for Suzanne to become aware of the Ohr Samayach branch located right next door to the place where she worked each day. That is when she joined Rabbi Akiva Tatz's Wednesday night shiur. From this weekly shiur, she continued on to learn in *Eretz Yisrael* in Nevei Yerushalayim.

It is not a simple journey to give up everything that is dear and familiar and instead embark on a new life with unfamiliar signposts, numerous obligations, and an altered outlook on life.

Suzanne was amazed. Only one year had passed — a difficult year, a wonderful year. A year that had wondrously taken her from sailing over the waves of the ocean, and hurled her, suddenly, to struggle through the waves of Torah. The reality seemed almost paradoxical, until she learned that Torah is compared to water.

LIFE'S LESSONS

The place I called home during the first part of my childhood was a tiny fourth-floor apartment. The front entrance opened straight into the ... dining room? Bedroom? Play room? Family room? It was a dining room, as indicated by the dining-room table in its center, though its actual function served as a great deal more than that. The four walls of that room were fully appropriated by the bookcase, the breakfront, a high-riser, a small refrigerator, a sewing machine, and a play-pen, although it was not in the least a large room. The effect was, I should say ... cozily cluttered, or something very close to that.

At first, the bed in there belonged to me. But when, due to its close proximity to the entrance door of our apartment, this evoked some disturbing night terrors, my brother offered to swap with me. In his usual good-natured manner, he graciously gave up his bed on the high-riser in the only children's bedroom. The lower bed of the high-riser in that little room could never be pulled up and out to its full size due to the lack of space in the room.

I remember when the high-riser was changed for a bunk bed. We kids jumped and romped about in ecstasy on every side of the workers, who were arduously assembling what to us was a capital piece of furniture. We believed we had acquired the most eccentric and exciting item any other child could only dream of. The room had no closet, and my mother's resourcefulness came to good use when she put up a rod in the bottom of the enclosed bookshelf in the dining room. Only after we outgrew those little dresses and the space in the book shelves proved to be too small were we forced to share the restricted space in our little bedroom with a high chest of drawers, which also included hanging space. Another major item enclosed in our little cubicle was the baby's crib. Snuggled in a perfect fit into the remaining space, it seemed almost as if the walls of the room had been custom-built around all the paraphernalia that needed to be there. Every inch of room was used to its maximum capacity. As for elbowroom for the inhabitants, well, let's just say that little people don't need that much space ….

My mother ingeniously expanded the limited space of our house by cleverly extending the boundaries, albeit invisibly, into the outside hall. This allotment of space was set aside for a playroom all to ourselves. In retrospect, I suppose we had something all those kids who consider themselves lucky today don't have. We had a whole flight of stairs to ourselves. Our own stairs actually lead to the roof of the house. (Of course the door to the roof was securely locked at all times.) We certainly enjoyed this larger-than-life fanciful toy. It was the perfect setting for playing school, affording the little "teacher" a wonderful view of all her "students." Alternatively, it was the best platform ever invented, used to stage the untold number of brilliant plays we performed. Indeed, we dreamed up an endless number of fantasy activities on those steps.

As for the kitchen in our home, it resembled more closely the looks of that popular toy we call the "kitchen center." On the whole, this miniature kitchen had to be used in shifts. What this means is that just about three people fit in there at any one time.

And that rule did not apply if one of them was standing and washing dishes. In that case, there was not even enough room to gain entry or even to take leave of our culinary alcove. Here again, my mother displayed her improvising abilities, increasing the mere twelve inches of counter space by utilizing the scanty space between the burners on the stove! "That was very important counter space," she recently recalled.

Among my rather amusing memories is that of my fairly aristocratic father verily climbing adroitly out of the window — the only entrance to our succah — which was a tiny 2-by-2 foot structure, built on the fire escape, all kidding aside. I remember standing and watching this comical spectacle, and reflecting on the apparent impishness of so regal a man.

Then one day the search started. For two years we children had the privilege of spending numerous nights in the company of our young aunts, whom we much adored, who came to babysit while our parents scoured the area in search of the right house. I still have fond memories of those special evenings, which forged the beginning of a lasting friendship between us. To their credit, it must be said that they were exceptionally warm and caring to us young charges, and very often entertained us with lots of special fun. (In retrospect, I realize that this was probably done at the expense of their homework time.) In addition, as young babysitters are apt to do, they would promise to buy us some treat for going to bed when the time arrived. Not once did they make an empty promise; they always kept their word. For some reason, this standard of theirs made a lasting impression on me.

Finally, a lot was purchased in partnership with family friends, and the construction of our house began. I was too young to be a part of all the struggles involved in building (which from my present perspective I can appreciate). To us kids this was all a great deal of fun.

Finally the great day arrived. Moving day.

We children frolicked about in the spacious new rooms — our old apartment in its entirety could practically have fit into the new dining room. We luxuriated and capered about in the vast open space of the backyard and porches we'd never had before. I distinctly recall how, in my mother's eyes, the large empty closets were her greatest delight.

Our new home was simply furnished in good taste, and I relished the novelty of it all. The smell of fresh paint and the recent parquet polish tingled my senses and enveloped me in delightful sensations of newness and fresh beginnings. To my innocent mind, there wasn't the slightest notion that new impressions are short-lived, and the concept that our new house would not remain new forever was entirely foreign to my childish fancies. However, it did not take long before I redefined this naïve belief and gained a greater awareness of how things work out in a world where such things don't last forever.

Purim turned out to be just a few short weeks after our momentous moving day. Many friends and acquaintances were understandably eager to come view our new residence, and come they did. A large number of people turned up in high-spirited anticipation to join us wholeheartedly in our Purim celebration that year. My mother's acclaimed savory dishes were passed around, delighting her guests with her delicious cuisine. My father distributed fine wine to please even the most discriminating tastes. The large new space afforded the various groups of men and *bachurim* room to dance and leap in uninhibited freedom. The whole atmosphere was invested with an elevated degree of *simchah* as family and friends locked hands in shared ecstasy.

One circle of joyous dancers in particular, swinging round and round in a vivacious circle of exuberance, their animated and heartfelt singing increasing in enthusiastic excitement, momentarily attracted everyone's attention.

Suddenly one member of this lively group of dancers slipped, feet soaring into the air and startling all those happy spectators into shocked silence. Then it happened — his long legs, in a struggle to touch safe ground, crashed into the brand-new wall, creating in it a large, gaping hole! The crescendo of cacophonous sound of just a minute ago fell into a sudden apprehensive silence. Not a single sound escaped from anyone in the immediate aftermath of this sorry performance, the sudden tense mood contrasting sharply to the exhilarating tumult of a minute ago. In unison, all eyes turned abruptly to stare at my mother. What would she say? How would she react to this obvious blow to her brand-new house?

My mother, in her usual composed demeanor, gently smiled and said softly, "It's okay, we'll have it repaired."

Indeed, the offending hole was duly plastered over, but that incident engraved a lasting imprint on my young heart and mind.

The amazing self-control and equanimity of my mother was nothing new to me. Neither was my fathers' cheerful acceptance of what he would always point out to us as being part of Hashem's grand master plan. What I did learn that year was that every hole can be fixed — every problem has a solution. And that nothing will stay new forever.

THE PERFECT HIDING PLACE

*L*eah hummed to herself as she was getting ready to leave the house. She was in a cheerful frame of mind; happy for the change of scenery a walk with her children would provide, and glad to give her children some fresh air. She was also looking forward to the "adult conversation" she was sure to enjoy with other mothers she would find walking outside.

In fact, this was the time of day when many busy young mothers could be found strolling the streets, youngsters in tow, looking as if they had not a care in the world.

She stirred the pot of soup just one more time, tasted it again just to be sure. Satisfied, she turned off the flame and wiped the counter one more time. She didn't like coming home to a messy house.

As she bent down to pick up the toys on the floor, little Ruthie started whining, "I wanna go awready!"

Leah eyed her active three-year-old with quiet understanding. Ruthie could never stay still for too long; she always had to be busy with something. Time spent waiting for her mother to get ready seemed interminable. Leah usually tried to withhold the news of an impending outing until the last minute in order to lessen the long wait for her child. Somehow she had miscalculated today. Perhaps it was because of the new baby, whose schedule was still so unpredictable, that the information had been imparted too much ahead of time.

As the last toys made their way into their rightful containers, Leah realized that Zevy, her one-and-a-half-year-old, needed a diaper change. *There, we are all ready*, she thought as she placed the diaper in the pail. All she still needed to do was slip on the baby's bunting and she was ready to leave. *Another minute*, she thought as she glanced at her watch. "What?" she gasped. "It's already three o'clock? How could that be? Where did the time fly?" She hadn't realized that a full hour had passed since she had started her preparation. Now her baby was almost due for a feeding. She couldn't simply leave now and soon have her baby screaming and wailing on the street. All eyes would be upon her. "Tsk, tsk," she imagined them all shaking their heads in sympathy. Oh, no, that was the last thing she wanted.

But what about Ruthie, who had meanwhile taken up her eager anticipation outside on the front lawn?

Ruthie wouldn't go anywhere on her own, Leah was sure of that. She would hop and jump and skip with all her youthful energy until Leah emerged, and then she would fasten her little hand onto the side of the double stroller and hop and skip some more. Besides, the front gate was securely closed.

As she fed the baby, she tried to relax, mentally reviewing her day, trying to figure out how had it passed so quickly.

At last she was ready and actually locking the door from the outside. Something was not right. She felt it before she even knew it. It was eerily quiet. Ruthie was nowhere in sight.

"Ruthie!" Leah called out. There was no answer.

"Ruthie! Ruthie!" Her tone went up an octave higher. The far-sounding echo of her voice was the only response.

Leah felt herself flooding with fear, inch by inch, vein by vein, artery by artery. An encompassing terror tightly gripped her heart. She could not breathe. She felt completely numb and stood rooted to the spot. The world seemed to stop.

In the distance she could hear a dog barking and a bus honking its horn. The sudden shrill wail of an ambulance siren brought her to her senses and sent her adrenaline into action full force. She broke out in a run. The front gate was locked. That discovery unsettled her for a moment. Ruthie couldn't have gone too far .... Still on the run, with a frantic prayer on her lips, she headed toward the back of the house, leaping over low bushes and trampling the neat rows of tulips on the way.

"Ruuuthieee!" she yelled at the top of her lungs. As she ran, she imagined little Ruthie clapping her chubby little hands and jumping in delight at some new discovery, golden tresses bouncing in the sunlight. Her imagination turned blank when she realized that there were no little hands or golden curls in her range of vision. She tried to calm down and think constructively. *Perhaps she somehow managed to get out of the yard and I will find her innocently playing with the neighbors' children next door.* Instantly, she hurried in that direction, hastily wheeling the carriage through the gate. It didn't take long for her to notice that all was still at the neighbors'. There was nobody home. She willed herself to block out her currently overactive imagination. The images her mind was entertaining were becoming more and more vivid. She realized that she couldn't just run around the block with her two little ones. She would use the telephone to help her in her frantic search.

It seemed to take forever until her trembling hand was finally able to insert the key into the lock, and finally she let herself in.

As she rushed down the hall toward the telephone, something odd caught her eyes as she flew past the children's room. She rapidly retraced her steps. Her eyes widened in shock when she saw that next to the bump under the fuzzy blanket were the dear golden curls framing the familiar heart-shaped face, finger securely inserted into the mouth. Her precious little girl, having grown tired of the long wait, had put herself to sleep in her own comfortable bed. Leah was overcome with gratitude to the One Who guards His children at all times, in all places.

We have all experienced the formidable feeling of misplacing an item; be it the car keys, a wallet, or other items. Many of us have experienced a "misplacement" of the above magnitude, given the natures of some of our children. This story really did happen and I sometimes reflect upon its message. We will run hither and thither and all over searching for the elusive item, or in the above case, the "missing child," when, in reality, it is sometimes right there, sitting or staring right into our face. Unless the One Who sees everything wants us to see, we are very much like a blind person groping in the dark. "*Hakol becheskas sumin ad she 'HaKadosh Baruch Hu meir es eineihem ....*"

Everyone is considered blind until Hashem enlightens their eyes.

This volume is part of
THE ARTSCROLL SERIES®
an ongoing project of
translations, commentaries and expositions
on Scripture, Mishnah, Talmud, Halachah,
liturgy, history, the classic Rabbinic writings,
biographies and thought.

For a brochure of current publications
visit your local Hebrew bookseller
or contact the publisher:

Mesorah Publications, ltd
4401 Second Avenue
Brooklyn, New York 11232
(718) 921-9000
www.artscroll.com